BLOOD YEAR

DAVID KILCULLEN

BLOOD YEAR

The Unraveling of
Western Counterterroism

OXFORD
UNIVERSITY PRESS

OXFORD
UNIVERSITY PRESS

Oxford University Press is a department of
the University of Oxford. It furthers the University's objective
of excellence in research, scholarship, and education
by publishing worldwide.

Oxford is a registered trade mark of Oxford University Press
in the UK and in certain other countries

Published in the United States of America by
Oxford University Press
198 Madison Avenue, New York, NY 10016

Published in the United Kingdom in 2016 by
C. Hurst & Co. (Publishers) Ltd.

Library of Congress Cataloging-in-Publication Data
is available from the Library of Congress

ISBN 978–0–19–060054–9

9 8 7 6 5 4 3 2 1

Printed in the United States of America
on acid-free paper

Whoever fights monsters should see to it that in the process he does not become a monster. And if you gaze for long into an abyss, the abyss also gazes into you.

Nietzsche, *Beyond Good and Evil*, 1886

CONTENTS

Preface   ix
Note on Sources   xi
Maps   xii

 1. Debacle   1
 2. Disaggregation   7
 3. Abyss   15
 4. Waterfall   37
 5. Crocodile   45
 6. Tsunami   53
 7. Rebirth   67
 8. Collapse   83
 9. Retribution   87
10. Rollback?   101
11. Internationale   111
12. Wilayat   127
13. Khilafah   133
14. Transformation   151
15. Spillover   167
16. Maskirovka   185
17. Age of Conflict   197

Epilogue   219

Notes   233
Index   259

PREFACE

In mid-2014 the Islamic State burst onto the global stage with a string of spectacular victories in Iraq, and a series of gruesome beheadings of journalists, aid workers and local civilians. For many—smart, well-educated people, who'd been paying attention but had no particular expertise or interest in the ins and outs of transnational terrorism—the rise of ISIS[1] was both baffling and deeply disappointing.

For years, their governments had been telling them that things were getting better. Western troops were out of Iraq, Osama bin Laden was dead, withdrawal from Afghanistan was on track, drones and special ops were handling the threat, militarized police and state surveillance were necessary evils that were keeping us safe, and—despite a few hiccups, like the fatal attack on a U.S. diplomatic compound in Benghazi in 2012—people were thinking and speaking of the bad old days of President George W. Bush's "Global War on Terror" in the past tense. In President Obama's soothing phrase, the nation's wars were ending.[2]

Now, seemingly overnight, we were back to square one, and people wanted to know why. The crisis of 2014 thus prompted a string of books, each more excellent than the last, by journalists and scholars documenting the rise of ISIS, its ideology, eschatology, objectives, motives and antecedents, and seeking to explain its attraction for certain kinds of people in our own and other societies.

This is not one of those books.

That is, it's not a book about ISIS: rather, it's about what the emergence of ISIS tells us about the broader War on Terrorism since 2001. This is linked to the rise of the Islamic State, to be sure, but it also connects the Arab Spring, the resurgence of confrontation with Russia, the Iranian nuclear deal, and the European refugee crisis. These may seem loosely linked, but as I argue in the narrative that follows, they're symptoms of the same problem.

Neither is this book a comprehensive history. On the contrary, it's a personal account, by a mid-level player in some of the key events of the past decade—the wars in Iraq and Afghanistan, the development and implementation of counterinsurgency and counterterrorism strategy in the United States and elsewhere—of how we came to get things so wrong, and what that tells us about the future.

PREFACE

Politicians of all stripes have an interest in turning terrorism into a partisan issue, rewriting history to protect their legacies, exploiting fear to further some agenda, or using terrorist incidents to attack opponents in the trench warfare that passes for political process. You can't blame them for that—politicians are politicians, you might as well blame a dog for barking. But partisan debate isn't objective reality, and to the extent that any of us think it is, we have bigger problems than ISIS. With that in mind, I should mention up front that I have no party political affiliation: I've never voted in a U.S. presidential election, donated money to any candidate or political organization, been a political appointee, or held elected office. My intention here is simply to explain things as I see them—with all the limitations that any one person's perspective inevitably implies.

As an Australian professional soldier, as a civilian intelligence officer, then as a U.S. government employee, I served during the Bush administration in Iraq, Afghanistan, Pakistan, the Horn of Africa and Southeast Asia. During the Obama administration, I served in many of the same places as an adviser and consultant to the U.S. Government, NATO and allied governments. I'm on record critiquing both administrations (for different reasons) in books, scholarly papers and congressional testimony. I mention this not to claim any particular expertise, just to illustrate that my outlook is professional not political.

I'm also not an academic expert on terrorism—my field is guerrilla and unconventional warfare, which though related, is not quite the same thing. In fact, in the *Lord of the Flies* world of academia, guerrilla warfare and terrorism studies people belong to different (often warring) tribes. So, if you're looking for a scholarly treatise on ISIS or on terrorism in general, there are better books to read. What I am, however, is an ordinary guy caught up in extraordinary events, a participant in parts of the story I'm about to tell, and someone who has been watching closely and keeping notes as this enormous slow-motion train wreck took place.

For what it's worth, then, this is my perspective on how we got here, where ISIS came from, what it all means, and what may happen next.

David Kilcullen
Washington D.C., November 2015

NOTE ON SOURCES

This account uses only open source information. To my knowledge, it makes no use of any classified material, in any form whatsoever, including information that was once classified but has since been leaked to the public (for example, material released by Wikileaks after 2010 or Edward Snowden in 2013). It *does* use material—such as CIA reports, court documents, congressional investigations or emails released to the public following court orders—that has been formally declassified and released in accordance with official government policy. This imposes inevitable limitations on some parts of the discussion; and of course, there's always the possibility that in thirty or fifty years—or next week—some hitherto classified information may emerge that changes parts of my analysis.

A limited amount of material in the second part of this account (and almost all of the first half) was previously published under my name, either in *Quarterly Essay*, Issue No. 58, May 2015, or as news analysis between July 2014 and September 2015. This material is used by permission of the copyright holder.

Finally, in discussing Syria, Iraq and North Africa, I've been fortunate to have access not only to my own personal notes from the field, but also to a stream of multiple-source reporting (all, again, unclassified) from people on the ground. For obvious reasons, I have an absolute obligation to protect the identities of these people, many now living in areas controlled by ISIS, the Taliban or the Assad regime. Whenever possible, I've sought to verify information from any field source with at least one other, and when a news organization or another analyst has published material that confirms or covers essentially the same information, I've chosen to quote that authority rather than mention my field source. When only one source is available, I've said so, and offered as much information on the source's identity as I can safely give.

To all of you—you know who you are—who helped me understand this war, who have suffered so much in it, and have shared so freely of your time and advice, I can only thank you, wish you and your families a speedy return to home, safety and peace, and acknowledge that while many contributed to this story, any errors and failings are mine alone.

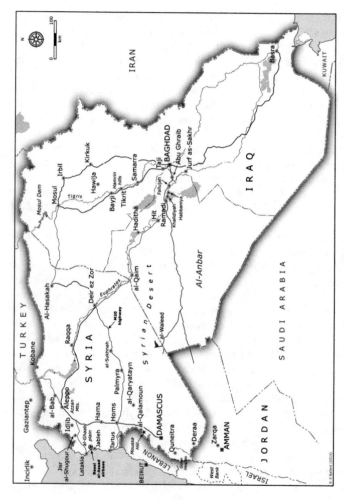

Map 1: Syria and Iraq

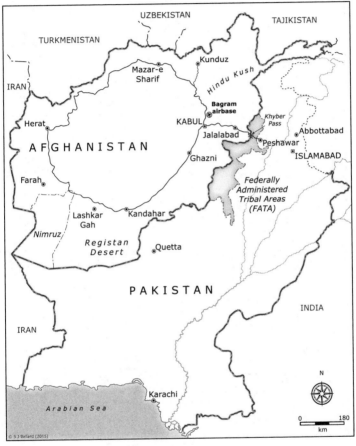

Map 2: Afghanistan and Pakistan

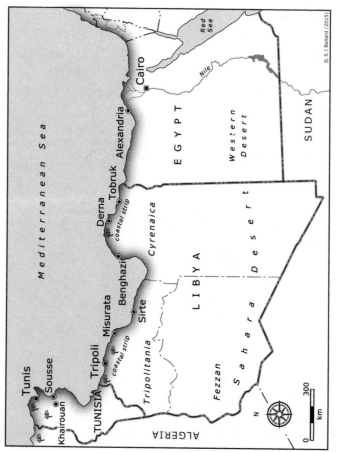

Map 3: North Africa

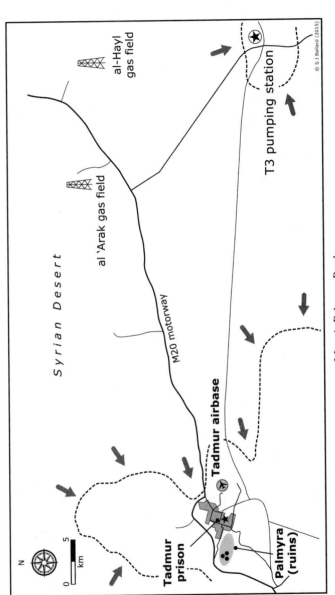

Map 4: Palmyra Battle

© S J Ballard (2015)

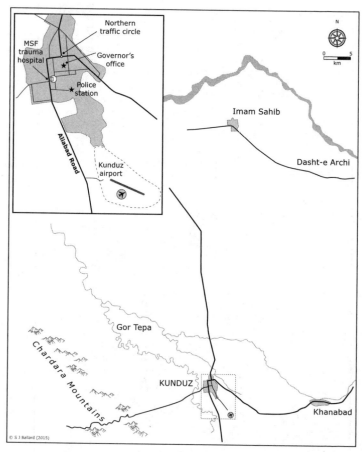

Map 5: Kunduz

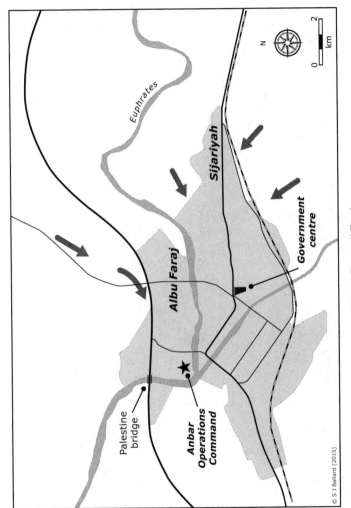

Map 6: Ramadi Battle

© S J Ballard (2015)

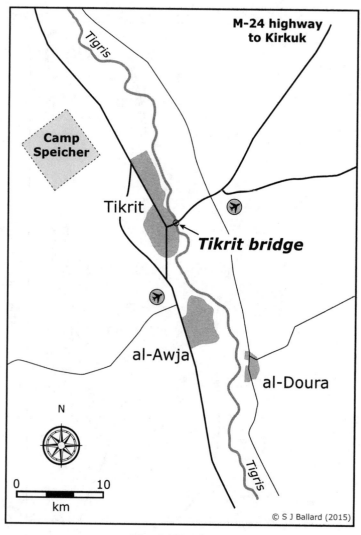

Map 7: Tikrit Battle

I

DEBACLE

United Arab Emirates, November 2014

My driver pulls up to a resort in the Empty Quarter. It's just after dawn, and we've been driving for hours across the desert from Abu Dhabi. We're near the Saudi border now; past this point the bare sand stretches for hundreds of empty miles. The place is all minarets and battlements—Classical Arabia as imagined by a hotel designer with grand tastes and an unlimited budget. We cross a causeway between dunes and snake into a courtyard past black BMWs, a silver Mercedes and two camouflaged jeeps.

Over the last mile we've been penetrating a series of increasingly overt security layers. Helicopters hover beyond the crest, search teams trawl the complex for bombs, and dogs bark from the perimeter checkpoint where police search cars and bags. All but one entrance is sealed; there are no other guests. Inside are more dogs, the buzz of radios and a counter-assault team: burly guys of indeterminate ethnicity, with dark glasses and skin-tone earpieces, holsters visible below grey suits, machine pistols discreetly within reach. Sentries step out of doorways to check credentials. A silver blimp glints overhead, packed with U.S.-made sensor technology designed for the Iraq War and positioned to detect the visual or heat signature of anyone approaching across the desert. The sponsor is taking no chances.

I'm rumpled from travel, freezing from the air-conditioned car, and could really do without all this drama. I stretch, climb out and

I

check my watch: still on Sydney time. I've been on the move for twenty-four hours, fifteen of those on the red-eye from Australia, and I'm in desperate need of a double espresso, some sunlight, and a piss.

However surreal the setting, this is deadly serious: a conference, long-scheduled, that has turned into a crisis meeting in a year of massacres and beheadings, fallen cities and collapsing states—the unraveling, in mere weeks, of a decade of Western strategy. Former prime ministers and presidents, current foreign ministers, generals, ambassadors and intelligence chiefs are here, with White House staffers, presidential envoys, and leaders from the Middle East and Africa. There are North Americans, Brits, Aussies, Iranians, Russians, Chinese and Indians. Two well-known journalists have agreed not to attribute what people say.

Beside the two dozen VIP delegates and their aides, a few scruffy field guys like me are hanging around the fringes to present research or brief the plenary sessions, though at such gatherings the real business gets done by grown-ups in bespoke suits, at side meetings we never see. The sessions have names like "Syria and Iraq: In Search of a Strategy," "North Africa in Crisis" and "Islamist Terrorism and the Region." Maybe it's my jetlag, but people look dazed to me—like morning-after partygoers. The hangover is a geopolitical one: after a wild decade of war and chaos, the rise of ISIS, the failure of the Arab Spring, the fracturing of Iraq and the spillover from Syria have suddenly, dangerously destabilized the Middle East and North Africa.

In the northern summer of 2014, in less than 100 days, ISIS launched its blitzkrieg in Iraq, Libya's government collapsed, civil war engulfed Yemen, a sometime small-town Iraqi preacher named Abu Bakr al-Baghdadi declared himself caliph, the latest Israel–Palestine peace initiative failed in a welter of violence that left more than 2,200 people (mostly Palestinian civilians) dead, and the United States and its allies, including the United Kingdom and Australia, sent troops and planes back to Iraq. Russia, a key sponsor of Bashar al-Assad's tyrannical regime in Damascus, reignited Cold War tensions by formally annexing Crimea (which Russian marines, politely masquerading as "green men," had not-so-stealthily seized in the spring), sent submarines and long-range bombers to intimidate its neighbors in their own seas and airspace, and armed and sponsored

Ukrainian rebels who shot down a Malaysian airliner with huge loss of innocent life. Iran continued its push to become a nuclear threshold power, supported Assad in Syria, and yet became a de facto ally of the United States in Iraq as Tehran and Washington sought, each for different reasons, to bolster the Baghdad government.

As this disastrous year closed, the fourth winter of war settled over Syria, and nine million displaced Syrians languished in freezing mountain camps with little prospect of ever going home. Half of Syria's twenty-three million people depended entirely on humanitarian aid. More than 200,000 had died; babies born in the camps that winter froze to death within days.[1] Refugees and displaced persons reached historically unprecedented numbers, fuelling a worldwide epidemic of suffering, people smuggling and exploitation of asylum-seekers. Across the increasingly imaginary Iraqi border, thousands had been displaced, decapitated, sold into sexual slavery, shot in the street or crucified for minor infractions of sharia law— as idiosyncratically interpreted by whatever local ISIS thug happened to make it his business. Panic pervaded Baghdad, and Irbil (capital of Iraqi Kurdistan) became a frontline city, within sound and occasional reach of the guns.

Islamist fighters from the Middle East, Europe, Australia, the Americas and all parts of Asia and Africa poured into Syria and Iraq at a rate twelve times higher than at the height of the anti-American war in 2007, swelling ISIS to more than 30,000 (for comparison, al-Qaeda, at its peak before 9/11, never had more than 25,000 full-time fighters). Thousands poured across Syria's frontier with Turkey, a NATO member that nonetheless tolerated relatively free movement to (or, increasingly, from) the conflict. ISIS provinces, or *wilayat*, appeared in Libya, Afghanistan, Pakistan, North Africa, the Caucasus and Egypt, and extremists in Indonesia, Malaysia and Nigeria swore allegiance to Baghdadi's caliphate. Attacks by ISIS-inspired terrorists hit Europe, America, Africa, Australia and the Middle East. Thirteen years, thousands of lives and billions of dollars after 9/11, any progress in the War on Terrorism had seemingly been swept away in a matter of weeks.

On 10 June 2014, ISIS seized Mosul, anchor of northern Iraq and home to more than two million. Twelve days before the city's fall, President Obama had betrayed no inkling of impending collapse in a speech at the United States Military Academy at West

Point, where he failed to mention ISIS at all (having earlier dismissed them as a "jayvee [junior varsity] team,"[2] wannabes lacking the capability of al-Qaeda) and spoke of what was once called the Global War on Terrorism as if it was winding down. "You are the first class to graduate since 9/11," the president said, "who may not be sent into combat in Iraq or Afghanistan."[3]

> When I first spoke at West Point in 2009, we still had more than 100,000 troops in Iraq. We were preparing to surge in Afghanistan. Our counter-terrorism efforts *were focused on al Qaeda's core leadership* ... Four and a half years later, as you graduate, the landscape has changed. We have removed our troops from Iraq. We are winding down our war in Afghanistan. Al Qaeda's leadership on the border region between Pakistan and Afghanistan has been decimated, and Osama bin Laden is no more ... [T]oday's principal threat *no longer comes from a centralized al Qaeda leadership. Instead, it comes from decentralized al Qaeda affiliates and extremists, many with agendas focused in countries where they operate.* And this lessens the possibility of large-scale 9/11-style attacks against the homeland. [emphasis added][4]

What happened? How could the president so misjudge the situation, days before the Mosul debacle? How did we get here? Can we recover, and what does a coherent strategy look like now?

Blood Year—which builds on, updates and expands a shorter essay published in April 2015—is my attempt to answer those questions. It draws on interviews with communities and combatants across the region, results from my own fieldwork, the work of my research teams on the ground in Iraq and Syria, and analysis by other well-informed observers and researchers. The answer, like many things in war, is hard but simple: it begins with the recognition that the West's strategy after 9/11—derailed by the invasion of Iraq, exacerbated by our addiction to killing terrorist leaders, hastened by precipitate withdrawal from Iraq and Afghanistan, opportunism in Libya, and passivity in the face of catastrophe in Syria—carried the seeds of disaster within it. And until that strategy changes, those disasters will continue.

President Obama's description of the strategy, italicized above, is quite accurate. We *did* focus on destroying the core of al-Qaeda (AQ) in Afghanistan–Pakistan, targeting the leaders around Osama bin Laden, and cutting links between his group and its affiliates in other countries. The goal was to dismantle AQ, breaking it apart into a series of smaller, regional groups that could then be dealt with by local governments, assisted by the international community through training, equipment, advisory efforts and targeted strikes.

This wasn't just an Obama strategy. In fact, the greatest change in U.S. strategy since 9/11 occurred between the first and second terms of President George W. Bush (that is, in 2005, rather than 2009, when President Obama took office), hence there's huge continuity between the Obama administration and the second, though not the first, Bush term. For political reasons, both Republicans and Democrats downplay these similarities, but they're striking all the same. The Obama administration's rhetoric differs, it makes more use of certain tools (especially drone strikes[5] and mass surveillance) and its focus has been on disengaging from the wars President Bush started in 2001–3. But all those things were also true of the Bush administration itself after 2005: in substance if not in rhetoric, for ten years the United States and its allies have followed much the same strategy.

I know this strategy intimately, because I was part of the team that devised it. So if this story is really a confession of failure, then it's my failure too. And if we want to comprehend how things went so awry in 2014, we must first admit our shortcomings, and then try to understand where the strategy came from, and how it went so badly wrong.

2

DISAGGREGATION

Canberra and Washington D.C., 2004–5

In October 2002 terrorists from al-Qaeda's Southeast Asian affiliate, Jemaah Islamiyah, bombed two nightclubs on the Indonesian island of Bali. They murdered 202 people, including eighty-eight Australians, and injured another 209, many blinded or maimed for life by horrific burns. Bali was the first mass-casualty hit by al-Qaeda or its affiliates after 9/11, a wake-up call that showed the terrorist threat was very much alive and close to home. It spurred the Australian government into increased action on counterterrorism.

A small group of officers, led by the ambassador for counter-terrorism, Les Luck, was selected from Australia's key national security agencies, given access to all available intelligence, and tasked to conduct a strategic assessment of the threat. In early 2004, as an infantry lieutenant colonel with a professional back-ground in guerrilla and unconventional warfare, several years' experience training and advising indigenous forces, and a PhD that included fieldwork with insurgents and Islamic extremists in Southeast Asia, I was pulled out of a desk job at Army Headquarters to join the team. Our efforts produced *Transnational Terrorism: The Threat to Australia*, the framework until 2011 for Australia's counter-terrorism strategy and for cooperation with regional partners and allies including the United States, the United Kingdom, Canada and New Zealand.

Looking at the threat in early 2004, we saw a pattern: the invasion of Afghanistan had scattered but not destroyed the original, hierarchical AQ structure that had existed before 9/11. Many of those fighting for AQ in Afghanistan in 2001 had been killed or captured, or had fled into Pakistan, Iran or Iraq. Osama bin Laden and his deputy, Ayman al-Zawahiri, were in hiding; Khalid Sheikh Mohammed (planner of 9/11 and mastermind of the Bali bombing) was in CIA custody at an undisclosed location. What was left of AQ's senior leadership was no longer a supreme command or organizational headquarters, but a clearing house for information, money and expertise, a propaganda hub, and the inspiration for a far-flung assortment of local movements, most of which pre-dated AQ. Al-Qaeda's "Centre of Gravity"—from which it drew its strength and freedom of action—was neither its numbers nor its combat capability (both of which were relatively small) but rather its ability to manipulate, mobilize and aggregate the effects of many diverse local groups across the world, none of which were natural allies to each other.

In this sense, AQ had much in common with traditional insurgent movements, which manipulate local, pre-existing grievances as a way to mobilize populations, creating a mass base of support for a relatively small force of fast-moving, lightly equipped guerrillas. These guerrillas work with numerically larger underground and auxiliary networks to target weak points such as government outposts, isolated police and military units, and poorly governed spaces. They might try to build "liberated" areas, forge coalitions of like-minded allies into a popular front, or transition to a conventional war of movement and thereby overthrow the state.

But unlike classical insurgents, who target one country or region, AQ was a worldwide movement with global goals. Thus, to succeed, bin Laden's people had to inject themselves into others' conflicts on a global scale, twist local grievances and exploit them for their own transnational ends. This meant that AQ's critical requirement, and its greatest vulnerability, was its need to unify many disparate groups—in Somalia, Indonesia, Chechnya, Nigeria, Yemen, the Philippines or half-a-dozen other places. Take away its ability to aggregate the effects of such groups, and AQ's threat would be hugely diminished, as would the risk of another 9/11. Bin Laden would be just one more extremist among many in Pakistan, not a global threat.

DISAGGREGATION

He and the AQ leadership would become strategically irrelevant: we could kill or capture them later, at our leisure—or not.

Out of this emerged a view of al-Qaeda as a form of globalized insurgency, and a strategy known as "Disaggregation." Writing for a military audience in late 2003, I laid it out like this:

> Dozens of local movements, grievances and issues have been aggregated (through regional and global players) into a global *jihad* against the West. These regional and global players prey upon, link and exploit local actors and issues that are pre-existing. What makes the *jihad* so dangerous is its global nature. Without the … ability to aggregate dozens of conflicts into a broad movement, the global *jihad* ceases to exist. It becomes simply a series of disparate local conflicts that are capable of being solved by nation-states and can be addressed at the regional or national level without interference from global enemies such as Al Qa'eda … A strategy of Disaggregation would seek to dismantle, or break up, the links that allow the *jihad* to function as a global entity.[1]

They say you should be careful what you wish for. In designing Disaggregation, our team was reacting against President Bush, who, through the invasion of Iraq, the "axis of evil" speech and statements like "Either you are with us, or you are with the terrorists,"[2] had (in our view) destabilized the greater Middle East and greatly inflated the danger of terrorism. The existing strategy had lumped together diverse threats, so that Washington ran the risk of creating new adversaries, and of fighting simultaneously enemies who could have been fought sequentially (or not at all). Practices instituted in the early years of the War on Terrorism, as a result of this "Aggregation" of threats, had proven strategically counterproductive and morally problematic.

For example, the U.S. and British practice of extraordinary rendition (dating back to the 1990s and involving seizing terrorism suspects in neutral or friendly territory, then deporting them for interrogation by regimes with sketchy humanitarian records, including Syria, Libya, Yemen and Egypt) undermined Western credibility on human rights and made it hard to pressure these regimes for reform. Cases like that of Maher Arar, for instance—a Canadian citizen detained during a stopover in New York in September 2002 on suspicion of being an AQ member, deported by U.S. authorities to Syria (where he was allegedly tortured for almost a year) but later declared innocent of any terrorist connection—made it hard for

American officials to pressure Bashar al-Assad on his atrocious human rights record.[3]

Likewise, naming Pakistan a "major non-NATO ally" in June 2004—even as some Pakistani intelligence officers continued to sponsor the Taliban and export terrorism across their region—hampered U.S. efforts to build ties with India and led to doublethink on the insurgency in Afghanistan. Similarly, President Bush's January 2002 "axis of evil" remarks in his first State of the Union address alienated Iranian leaders (who had been quietly cooperating against the Taliban and detaining AQ members).

Most egregiously, the manipulation of intelligence to justify the invasion of Iraq—which had no known connection with 9/11 and turned out to have no current weapons of mass destruction (WMD) programs—hugely undermined Western credibility. The failure to turn up expected stockpiles after the invasion discredited the U.S. claim of active weapons programs, and contradicted the British government's assertion that Iraqi forces could launch WMD within forty-five minutes of an order to do so. Subsequent evidence of political spin on American intelligence destroyed the reputation of U.S. Secretary of State Colin Powell, who had relied on that intelligence in making the case for war to the United Nations. In Australia, Andrew Wilkie, an analyst at the Office of National Assessments (Australia's strategic intelligence agency, reporting directly to the prime minister) resigned a week before the invasion, protesting the politicization of intelligence and creating a crisis for the Howard government. In the UK, a media furor over the forty-five minutes claim led to the death of Dr David Kelly, a British bioweapons expert. Kelly was publicly hauled over the coals by the House of Commons foreign affairs committee in July 2003, and found dead in an apparent suicide—under controversial circumstances—two days later.

The Iraq invasion alienated traditional allies like France and Germany, made potential partners unwilling to work with us, and dramatically raised the standard of proof for subsequent intelligence assessments, such as those on Bashar al-Assad's use of chemical weapons in Syria and for the Iranian nuclear program. All this helped AQ further its agenda of aggregating disparate local groups by creating the perception of a global "War on Islam" led by the United States, while making it harder for the U.S. or allies like Australia to build regional partnerships against terrorism.

In short, the aggregation strategy was killing us. As I wrote in the same 2003 military paper, "such a strategy undermines U.S. legitimacy ... because it tends to link obviously disparate conflicts, giving the appearance that the U.S. is using the War as an excuse to settle old scores. Similarly, it causes the U.S. to support morally dubious regimes and (by creating suspicion as to U.S. motives) undermines opportunities for common cause with other democracies—notably the Europeans."[4]

It turned out that plenty of people in the U.S. government felt the same way. Shortly after the Australian strategy came out in September 2004, Canberra received a request from Paul Wolfowitz, deputy secretary of defense, for me to join the team writing the 2006 Quadrennial Defense Review (QDR), a strategic assessment that the Pentagon produces every four years for Congress. After some back and forth—Australia offered a general instead, while the Americans politely reiterated their request for the guy who'd written the Disaggregation paper—I was on my way to Washington, D.C., embedded in the QDR team from December 2004.

The job took me to the Pentagon, the State Department, the Central Intelligence Agency, the Department of Homeland Security, U.S. Special Operations Command, U.S. Central Command, the RAND Corporation and the newly created National Counterterrorism Center (NCTC). In all these places I encountered people whose critique of the past three years was much like mine. To anyone who'd deployed in the War on Terror—or had merely been paying attention since 9/11—it was nothing more than a statement of the obvious. Many people were thinking about variants of Disaggregation, but I could speak more bluntly than most, since I had neither a political affiliation nor a career in the U.S. government, and since the Australian accent (for reasons I've never quite been able to fathom) affords the speaker a measure of amused indulgence in Washington.

Disaggregation, through the combined efforts of all these people, and under several different names, became central to Western counterterrorism strategy in the decade after 2005. In essence, it was an attempt to reverse the lumping together of disparate threats after 9/11, to break the links among groups within the AQ network, target the central players' ability to control their franchises, and partner with local governments to defeat threats in their own jurisdictions.

Several U.S. counterterrorism documents—NCTC's *National Implementation Plan for the War on Terror*, the White House's 2006 *National Security Strategy of the United States of America*, the Joint Staff's 2006 *National Military Strategic Plan for the War on Terrorism* and Special Operations Command's *Campaign Support Plan* (known informally as CONPLAN 7500)—draw on this set of ideas.[5] Admiral Eric Olson, Commander of Special Operations Command, expressed the approach most clearly when he described the goal as being to "isolate the threat," "defeat the isolated threat" and then "prevent its re-emergence."[6] Likewise, the UK's Contest strategy evolved toward Disaggregation from 2006 to 2015, as did Australia's approach.[7]

The working hypothesis of all these strategies—in military parlance, the "theory of victory" on which they were based—was precisely as outlined by President Obama in his 2014 West Point speech: that terrorism could be reduced to a manageable level by dismantling core AQ; maintaining pressure on its leaders so as to cut them off from regional franchises; helping governments deal with those franchises, once localized, through carefully calibrated capability-building efforts; countering the ideology that fuels militancy; and addressing the conditions that create fertile ground for terrorism. This, after 2005, became the consensus view of most Western governments and counterterrorism strategists on how to deal with AQ.

It seems sensible. It was certainly better than what we *had* been doing. And, except for two factors I'll discuss shortly, I still believe the strategy could have worked. But it didn't—as any Iraqi, Syrian, Afghan, Somali or Yemeni can tell you, and as people in Sydney, London, Ottawa, Paris and Copenhagen have been gruesomely reminded of.

Back in 2004, though, when Disaggregation was first mooted, the key challenge was bureaucratic resistance to the notion of AQ as a form of globalized insurgency. It's hard to remember now, more than a decade later, how intense was the official discouragement of counterinsurgency—the theory, its techniques, even the word—at this time. The secretary of defense was still Donald Rumsfeld, the man who'd side-lined the chief of staff of the army, General Eric Shinseki, for having the temerity to suggest that Iraq might be something other than a cakewalk, who'd overridden the objections of his war planners and structured the invasion force in such a way that it had enough firepower to unseat Saddam Hussein but not enough manpower to ensure something stable would replace him.[8]

Rumsfeld's preferred number for the invasion and post-conflict stabilization of Iraq was only 75,000 troops, even though Pentagon war planners estimated that 400,000 Americans, and as many allied troops as possible, would be needed.[9] After a sharp tussle between professionals and political appointees in the Pentagon (during which one senior officer retired early in protest rather than execute a plan he knew to be disastrously flawed) the force that invaded Iraq was just over 200,000—sufficient to defeat Iraq's regular military, but criminally inadequate to contain the chaos after the fall of Saddam, or counter the escalating insurgency once the lid came off his regime.[10]

After Saddam fell, Rumsfeld insisted on leaving the absolute minimum force in Iraq, then oversaw Ambassador L. Paul "Jerry" Bremer's disastrous de-Ba'athification edict and the disbanding of the Iraqi Army, two critical early missteps that put 400,000 fighting men—along with middle-class Iraqis who'd been nominal party members, as many had to be if they wanted a job—out on the street with no future, homicidally intense grievances and all their weapons.

In Anbar province, the heartland of Sunni Iraq, whole units of the Iraqi Army, with their weapons, equipment and command structure intact, were sitting on the side-lines during the first few weeks after the invasion, observing developments, reluctant to join the resistance but seeing fewer and fewer alternatives as time went on. Periodically, in the early days, their leaders would approach coalition commanders to explain that they were ready and able to help.[11] The lucky ones would be rebuffed or told to go join the lines at the recruiting office like everyone else; the unlucky were arrested or even killed. Many had expected—had been *told* to expect, over many years, through carefully constructed messages delivered by U.S. intelligence—that if they stood aside in the event of an invasion, they'd play a key role in stabilizing post-Saddam Iraq and retain their influence.[12] When reality turned out to be the opposite, these Iraqi officers and their troops saw Bremer's policies as outright treachery, and their anger at the betrayal boiled over.

When these men joined the armed resistance, and the war promptly went critical, Rumsfeld denied reality and contradicted

General John Abizaid, commander of U.S. Central Command, who'd told Congress the insurgency was far from fading.[13] But senior military officers, as well as many influential civilians, were painfully aware of the lives (American, allied and Iraqi) being lost through Rumsfeld's obstinacy. They began pushing for change: Major General David Petraeus led the effort to develop a counterinsurgency doctrine, while General Jack Keane, Dr. Frederick Kagan, Colonel H.R. McMaster and Professor Eliot Cohen argued for what eventually became the 2007 "Surge"—though it couldn't be implemented until President Bush finally fired Rumsfeld in late 2006. Hank Crumpton, a CIA officer with decades of experience in clandestine operations, who had overseen the intelligence agency's outstandingly successful unconventional warfare campaign against the Taliban in 2001, was appointed ambassador for counterterrorism in late 2005. As the QDR wrapped up, Crumpton asked Canberra to second me to the State Department as his chief strategist.

Less than a month later, as a newly minted civilian official, feeling faintly ridiculous in my still-unstained body armor, with a brand new encrypted cellphone and one of those funky, retro briefcases that chains to your wrist, I stepped off a helicopter into the heat, noise and dust of Landing Zone Washington in the Green Zone, the fortified compound in downtown Baghdad that had become Ground Zero for the greatest strategic screw-up since Hitler's invasion of Russia.

3

ABYSS

Iraq and Afghanistan, 2005–6

I mentioned two factors that undermined Disaggregation; the first, clearly, was Iraq. When I arrived on that first trip in 2005, Baghdad was not yet as horrific as it later became. People still lazed on white plastic sun-lounges by the swimming pool at the U.S. Embassy— once Saddam's Presidential Palace and, like his other palaces, furnished in a head-scratchingly bizarre style, ornate yet shoddy, best described as "Mesopotamian Fascist." Near the pool was a sign reading "No Drinking While Armed," and in the cafeteria people who'd served under Bremer had coffee mugs that said, "Iraq: We Were Winning When I Left." We hadn't left, of course: as soon as I ventured outside the wire to meet community leaders and work with our counterterrorism teams, it was clear that by any objective standard Iraq was a mess. Hundreds of civilians were being killed every week—1,059 in the first three weeks of 2006 alone.[1] Every day, oily black pillars of car-bomb smoke rolled up from across Baghdad, and you could hear the dull sound of an AK-47 or the whump of a grenade from any point on the horizon, any night of the week.

One of those nights, I was outside the bar that some CIA officers had built in a bombed-out house near the Palace, sitting in the dark, the night air cooling my sunburn after a few days with a light infantry unit working the "belts," the zone of agricultural settlement and satellite towns around Baghdad that had become an incubator for the insurgency. Abruptly, two helicopters roared a few hundred feet overhead, popping decoy flares to confuse heat-seeking missiles. It was the coalition force commander, General George Casey, returning from Camp Victory, the vast base complex near Baghdad International Airport. I flinched as the noise washed over me. Then it hit me—as if I'd been punched, as if one of the flares had fallen into my lap—that we were losing the war. How else, three years into the occupation, with 160,000 American troops on the ground,[2] could the commanding general still not move 10 miles across downtown Baghdad without such precautions? How could we stabilize Iraq if we couldn't even secure its capital? (Later in the war a friend of mine, a U.S. Army general with a famously dry sense of humor, signed off an email "Note to Self: consider renaming Camp Victory.")

Earlier I likened President Bush's decision to invade Iraq to Hitler's invasion of Russia, and that's no exaggeration: the two blunders were exactly equivalent. It should go without saying that Western powers in Iraq were in no way comparable to Nazi Germany in their ideology, treatment of civilians or strategic objectives—quite the reverse. Yet in invading Iraq with the job still unfinished in Afghanistan, President Bush made precisely the same strategic error as Hitler did in invading the Soviet Union. In 1940 Hitler conquered Western Europe, leaving Britain isolated and heavily damaged, so that it seemed inevitable that Churchill would eventually sue for peace. The Soviet Union was a long-term adversary, contained by treaty and posing no immediate threat, but in mid-1941 the moment seemed right for an invasion, which was expected to be a pushover. When it wasn't, Hitler was caught between two fires. The Russian quagmire trapped him, Britain recovered, America joined the war, resistance spread through German-occupied Europe, and the second front opened in Normandy; and once the Soviet Union began its series of ferocious counter-offensives on the Eastern Front, Hitler's defeat became, if not inevitable, then a matter of time, effort, and will.

Likewise, as early as December 2001, with the Battle of Tora Bora still raging on the Afghan–Pakistani border, U.S. Central Command, on direction from Washington, began transferring assets from Afghanistan, rebalancing for a future invasion of Iraq. The job was far from finished in Afghanistan: bin Laden's location was still unknown, the Bonn Conference (the UN-sponsored talks to create a future Republic of Afghanistan) had just ended, and the effort to stand up a stable government to guard the country against a Taliban return had barely begun. When bin Laden and Zawahiri resurfaced in Pakistan later in 2002, there was the complex problem of how to deal with them, and the thornier issue of Pakistani complicity with the Taliban. Rather than face this question—the classic twenty-first-century problem of how to wage war on non-state actors who hide in countries with which you're technically at peace—President Bush and his team turned to the seemingly simpler (because state-based) problem of Iraq.

Like Stalin's Russia in 1941, Saddam's Iraq was a long-term adversary: President Bush's father, George H.W. Bush (with Dick Cheney as his secretary of defense and Colin Powell as Chairman of the Joint Chiefs of Staff), had fought Saddam in the First Gulf War in 1990–91. President Bill Clinton had launched two follow-on operations against him, including multinational airstrikes in 1993 and 1998. Clinton had also approved a CIA effort to sponsor a revolt against Saddam by Kurdish guerrillas and members of Ahmad Chalabi's Iraqi National Congress in 1995.[3] After the revolt failed, President Clinton maintained sanctions and no-fly zones over Iraq, at great expense and risk for U.S. aircrews, and signed into law, in 1998, an act of Congress (the Iraq Liberation Act) that made regime change in Iraq a formal U.S. goal.

By the end of the Clinton administration, though regime change in Iraq remained official American policy, Saddam was partially contained by sanctions and posed no immediate threat to his neighbors, while more than a decade of international embargoes and no-fly zones had seriously eroded his military effectiveness—Vice Admiral Thomas R. Wilson, head of the Defense Intelligence Agency, testified as much (in so many words) before the Senate Armed Services Committee on 19 March 2002, exactly one year before the war began.[4] Precisely because the Iraqi military was seen as so weak, the invasion was expected to be a pushover, and the lightning march to Baghdad in March–April 2003, along with the spectacular rout of Saddam's elite Republican Guard, seemed to confirm this. Then things fell apart.

The bare-bones invasion force Rumsfeld had insisted upon was enough to push Saddam off his perch, but not to contain the chaos of his fall. And senior leaders in the administration had given little thought to post-war stabilization. In part this was a side-effect of the incredible tempo of the coalition's advance: Iraqis weren't the only ones disoriented by the speed of the invasion, which went from Kuwait to Kurdistan in just three weeks, giving post-conflict stabilization teams (under retired U.S. Army Lieutenant General Jay Garner) little time to get a grip on a chaotic, constantly-changing situation. During the first days of the occupation, my friend and colleague Nate Fick—commanding an elite U.S. Marine Corps Force Reconnaissance platoon that had spearheaded the advance to Baghdad—assessed any meaningful reconstruction effort as totally absent, and the U.S. impact on establishing order as "just about zero."[5] And things only went downhill from there.

In another sense, though, the failure to prepare for post-war problems was no accident, since the plan (at least for Cheney, now vice president, and within Rumsfeld's coterie of political appointees at the Pentagon) was emphatically *not* for a long-term effort to occupy and stabilize Iraq, but rather for a quick-in, quick-out operation in which the Americans would topple Saddam, hand power to a designated successor, and ride victorious into the sunset. In part, the lack of postwar planning occurred because looking too closely at post-conflict costs or risks might have undermined the argument for war: "postwar planning was an impediment to war … because detailed thought about the postwar situation meant facing costs and potential problems, and thus weakened the case for launching a 'war of choice.'"[6] Likewise, as intelligence agencies gathered information on the situation in Iraq, much of their effort was beside the point, since "Bush and his aides were looking for intelligence not to guide their policy on Iraq but to market it. The intelligence would be the basis not for launching a war but for selling it."[7]

In part also, Rumsfeld was trying to repeat the light-footprint, rapid success of 2001 in Afghanistan, when overthrowing the Taliban cost very few American lives and brought a smooth transition to an internationally recognized interim administration under Hamid Karzai. The swift success of 2001 was not only a victory over the Taliban, but also a vindication of Secretary Rumsfeld's ideas in the face of opposition from the Joint Chiefs of Staff, whom Rumsfeld considered hidebound and conventional. It gave rise to a genuine, triumphalist—if utterly and tragically mistaken—belief that a "New American Way of War," characterized by precision weapons, advanced intelligence surveillance and reconnaissance (ISR), and a high-tech "system of systems" (a suite of capabilities known to insiders as "Transformation" or the "Revolution in Military Affairs" and to the public as "Shock and Awe"), had changed the rules of the game, so that the risk and cost considerations inherent in war, familiar to every professional soldier and field operator, no longer applied, and could safely be ignored by civilian policy-makers and pundits who knew better.[8] Afghanistan (which still looked like a success as Iraq was being planned in 2002) seemed to prove that the United States and its allies were effectively invincible when applying this new way of war: opposition to Rumsfeld's light-footprint invasion plan thus seemed like old-think, especially when it emanated from the same Joint Staff whose caution had proven so unfounded in Afghanistan.

Journalist James Fallows cited the willful naïveté of the group of policy-makers around Secretary Rumsfeld and Vice President Cheney at this time. Fallows wrote that the Bush administration went "Blind Into Baghdad"—arguing that the occupation became "a debacle not because the government did no planning but because a vast amount of expert planning was willfully ignored by the people in charge ... U.S. government predictions about postwar Iraq's problems have proved as accurate as the assessments of pre-war Iraq's strategic threat have proved flawed. But the administration will be condemned for what it did with what was known. The problems the United States has encountered are precisely the ones its own expert agencies warned against."[9]

Fallows' analysis rings true for me, given what I know of the counterinsurgency advice offered to the United States and allied governments before the invasion. As I said, "counterinsurgency" was a dirty word at this time among higher-ups in the Pentagon. Still, as Fallows notes, the insurgency that emerged after the occupation wasn't just predictable, it was *predicted* in a series of increasingly strident papers, briefings and memos by experts in guerrilla warfare, counterinsurgency and stabilization operations—a slew of specialists at the RAND Corporation, the CIA, the U.S. Army War College, the Marine Corps University and the Center for Strategic and International Studies (CSIS). I can't recall one reputable expert in guerrilla warfare who didn't predict—clearly, though not always publicly—some version of the disaster that followed. All warned of the risk of armed resistance and a long and difficult occupation in the face of insurgency; all were ignored.

In the event, the late Ahmad Chalabi, Rumsfeld's chosen successor to Saddam, failed to gain the military or political support needed to control the situation. Unlike Hamid Karzai—a credible anti-Taliban leader with decades of experience, thousands of fighters, and political support from inside and outside Afghanistan—Chalabi turned up with fewer than 100 fighters, a mixed reputation (at best) among the few Iraqis who'd even heard of him, a checkered and possibly criminal past in Jordan, and no support outside neo-conservative think-tanks in Washington D.C. and Douglas Feith's Office of Special Plans at the Pentagon.[10] The Afghan model—light-footprint invasion, quick transition to an internationally endorsed interim government, elections as soon as the country was stable enough, and then head for home—failed in the utterly different conditions of Iraq.

By comparison to Afghanistan, which was a strong society with a weak state and virtually no infrastructure, Iraq—with its factories, freeways, universities and hospitals—was a developed country. But it was a weak society: Iraqis had suffered a generation of traumatic abuse under Saddam, who systematically culled the nation's intelligentsia, destroying anyone with the vision and leadership to threaten the regime, promoting self-interested conformists, and dividing elites along ethnic, religious, tribal, class and urban–rural lines. Iraqi leaders—those who'd survived Saddam's bloodbath—were fractious, fearful and riven by sectarian and factional dissent, while the population at large was suffering something akin to a national post-traumatic stress disorder.

Now, as Saddam's dictatorship dissolved, what was left of the elites fell into squabbling. An authority vacuum developed at the top of Iraqi politics, while resistance festered on the street and the country burned. Citizen safety evaporated: revenge killing, theft and score-settling escalated, while coalition troops stood by without orders to intervene. People looted every last toilet seat, pencil sharpener and light bulb from the office buildings of a government that had systematically stolen from them for decades, and then turned against their neighbors. The breakdown of order in Iraq's cities was a terrifying shock to a population brought up under Saddam's authoritarianism, and the failure of essential services (food, water, electricity, sanitation) undermined public confidence among people conditioned by long experience to be utterly dependent on the state. Heavy-handed coalition efforts to counter the resistance alienated ordinary Iraqis, creating thousands of what I later described as "accidental guerrillas,"[11] and by late 2003 we were bogged down in our own two-front war.

At this point, jihadists like Abu Musab al-Zarqawi came out of the woodwork. Zarqawi, born in 1966 as Ahmad Fadil Nazzal al-Khalayleh, grew up in the Jordanian industrial town of Zarqa, north of Amman. As an adolescent, he became a small-time criminal and drug dealer. He embraced militant Islam after several run-ins with the local police, and travelled to Afghanistan in 1989, just as the Soviet–Afghan War was ending. On returning to Jordan he did time in prison for forming a terrorist group to overthrow the Jordanian government. After his release under a general amnesty in 1999, he returned to Afghanistan where he formed a new group, at-Tawhid wa'l-Jihad ("Monotheism and Jihad"), established a terrorist training camp in the far-western Afghan province of Herat, and fought in loose alliance with AQ (though never under its formal authority) against the U.S.-led invasion of 2001.

After the Taliban fell, Zarqawi (who'd been wounded in the chest during the invasion) fled westward into neighboring Iran for medical treatment, and then made his way to Iraq to organize resistance against the expected invasion. He was probably in Iraq at least nine months before the coalition invaded, recruiting underground cells, building an auxiliary network and establishing a system of weapons caches and safe houses—the critical supporting infrastructure for a future guerrilla campaign—but his relationship with Saddam remains unclear. According to a CIA report that was only fully declassified in April 2015, the Iraqi government knew by June 2002 that Zarqawi was present in Iraq under an assumed name (a fact also known to U.S. intelligence at the time, and which Vice President Cheney, Secretary of State Colin Powell and others advanced as proof that Saddam was in league with AQ).[12] On the other hand, Jordanian intelligence and court documents suggest Zarqawi was in Syria in 2002, and only entered Iraq later.[13] In either case, on balance, it seems probable Zarqawi had no direct relationship with the Ba'athists until *after* the invasion.

Likewise, as far as we know, Zarqawi was never under AQ authority before the Iraq war. Mustafa Hamid—a leading militant who fought in Afghanistan, visited Zarqawi in his camp near Herat, and (like him) escaped into Iran after 2001—told Australian counterterrorism expert Leah Farrell that "from the beginning, Abu Musab al-Zarqawi was very independent ... he was not under the control of al-Qaeda at all, but he had a good friendly relationship with them."[14] Zarqawi did eventually pledge *bayat* (allegiance) to bin Laden, bringing his group under nominal AQ authority in October 2004 as Tanzim Qaidat al-Jihad fi'l Bilad al-Rafidayn, "the Organisation of the Base of Jihad [i.e. al-Qaeda] in Mesopotamia," usually Anglicized as al-Qaeda in Iraq (AQI). But this was largely a matter of marketing—a propaganda move rather than a formal command relationship. Even after the rebranding, Zarqawi remained financially and operationally independent, and the relationship between him and the AQ leaders would soon collapse.

Now, exploiting the post-invasion insecurity, Zarqawi and his nascent jihadist guerrilla movement set out to foster conflict between the occupation force and the population.[15] Zarqawi's cells were behind several early confrontations, which were portrayed at the time as spontaneous acts of protest that turned violent through Western naïveté and heavy-handedness. In fact, these were provocations: as insurgents do, Zarqawi was manufacturing incidents and manipulating the resulting grievances, his group acting as a catalyst to turn chaos into uprising. By summer 2003—through provocations like these, and spectacular attacks like the massive truck bomb at the Canal Hotel in Baghdad with which Zarqawi murdered Sérgio Vieira de Mello, Special Representative of the UN Secretary-General, and twenty others—he and those like him had forced the international community behind blast walls and inside armored vehicles, separating them from ordinary Iraqis and turning wary cooperation into open resistance. As Osama bin Laden's deputy, Ayman al-Zawahiri, said in September 2004, the insurgency "turned America's plan upside down. The defeat of America in Iraq and Afghanistan has become just a matter of time, with God's help. The Americans in both countries are between two fires. If they carry on, they will bleed to death—and if they pull out, they lose everything."[16]

By October 2003 the Taliban, recovering from their defeat of 2001, had formed a new government-in-exile (the Quetta Shura) in Pakistan, and launched an insurgency in Afghanistan. By mid-2004 a renewed Taliban insurgency was in full swing, and this two-front dynamic—not one but two simultaneous large-scale land wars in Asia—became a hole in the heart of Western strategy: the cost, in human life, credibility, money and time, of extracting ourselves from the unforced error of Iraq weakened our efforts to stop the rot in Afghanistan, and fatally undermined the broader impact of Disaggregation.

Indeed, as U.S. counterterrorism strategist Audrey Kurth Cronin commented in her response to an earlier version of this argument, the effect of Iraq on Disaggregation was so dire that the strategy may have been dead on arrival, given that it didn't emerge as official policy until 2005, when much of the damage had been done and things were already deteriorating rapidly in Iraq and Afghanistan.[17] Disaggregation, in hindsight, may have been the right strategy too late—a fitting approach for a situation that no longer existed.

In any case, once the insurgency in Iraq really hit its stride after March 2004, the demand for resources created by the escalating conflict, like the cost in lives lost and ruined, was stupendous, as was the drain on policy-makers' attention. It was impossible to get leaders to focus on resurgent violence in Afghanistan, the emergence of al-Shabaab in Somalia, the growing Pakistani Taliban, rising anti-Americanism in countries subjected to drone strikes, proliferating terror cells in Europe, AQ franchises on other continents, or any of the other issues we could have addressed—and perhaps prevented—had the United States and its allies (including Australia and the UK) not been mired in Iraq.

Perhaps most crucially, the crisis atmosphere made U.S. policymakers reluctant to press for reforms among authoritarian regimes—many of which were American allies—in the Middle East and North Africa, even though anyone who'd spent time in the region recognized these regimes' oppressiveness was a driver of terrorism and an exploitable grievance for AQ. Of all the members of President Bush's cabinet, it was the secretary of state, Condoleezza Rice, who called most clearly for change. In June 2005, in a speech at the American University in Cairo, she said:

For 60 years, my country, the United States, pursued stability at the expense of democracy in this region, here in the Middle East—and we achieved neither. Now, we are taking a different course. We are supporting the democratic aspirations of all people ... As President Bush said in his Second Inaugural Address: "America will not impose our style of government on the unwilling. Our goal instead is to help others find their own voice, to attain their own freedom, and to make their own way." We know these advances will not come easily, or all at once. We know that different societies will find forms of democracy that work for them. When we talk about democracy, though, we are referring to governments that protect certain basic rights for all their citizens—among these, the right to speak freely, the right to associate, the right to worship as you wish, the freedom to educate your children—boys and girls—and freedom from the midnight knock of the secret police. Securing these rights is the hope of every citizen, and the duty of every government.[18]

But as violence escalated in Iraq, and foreign fighters flocked to the conflict from Saudi Arabia, Syria, Jordan and Egypt, Secretary Rice—and Hank Crumpton, the counterterrorism ambassador—were forced to focus on short-term efforts to stabilize pro-Western (albeit often feckless or authoritarian) regimes, rather than on the long-term democratic reforms Rice believed were ultimately the only way to break the endless cycle of terrorism and oppression.

As Crumpton's chief strategist, I spent weeks in one war zone or another—traveling to Iraq, Pakistan, Afghanistan, the Horn of Africa and Southeast Asia—gathering data, helping to set up joint counterterrorism operations, collating field reports that consistently showed a deteriorating situation. In mid-2006, after spending time in and around a series of frontier outposts in Afghanistan and Pakistan, I wrote a detailed assessment for Secretary Rice, laying out our lack of progress against the growing cross-border insurgency. This was entirely obvious to anyone with even the slightest knowledge of conditions there, and all my bosses agreed—in principle—but that didn't mean they had the resources or the attention span to do anything about it. Iraq overwhelmed even the U.S. government's organizational capacity: it was so big, so bad, and so politically problematic that it crowded out everything else.

Robert Gates, Rumsfeld's successor as secretary of defense (and his mirror image in virtually every way), understood the opportunity cost of this tunnel vision: asked during his Congressional confirmation hearing what his priorities would be as Secretary of

Defense, Gates said "Iraq, Iraq and Iraq."[19] He was completely correct—Iraq *had* to be at the top of the to-do list, given the disaster that had developed on his predecessor's watch. Nevertheless, in digging ourselves out of our hole in Iraq, we were burning irreplaceable time, sapping political will, exhausting public patience, squandering financial and human resources, drawing attention and effort away from other critical problems, and creating a new monster—Zarqawi's group, later to become ISIS.

And Zarqawi was far from the only threat. If we extend the World War II analogy, Hitler faced a war on two fronts after 1941, but at least he was operating on what strategists call "interior lines": he held one central block of territory, could shift assets from one front to another, his supply lines were entirely within territory he controlled, and as the conflict continued his forces were pushed closer to their bases, making them increasingly easy to supply and support. By contrast, Western powers after 2003 operated on exterior lines—dealing with two major wars that were widely separated geographically, so that they had to be approached from extended supply routes through hostile regions (one through Pakistan, one through Russia and Central Asia, and one running the gauntlet from Kuwait to Baghdad). And these supply lines grew even longer, more costly and less secure as the twin conflicts continued, limiting the coalition's ability to shift resources from one front to another.

If any player had the interior-lines advantage at this time, it was Iran, sitting in a central position with Afghanistan to its east and Iraq to its west. Tehran hastened to capitalize on this geographical advantage. Iranian forces sponsored Shi'a militias like the Mahdi Army of Muqtada al-Sadr, the Badr Organisation, the Hizbollah Brigades, and several other Iraqi clandestine groups. Iran sent operatives from the Quds Force, the covert action arm of the Iranian Revolutionary Guards Corps (IRGC) under the command of General Qasem Soleimani, into Iraq to sponsor attacks by these "special groups" as part of the diversifying insurgency.

Although those of us who served in Iraq always saw Iranian actions as aggressive—understandably, I guess, since they were doing their best to kill us—it's worth mentioning that Tehran's motivation to acquire nuclear weapons, sponsor terrorists, launch covert operations, and expand its influence across the region may partly have been a completely rational defensive reaction to early U.S. moves in the War on Terror. To be clear, Iran's clerical–authoritarian regime has a pattern of aggression and subversion stretching back to the Tehran embassy hostage ordeal in 1979–81, the Beirut embassy and Marine barracks bombings of 1983, support for terrorism against Israel and engagement with organized crime and terrorist networks across Latin America, Africa and the Middle East. U.S. actions after 2001 didn't cause or justify this behavior—which long pre-dated 9/11—any more than they excused the atrocities Soleimani and his cells later sponsored in Iraq, Lebanon, Israel, Yemen and Syria. But by creating a crisis atmosphere, Western actions strengthened hard-liners and gave even moderates in the Iranian regime sound, rational reasons to continue and escalate this behavior.

Think for a moment about how things appeared from Tehran. Looking back, many Iranians (even members of the country's vast, well-educated, liberal younger generation) saw a history of *Western* aggression, ranging from the 1953 British–American plot to over-throw Iran's elected prime minister, Mohammad Mossadegh, through support for the Shah's regime (including, by the way, his nuclear program—the United States gave Iran its first reactor in 1959, France and Germany transferred nuclear technology in the 1970s, and the Shah's nuclear scientists trained at the Massachusetts Institute of Technology), to the 1980 Desert One raid, the "tanker war" of the 1980s, the 1988 shoot-down of an Iranian airliner by an American warship and—worst of all—Western support for Saddam during the Iran–Iraq War.[20]

Iran, like Russia, had a long-standing relationship with the anti-Taliban Northern Alliance in Afghanistan, and after U.S. forces partnered with the Northern Alliance during the invasion of 2001 there was a brief period of cooperation between Washington and Tehran against AQ. But in January 2002, President Bush named Iran, Iraq and North Korea as the "Axis of Evil." Fifteen months later, Saddam's regime was swept away, Saddam himself was left cowering in the spider-hole near ad-Dawr, a town near Tikrit from which he'd be hauled out to prison and eventual death, and Iraq was under American occupation. Two weeks after Baghdad fell, Charles Krauthammer—a conservative columnist close to figures in the administration—said "We are in a position, after the shock and awe of this war, of influencing the behavior if not the composition of regimes in Iran, Syria and elsewhere."[21] Other public and political leaders made similar comments. For anyone watching from Tehran the message was clear: "You're next." The drive for nuclear weapons—or, better (because vaguer and less likely to draw a sharp response), to become a nuclear threshold power—became Tehran's insurance policy against regime change, a way of deterring a U.S. move against Iran in the wake of the Iraq War.

And as the occupation soured, the build-up of U.S. troops into Iraq and Afghanistan offered Iran both grave danger and great opportunity. On the one hand, should these countries ever fully stabilize, the United States would be ideally positioned to use them as a base from which to invade Iran across one or both frontiers or, even worse from the regime's standpoint, to sponsor unrest among Iran's change-hungry youth and its jumpy Kurdish, Baluch and Arab minorities. On the other hand, Iran was now perfectly placed to destabilize these same neighboring countries: many key players in Iraqi politics (including Ahmad Chalabi, now heading the de-Ba'athification program in Baghdad) had close ties to Tehran, the Iranians had a long-standing relationship with the Iraqi Kurds, several Shi'a militant groups and political movements were funded by the Quds Force, and it was easy to manipulate the post-occupation chaos.

Likewise, in Afghanistan, Iran established close ties to the new Afghan leaders, maintained its influence with Northern Alliance warlords who'd been strengthened by the invasion, deepened its economic reach, and began sponsoring armed groups. In combination with the push for nuclear capability, keeping Iraq and Afghanistan unstable—and the U.S. and its allies bogged down—became key pillars of an Iranian security strategy to deter any U.S. move against Iran. With the Iranians now backing Shi'a militants, from March 2004 onward there was not one insurgency in Iraq, but at least six.

On the Shi'a side were communitarian militias, Iranian proxies, and the Sadrists of the Mahdi Army, a movement of poor, pious Shi'a, engaged as much in social revolution as in sectarian warfare. On the Sunni side were jihadists like Zarqawi, secular Sunni nationalists, who rejected the transformation of Iraq into what they saw as an Iranian satellite, and former regime elements.

There were significant overlaps among these six basic groups. For example, Izzat Ibrahim al-Douri—vice-chairman of Saddam Hussein's

Revolutionary Command Council, "King of Clubs" on the famous deck of cards issued to help invasion troops identify regime leaders, and the most senior Ba'athist to evade capture in 2003—was running a resistance network of religious groups and former officers which he'd organized before the war, using attack plans, safe houses, support networks and weapons caches established years earlier, and was all too ready to cooperate with Sunni nationalists and jihadists if it would further his goal of kicking the occupiers out.[22] Indeed, al-Douri was part of a Salafized (militantly religious) faction within Saddam's military, which Saddam himself had sponsored as part of a so-called "Faith Campaign" after his defeat in the 1991 Gulf War, as a way of ensuring the loyalty of his officers and unifying Iraqi society around a Sunni-dominated, more overtly religious, vision for Iraq. Thus, for Ba'athists like al-Douri and his underground cells, there was little difference between support for the regime, allegiance to a Sunni nationalist Iraqi identity, and jihad.

Not everyone was so ideological. As well as the politically-motivated groups, criminal networks—built on pre-war tribal or business relationships—fostered a shady cast of characters, "conflict entrepreneurs" who used classic guerrilla tactics but fought not for victory (to end the war on terms favorable to their side) but rather to perpetuate the violence, because it brought them riches, power and status. Each group had its factions, and its factions-within-factions—I counted more than 150 separate militant groups at one point in 2007.

And then there were the Kurds, an entire third of Iraq that had risen against Saddam in the early 1990s to carve out its own well-armed autonomous region, and one of the few places in the whole country where most people didn't actively despise us, but which was clearly not likely to accept central government authority any time soon. After expelling Saddam's government from their territory in the 1980s and early 1990s the two major Kurdish political groupings—the Kurdish Democratic Party (KDP) and the People's Union of Kurdistan (PUK)—had fought a brief civil war, but then managed to maintain a delicate balance of power, resulting in political stability that enabled economic growth and made Kurdistan one of the safest and most developed areas in the country. But the Kurds' national project was fundamentally destabilizing to their neighbors—significant Kurdish minorities existed in Syria, Turkey and

Iran, and the Turks were fighting a protracted campaign against the left-wing Kurdish separatist movement, the Kurdistan Workers' Party (Partiya Karkerên Kurdistanê, PKK). Moreover, jihadist groups such as Ansar al-Islam—along with several AQ cells—were active in the Kurdish region. In any case, whatever their attitude to the international community, the Kurds remained wary of Baghdad, relations with the new Iraqi government were fraught, and sporadic incidents of violence broke out along the Kurdish—Arab frontier and in disputed territories such as the area around Kirkuk.

Within this crowded conflict space, external players extended their influence. Iran backed the Shi'a militias, sent Quds Force operatives to ensure its dominance, paid off politicians, sponsored political parties, engaged in economic warfare, gave its proxies the deadliest explosive devices seen in the war (EFPs, explosively-formed projectiles that converted a copper slug into a jet of plasma that could punch through armored vehicles like a blowtorch through butter) and ran covert operations to bog coalition forces down. For their part, some Sunni Arab states turned a blind eye to fighters travelling from or through their territory, from North Africa, the Middle East, and (in smaller numbers than today) Asia and Europe. This sectarian dynamic—soon amounting to a proxy war between Shi'a Iran and the Sunni states—made the conflict increasingly violent and destabilizing as it went on, and began to draw in regional players like Turkey, Saudi Arabia and Israel, each of whom considered Iran's expansion at least as big a threat as AQ or Zarqawi.

Zarqawi's group specialized in exploiting this sectarian violence, and the war took an extraordinarily nasty turn after February 2006, when his cells bombed one of the holiest sites in Shi'a Islam, the al-Askari shrine at Samarra, unleashing a full-scale religious war as Shi'a groups hit the streets seeking revenge against Sunnis. By September 2006, hundreds of civilians were being killed every week, mostly in Baghdad and the belts,[23] in a cycle of kidnapping, assassination and tit-for-tat atrocities that the occupation force seemed powerless to stop.

Shi'a groups operated mainly defensively, protecting their communities against jihadists and Sunni nationalists, but this didn't stop them kidnapping, torturing and killing Sunni civilians when they could. Because Sunnis had boycotted the January 2005 parliamentary elections—turnout was only 2 per cent in Anbar, for example—Shi'a parties controlled the government ministries responsible for essential services. Hadi al-Ameri, a Shi'a militia leader and head of the Iranian-sponsored Badr Organization, became Iraq's transport minister. He stacked the institutions he controlled with loyalists, while stockpiling international assistance money (intended for reconstruction and essential services) as a war chest against the inevitable day of conflict with his rivals. Likewise, Bayan Jabr, minister of the interior, later finance minister, and another Badr commander, was accused by John Pace, the senior UN human rights official in Iraq, of torturing hundreds of Sunnis to death every month in Baghdad alone, using killing rooms inside the Ministry of the Interior building.[24] Pace told British journalists Andrew Buncombe and Patrick Cockburn "that up to three-quarters of the corpses stacked in the city's mortuary show evidence of gunshot wounds to the head or injuries caused by drill-bits or burning cigarettes. Much of the killing, he said, was carried out by Shia Muslim groups under the control of the Ministry of the Interior."[25] And over at the Health Ministry, the Sadrist Deputy Minister, Hakim al-Zamili, was accused of using ambulances to ferry weapons and ammunition for death squads that kidnapped and killed Sunnis.[26]

Besides the direct killing of Sunnis, sectarian Shi'a leaders could manipulate access to essential services in order to force people to flee Baghdad's few remaining Sunni enclaves, a subtle but effective form of "ethnic cleansing." In mid-2006, for example, many Shi'a areas had constant electricity while Sunni districts were lucky to get four hours a day[27]—this in a place where water and sewage systems are electrically powered, so that a power outage often means a water outage as well. Banks and financial institutions serving Sunnis were also frequently bombed or shut down, so that Sunnis had little choice but to keep their money under the mattress at home, making them vulnerable to robberies and home invasions, as well as to snap searches by Shi'a police who might confiscate funds and accuse families of stockpiling money to help the insurgency. Likewise, Sunnis—most of whom believed Shi'a death squads were running the ambulances and hospitals—had little or no access to the health system. Many took the hint and left.

For its part, AQI sought to provoke the Shi'a paramilitaries (and the Shi'a-dominated Iraqi Police and Army) against the Sunni community, trying to inflict as much pain as possible on its own people. It took me a while to figure out the reason for this, but the difference in tactics was clear from the start. For example, you might be driving down a narrow street in a Shi'a neighbourhood and feel a sudden chill—no kids on the street, windows open, people stepping into doorways as you passed. You'd get that prickly feeling in the back of your neck and know you were about to be hit. People would pull children into houses, and open windows so the blast wouldn't break them, because they knew an attack was coming—the insurgents had warned them, because their goal was to protect their own population.

By contrast, in Sunni areas, AQI would rock and roll with no warning, launching ambushes or detonating car bombs without compunction, in streets packed with their own people. This was more than mere callousness: it was a deliberate strategy of hurting their own. On 19 March 2007, in the mainly Sunni district of Adhamiyah, for example, a man drove a car into a market with two children—a boy and a girl, aged six or seven—in the back seat. The guards let them through, since they were clearly a family. Once inside, the driver jumped out, the children began screaming in terror, and the car detonated with a blast that tore them apart and killed several shoppers. This was one of only three enemy actions in my whole time in Iraq that made me cry actual tears. *Who would do that to a child?*

I wanted to scream. I wanted to hunt down the human filth responsible for this, look them in the eyes, and shoot them on the spot. At that moment I knew the hatred every Iraqi parent felt—and provoking that loathing in the Shi'a, and directing it against Sunnis in a cycle of escalating violence and fear, was the twisted genius of AQI.

For AQI's atrocities were driven by a brutal political logic: in provoking the Shi'a, Zarqawi hoped to bring such heavy retaliatory violence down on the Sunni community that they would be backed into a corner, where his group would be all that stood between Sunnis and the Shi'a death squads, giving people no choice but to support AQI, whatever they thought of its ideology. This utterly cynical strategy—founded on a tacit recognition that AQI's beliefs were so alien to most Iraqis that they'd never find many takers unless backed by trickery and force—meant that Shi'a killing Sunni was, paradoxically, *good* for AQI, and so Zarqawi's people would go out of their way to provoke the most horrific violence against their own people.

For example, fighters from an AQI cell might establish a safe house in a Sunni neighbourhood, creating a hideout in an abandoned row of buildings, fortifying compounds and mouse-holing connecting walls so they could move freely.[28] Then they'd assassinate a few local Sunnis in spectacularly brutal fashion to remind everyone else to keep their eyes down and their mouths shut. Once they'd created a safe base for their operations, AQI would begin to scout the neighboring Shi'a community, cruising the streets in groups of three or four, riding in vans, orange-and-white Baghdad taxis, or (their trademark) BMW sedans with the windows blacked out. They would kidnap young boys, torture them to death and dump the bodies—eyes gouged out, ears, little limbs and genitals hacked off, cigarette and blowtorch burns all over them or (an AQI trademark) the tops of their heads sliced open and electric drills thrust into their brains—back on the street in front of their houses.[29]

This is not a theoretical example, by the way—it's just a straight-up description of what they did to the twelve-year-old brother of a translator who worked with me in Baghdad. The goal was to trigger outrage and retaliation which, of course, would fall on the Sunnis in the neighboring district, not on the AQI cell that was actually responsible for the horror. Do this enough times, they reasoned, and the cycle of violence would become self-sustaining. Their goal was to provoke a sectarian conflict that would force Sunnis to close ranks in an AQI-led proto-state—which, by October 2006, they were already calling ad-Dawlah al-'Iraq al-Islamiyah—the Islamic State of Iraq (ISI). Like gangsters running a protection racket, they themselves created the violence from which they offered to protect people. Why leave it to chance?

And Shi'a groups, already nursing decades of grievance against the Sunnis who had dominated Iraq under Saddam and before, were all too happy to oblige. Besides the formal paramilitary groups like Badr and the other Iranian-backed organizations linked closely to Iraqi government institutions such as the Interior Ministry, free-lance and irregular Shi'a groups participated too. Abu Deraa, for example, a Shi'a militant in the slums of Sadr City on Baghdad's east side, became infamous for killing hundreds of Sunnis in this period, devising increasingly gruesome methods of slaughter—like any drug, blood-lust demands progressively bigger hits to satisfy its addicts—and earning himself the nickname "the Shi'ite Zarqawi." A YouTube video of June 2006 showed Abu Deraa fattening a young camel on a bottle of Coca-Cola, promising to butcher it and distribute the meat to the poor in Sadr City once he'd killed Tariq al-Hashimi, Iraq's Sunni vice president.[30]

The conflict entrepreneurs got in on the act too, with commercial kidnapping gangs auctioning off terrified children for slaughter, in a makeshift night market that operated under lights near the soccer stadium.[31] A whole underground industry grew up around the making of sectarian snuff videos—a light infantry unit I worked with in June 2007 found a makeshift studio in an abandoned industrial site south of Baghdad, with the Klieg lights and the video editing suite still set up, blood coagulating in dark pools on the floor and sprayed above head height on the walls.[32] All this was happening under our noses: coalition policy was to hand over to the Iraqi government as fast as possible, keep U.S. troops out of the cities, and live on large self-contained bases rather than among the people. The country was tearing itself apart while we kept our eyes on the exit.

As AQI was provoking and exploiting this vicious sectarian war, the central AQ leaders around bin Laden and Zawahiri, looking on from their Pakistani safe haven, were appalled. Not on humanitarian grounds: it was just that they had a different strategy in mind. Senior AQ leaders detested the Shi'a as heretics, but they viewed America and its allies as the main, and by far the more important, enemy. They sought a global Islamic uprising against the West, using an attrition strategy—bleeding the United States and its allies dry—to force Western influence out of the Muslim world, after which they planned to inherit the wreckage. As Zawahiri explained in a 2005 letter to Zarqawi, this strategy had four phases:

> The first stage: Expel the Americans from Iraq. The second stage: Establish an Islamic authority or emirate, then develop it and support it until it achieves the level of a caliphate over as much territory as you can, to spread its power in Iraq, i.e., in Sunni areas, in order to fill the void stemming from the departure of the Americans, immediately upon their exit … The third stage: Extend the jihad wave to the secular countries neighboring Iraq. The fourth stage: It may coincide with what came before: the clash with Israel, because Israel was established only to challenge any new Islamic entity.[33]

The goal of this approach—which, remember, came from AQ leaders in Pakistan, not from Zarqawi in Iraq—was to defeat the occupation through a mass uprising, and to do this they pursued what Marxist guerrillas would call a popular front strategy. For core leaders in AQ, a Shi'a–Sunni civil war in Iraq was, at best, a distraction from the main effort. As Zawahiri reassured Zarqawi, once the Americans were gone, they could always deal with the Shi'a and the apostates later.

Later in the same letter, Zawahiri—in a schoolmasterly, passive-aggressive tone that must have infuriated the hot-tempered Zarqawi, if he ever read it—posed a series of pointed questions about AQI's war on the Shi'a:

> Indeed, questions will circulate among mujahedeen circles and their opinion makers about the correctness of this conflict with the Shia at this time. Is it something that is unavoidable? Or, is it something can be put off until the force of the mujahed movement in Iraq gets stronger? And if some of the operations were necessary for self-defense, were all of the operations necessary? Or, were there some operations that weren't called for? And is the opening of another front now in addition to the front against the Americans and the government a wise decision? Or, does this conflict with the Shia lift the burden from the Americans by diverting the mujahedeen to the Shia, while the Americans continue to control matters from afar? And if the attacks on Shia leaders were necessary to put a stop to their plans, then why were there attacks on ordinary Shia? Won't this lead to reinforcing false ideas in their minds, even as it is incumbent on us to preach the call of Islam to them and explain and communicate to guide them to the truth? And can the mujahedeen kill all of the Shia in Iraq? Has any Islamic state in history ever tried that? And why kill ordinary Shia considering that they are forgiven because of their ignorance? And what loss will befall us if we did not attack the Shia?
>
> And do the brothers forget that we have more than one hundred prisoners—many of whom are from the leadership who are wanted in their countries—in the custody of the Iranians?
>
> And even if we attack the Shia out of necessity, then why do you announce this matter and make it public, which compels the Iranians to take counter-measures? And do the brothers forget that both we and the Iranians need to refrain from harming each other at this time in which the Americans are targeting us?[34]

The message was clear: Zarqawi's brutality was undermining AQ's popular front strategy, turning off supporters and alienating potential allies. Zarqawi was literally giving terrorism a bad name—and he was really starting to infuriate Zawahiri and the other AQ leaders.

Unlike Zawahiri, Zarqawi's group saw (and ISIS still sees) the Shi'a as the main enemy, not a distraction. AQI had an apocalyptic worldview, regarded the West and Iran as being in a de facto alliance against the true faith, and considered Shi'a domination the greatest threat. They perceived a four-fold opportunity: create such a horrendous sectarian conflict that Iraq would become ungovernable, cement AQI's control over the Sunnis, allow them to create an Islamic State, and help draw other Sunni states into a unified caliphate. For senior AQ figures like Zawahiri, the caliphate was a vague, utopian ideal that helped unify disparate groups precisely because it was so far off in the future.[35] By contrast, for Zarqawi and AQI—as for ISIS later—the caliphate was an immediate, real-world objective, and a sectarian war with the Shi'a was the quickest road to it.

This disagreement may have proven fatal for Zarqawi. Predictably, given the haughty, independent streak he'd shown from the start, he ignored Zawahiri, escalating his slaughter of the Shi'a and triggering a permanent rupture between AQI and the central AQ leaders. Zarqawi was killed on 7 June 2006 in a U.S. airstrike on his safe house in a palm plantation near Baqubah, a town north of Baghdad, after an intelligence tip-off and amid persistent rumors that AQ leaders had sold him out. But as Zarqawi fully intended, the slaughter outlived its instigator—like most ethnic and sectarian conflicts, once rolling, it took on a life of its own.

By November 2006 the violence had massively escalated, and U.S. public support for the occupation had plummeted, to the point where President Bush was forced to make a change. He replaced Rumsfeld, pushed Vice President Cheney aside and took direct charge of the war himself, appointing General Petraeus to command in Iraq. He then launched the Surge—a wholehearted attempt to apply Petraeus's counterinsurgency doctrine, along with more troops and a larger civilian effort on the ground to achieve greater political leverage and force an end to the conflict. This escalation of involvement was intended to protect the population, break AQI's hold of fear over the Sunni community, stop the cycle of sectarian violence, force the Iraqi government to be more inclusive

and less sectarian, and reduce civilian casualties. On a more fundamental level, President Bush's actions made it clear to Iraqis,
Americans and allies that his goal was to win, not just to leave. He
was belatedly recognizing an enduring truth; it's far better to avoid
getting dragged into counterinsurgency warfare in the first place,
but once you're there you have only two choices: you can leave
early, or you can leave well.

I'd worked with Petraeus throughout 2006 and had enormous
confidence in his ability to turn things around in Iraq. Not that I
necessarily thought that was possible—in fact, from what I'd seen
in Iraq over the preceding year, I gave the Surge a one-in-three
chance at best. But I felt that, hard though it would be, if Petraeus
couldn't do it, nobody could. A few days after President Bush's
speech launching the Surge, Petraeus asked Secretary Rice to lend
me to the U.S. Army, to serve on his personal staff in Baghdad as
Senior Counterinsurgency Advisor.

Before deploying, I flew to Australia for briefings and, late one hot
Canberra night in February 2007, was called to Prime Minister John
Howard's suite in Parliament House. I'd met him once before, in
1999, the night before Australia's military intervention in East Timor,
when—accompanied by Kim Beazley, Leader of the Opposition, in
a move of genuine bipartisan support—he'd visited our base in
Townsville to speak to the combat troops (including my infantry com-
pany) who'd be on the first planes in. Now, sitting in a green leather
armchair in his office, he talked about Australia's commitment to the
U.S. alliance, the need to play our part in freeing Iraq of terrorism,
how it was impossible for a multicultural, maritime trading nation
like Australia to be secure in an insecure world. At the end, in his
quiet, concise way, he gave me his personal guidance for the mission,
which I scribbled inside the cover of my field notebook: "You have
our 100% support. We're committed to making this work. Do whatever it takes to help P succeed. Keep me informed."

A week later I was back in Baghdad.

4

WATERFALL

Baghdad and the Belts, 2007

This time things were much, much worse. As I flew in on a C-130 troop transport from an airbase in Jordan, we had to circle for almost an hour above Baghdad International Airport. Shouting over the engine, the loadmaster told me the airspace over the city was closed, a fire-fight was raging on the edge of the Green Zone and F-16s were hitting snipers less than a thousand yards from the embassy, pulling gun runs directly over the Palace. We eventually landed, but had to wait five hours for permission to move to the Green Zone along Route Irish, then the most dangerous ten-mile stretch of road in the world. We made the run in a stiflingly claustrophobic armored bus known as the Rhino, buttoned up in body armor, blast-protective goggles and helmets, escorted by young cavalry troopers in armored vehicles, heads swiveling from side to side every ten seconds as we sped through the darkened, deserted streets of a battered city under military curfew. I reached my sandbagged trailer behind the embassy well after midnight, soaked in sweat and just in time for a rocket attack, the fifth that day.

Despite the title, my job wasn't to advise General Petraeus—he didn't need any advice on counterinsurgency, least of all from me—but rather to help coalition and Iraqi military units, aid agencies and civilian personnel adapt to the new strategy. You might think of it as a variation (a very peculiar one, to be sure) of "change management": helping a big, failing enterprise turn itself around. I'd spend a day or so in the Palace among Saddam's Byzantine floors, gargantuan helmeted heads and phallic Scud Missile murals, absorbing reams of intelligence data between rocket attacks, before escaping back to the field. I'd accompany patrols, sit in on meetings with community leaders, develop an understanding of people's problems and work with them to develop a fix—new tactics, new technology, re-purposing a particular piece of kit, whatever it might be.

As Iraqi and coalition units got to know me, and realized that I could offer support and relay their concerns, but wouldn't carry tales to Baghdad unasked, we developed a close rapport. And since most people in Iraq, even in remote outposts, had email, I was soon plugged into a network of junior leaders who'd tell me their problems and offer brutally frank advice on how we could better handle the battle. I connected them with each other, so that they began to pass information across units and districts, sharing lessons and helping the organization adapt more quickly. Working closely with Colonel Pete Mansoor (General Petraeus's executive officer) and Emma Sky (political adviser to General Odierno, the corps commander, commanding the maneuver units in direct combat against AQI) I used this network to field-test a set of best practices, later codified as *Multi-National Force Iraq Commander's Counterinsurgency Guidance*, the tactical blueprint for the Surge.[1]

Four months in, it was far from clear that the Surge was going to work. By then I was intimately aware of how difficult and dangerous it was proving to be for the troops who had to execute it. We'd gotten off the bases and built a network of combat outposts across Baghdad. The plan was to foster trust and begin *really* listening to the Iraqis, working with them to co-design solutions, and figuring out Iraqi ways to get things done that were obvious to them but that we might never have considered. We expanded "district-hardening" programs—blast walls, checkpoints and neighbourhood-watch committees—that had been started the previous year, trying to break the cycle of tit-for-tat sectarian slaughter. We instituted controls on the abuses of Iraqi police and military units—the "death squads" John Pace and others had warned about—mainly by accompanying them everywhere, embedding advisers at every level, and second-guessing their every move. We reduced civilian losses a little, and generated better intelligence through tip-offs from the community.

WATERFALL

But our casualties were still too high—the highest in the war so far—and the rate of suicide bombings, sniper attacks, roadside bombs and mortar hits was up, not down. I would lie awake in my sandbagged trailer all night, listening to the Blackhawks bringing the wounded in from the Belts, as they turned directly over our compound to land at the nearby surgical hospital—every helicopter carrying one or more desperately injured American soldier. Those helicopters would fill my nightmares for years afterward: one more reason, on top of the rockets, to stay out of the Green Zone as much as possible.

I think I've made it clear by this point that I was no fan of President Bush, whose actions of the past four years had led us to this desperate position. I thought the War on Terror had been mishandled from the outset: through aggregating threats, through the diversion into Iraq, then through failure to manage the occupation properly while other theatres languished. But in spite of myself, when the president took personal charge in 2007, I found myself hugely impressed by the man's leadership, willpower and grasp of detail. Two things epitomized this for me: the first was his performance at a conference in Tampa, Florida, on 1 May 2007.

Tampa was a coalition conference—almost fifty countries represented—and the president spoke after lunch on the first day. He was singularly unimpressive at first: folksy, shallow and upbeat in a way that facts on the ground simply didn't justify. But then he finished his remarks and asked the reporters and television cameras to leave. As soon as the doors closed his voice changed, his body language became more alert, and he began to talk in a concrete, specific, realistic way. He showed a comprehensive grasp of both tactical-level detail and the big picture, and—what impressed me most—a clear understanding of exactly what was, and was not, working on the ground. (I found myself wondering why he felt he needed to conceal this side of himself from the media: I, for one, would have found it far more reassuring than his relentlessly positive public persona.) Then he began to appeal to coalition members to raise their commitment—and in so doing demonstrated a level of emotional intelligence, as well as a deep knowledge of what nations were already providing and of the political constraints on their contributions. It was a *tour de force* of coalition leadership, and by the end of it, he'd converted my skepticism into a grudging acceptance that we *might* just get it done.

The second illustration of the president's leadership was his focused engagement, epitomized by near-daily phone calls and weekly videoconferences with General Petraeus, Ambassador Ryan Crocker and Iraqi leaders. On the Iraqi side, President Bush made it clear to Nouri al-Maliki, the Iraqi prime minister, that he was paying close attention, that Maliki had his support, but that the United States would insist on a fair distribution of power among Sunnis, Kurds and Shi'a and prevent any one group from exploiting its opponents. This was a message only the president could credibly send, and it had to be sent again and again. The president's engagement was critical in encouraging Maliki to act more inclusively during this period, and in restraining some of his officials.

However good President Bush's performance during the Surge, we should never have been there, of course. Even taking the invasion as a given, he should never have let things get this bad. He shouldn't have waited three years to fire Secretary Rumsfeld, sideline Vice President Cheney and take personal charge—and above all, he should have thought the invasion through. And while his sustained attention was central to the improvement we started to see in 2007, it made the overall strategic tunnel vision—the focus on Iraq to the exclusion of pressing problems elsewhere—even worse. It would have been far preferable if we'd never invaded at all. But here we were, and with the president's engagement, Petraeus's leadership and the talent of commanders like General Raymond Odierno and people at every level below him, we were finally getting out of the hole we'd dug for ourselves. And by June a new factor had emerged: the Anbar Awakening.

As I've pointed out, AQI's beliefs (and the contempt and violence with which Zarqawi and his people treated their own community) were alien to most Iraqis, none more so than the Sunni tribes who dominate the country's vast western desert, with its remote frontier crossings, dusty supply routes and ancient smuggling trails. The tribes had always been an authority unto themselves. They were conflict entrepreneurs from way back—their interests had a purely coincidental relationship with legality at the best of times—and they were no friends of Baghdad. But AQI was bad for business, grabbing the most lucrative smuggling routes, skimming money off the tribes' earnings, bringing violence that shut down trade and coming in as mostly urban outsiders to impose a virtually unrecognizable version of Islam.

Early in the war several tribal leaders had approached U.S. Special Forces in Anbar, proposing that they work together, only to be snubbed by higher headquarters.[2] By 2005 some tribes—the Albu Mahal, the ar-Rishawi, the al-Fahd—were rising against AQI in a series of rebellions, which the terrorists crushed with a brutality breathtaking even for them. AQI slaughtered tribal leaders, raped and enslaved women, beheaded and disemboweled children in front of their own parents, burned houses with whole families in them, but still the tribes rose, again and again.

It's a persistent myth, mainly among people who weren't in Iraq at the time, that the Surge only worked because of the lucky accident of the Awakening. Actually, the reverse is true: 2007 was the tribes' fifth attempt to throw off AQI, and the reason this attempt succeeded, where the previous four failed, was the Surge. This time around, we finally had enough troops to protect people where they slept, led by commanders willing, able, funded and authorized to reconcile and partner with them. We had a command team and a doctrine that encouraged such partnership, and—not least—we had support from the White House to do whatever it took to end the violence. Each element had existed at some point beforehand, but never all at the same time, and that bottom-to-top alignment of factors made all the difference.

By September 2007 the carnage was slowing dramatically. Along with political and economic pressure to convince the Iraqi government and Shi'a militias to call off their death squads, this triggered a tipping point, with precipitous drops in all conflict indicators: roadside bombs, civilian deaths, coalition casualties, sectarian killings, numbers of incidents. Petraeus briefed a skeptical Congress that September, using a PowerPoint image we nicknamed the "waterfall slide" because the plummeting violence, represented graphically, looked like Niagara Falls. Against all odds, the Surge was working.[3]

The ultimate reason for the turn-around wasn't the new counterinsurgency doctrine, the president's engagement or the extra troops (though of course all these things played a key role). Rather, the decisive factor was the partnership we finally achieved with Iraqis and the measures we took to make ordinary civilians safe, which by extension reduced our own losses. The horror of the preceding eighteen months, the most violent in the entire modern history of Iraq, helped us. Iraqis gazed into the abyss: the abyss looked back into them, they blinked and looked away.

But of course, the turn-around was fleeting, since it was founded on a scale of American troop presence, and thus a degree of U.S. government leverage, that was not to be sustained.

By October 2007, after a month or so in Australia, I was back in Washington, now a U.S. foreign service national serving on Secretary Rice's personal staff as senior adviser for counterinsurgency, and with a new focus: Afghanistan. Just as she had been the most outspoken about the need to promote democratic reforms among the region's authoritarian regimes, Secretary Rice was the first of President Bush's cabinet to lift her eyes from Iraq to the bigger picture, to break the tunnel vision and try to get a grip of problems that had festered while we were distracted there. The most important of these was Afghanistan, and by late 2007, at her direction, I was back out among the same outposts along the Afghanistan–Pakistan frontier, working the same forested hills of Kunar and Nuristan, helping to stand up the civilian counterinsurgency effort of the "Other War"—one that had taken a decided turn for the worse. Afghanistan remained my focus for the rest of my service in government, both in the field and while in Washington.

But I still had friends in Iraq. I'd wake up five times a night, soaked in sweat from thinking about it, and tense up when I heard a truck's airbrakes (which sound exactly like an incoming rocket). I'd swerve when I saw a random piece of debris on the road and tremble when I heard a helicopter, ambulance or fire truck. I'd obsessively scan the news and the intelligence feed multiple times a day, looking for people, places and units I knew. This preoccupation made me watch the 2008 presidential election very closely.

Through 2007 and 2008, Senator Barack Obama (a strong opponent of the Surge and one of the last members of Congress to admit that it was working) campaigned on getting out of Iraq to focus on Afghanistan and Pakistan. He was in a stronger position than more experienced politicians because, being so junior, he hadn't been in Congress for the vote to authorize the use of military force in Iraq in 2002. Senators Biden, Clinton and Kerry had all voted for the war, a popular choice at the time, which came back to bite them once Iraq became political kryptonite. Senator Obama, on the other hand, was free to present himself as principled and consistent since he'd yet to accumulate any baggage on Iraq.

As a technical specialist with no partisan allegiance, I happened to agree entirely with Senator Obama that Iraq was a bad idea from the outset and that the occupation had been bungled. I also fully endorsed the second part of his argument—the need to stop the rot in Afghanistan. But the first part—the bit about leaving Iraq—had me extremely worried, and as President Obama took office in January 2009 these worries intensified.

I felt the new president and his team were confusing talk with action—as if a well-crafted narrative on some issue, or a well-turned phrase in some speech, equated to handling it. If speeches could have fixed our problems in Iraq, then Rumsfeld, Bremer and President Bush could have seen off the insurgency in 2003 with mere rhetoric. Too many of the new administration's statements sounded more like poses than policies to me. The new team also talked about what they'd "inherited," as if Iraq had been foisted on them rather than being a problem that they had (in theory) been thinking about and campaigning on for years, had actively sought responsibility for, and that Americans had elected them to solve. They seemed to spend as much energy blaming others as taking responsibility for next steps. Of course, there *was* a huge amount of blame to go around—virtually all of it, at this early stage of the Obama administration, attaching by definition to the previous administration—but that didn't change realities on the ground. Most seriously, I felt they were conflating *leaving* Iraq with *ending* the war.

Indeed, for years after the complete departure of U.S. forces from Iraq—throughout the 2012 election campaign, and right up until almost the fall of Mosul, in fact—the president and others would proudly claim as a foreign policy achievement the fact that they had "ended the war in Iraq," seemingly not noticing that the war was far from over, and that the hard-won peace achieved during the Surge was slipping away. As I said earlier, the harsh reality is that once you're in a full-blown insurgency, your choices are tightly constrained: you either leave well, or you leave quickly. And as the Obama administration took the reins, all signs pointed to the latter.

5

CROCODILE

Iraq after the Surge

It's worth pausing for a moment to consider how Iraq stood in January 2009 as President Obama took office. AQI had been virtually destroyed, its leaders describing it as being in "extraordinary crisis."[1] Violence was down dramatically. According to an independent assessment by Iraq Body Count, an NGO, in July 2007 (the first full month all Surge forces were in place) 2,693 civilians died; by January 2009 the figure was down to 372, an 86 per cent reduction.[2] In that same year and a half, monthly incidents fell 79 per cent, from 908 to 195, U.S. troops killed per month fell from 101 to fourteen (an 86 per cent drop), while wounded per month were down 90 per cent, from 756 to seventy-three.[3] These statistics give a sense of how dramatically the security situation had been transformed, but the most important things were harder to quantify.

At the street level, business confidence was up, kids were back at school and people were getting on with their lives. The trickle of intelligence from ordinary Iraqis had become a torrent, reflecting improved trust between the community and security forces. Muqtada al-Sadr, after losing several key lieutenants, had declared a ceasefire and exiled himself to Iran, so that violence from Shi'a militias also dropped dramatically.

Prime Minister Maliki was being more inclusive (albeit off an extremely low baseline) towards Sunnis and Kurds. He'd personally led Iraqi forces against Shi'a militias in Basra, Iraq's main southern city, in March 2008—a hard-fought military action that was even tougher for a politician from a Shi'a sectarian party. He'd cleaned up some of his government's abuses, removing corrupt officials in the finance and interior ministries, though, in many cases, abusive ministers were reshuffled rather than dismissed from office. The police had improved (again, off a shockingly low base) and the army was more capable, with competent Special Operations Forces, some excellent infantry units, improved combat skills, and better equipment, logistics and maintenance. At the insistence of embedded advisers from the coalition, competent non-sectarian officers had been promoted in the armed forces, and Sunni police or mixed-sect military units were protecting some Sunni-majority districts.

The Sons of Iraq (successors to the tribal Awakening) had expanded massively: 110,000 young Sunni men were now being paid to protect (and, incidentally, deterring government abuse of) their communities. These men and their families—another half-million people, since most Iraqi families had four-to-five kids[4]—were partnering with the coalition, when they would otherwise have been in the recruiting base for the insurgency. The money they were paid helped their families, gave them a sense of personal honor and worth, and kept them out of other, less positive, pursuits. All this had a huge impact on confidence in the Sunni community, which was no longer so subject to AQI terror or hostile Shi'a occupation.

These improvements led some external observers, then and later, to describe the Surge as a U.S. victory.[5] This was way off the mark.

First, even if the Surge had been a total success—it wasn't, but even if it had been—at the grand-strategic level (i.e. the war against terrorism beyond Iraq) it did nothing to advance the overall Disaggregation strategy on which our plan to defeat AQ hinged, and from which we'd been distracted by the long and bloody detour to Baghdad. Second, as I've noted, President Bush's personal attention on Iraq was extremely welcome, but it tightened the tunnel vision so that other crises received even less attention. Third, the drop in violence—purchased with the blood of American, allied and Iraqi troops—created the essential breathing space for Iraq's self-serving politicians to resolve their differences, but they didn't use that space to do so. Ultimately it was the presence of international troops, money and advisers that compelled Baghdad to act more inclusively: Maliki had reluctantly accepted the existence of the Sons of Iraq, under duress from U.S. leaders, but there was no way he would continue to do so once we left. (During a meeting at his office one evening in 2007, at the height of the Awakening, Maliki exclaimed to a coalition officer, "You've taken a crocodile as a pet!" only to be told, "It's not *our* crocodile.")[6] Fourth, and most importantly, calling the Surge a victory made us think we could finally leave. This, of course, had been the goal ever since the quick-in, quick-out fantasy of Rumsfeld's invasion plan. It had been the strategy before the Surge, when we kept our eyes on the door even as the country fell apart. Now that we could convince ourselves we'd "won," that undertow reasserted itself.

President Bush, in his final months in office, settled with Maliki on a timeline that saw U.S. troops out of Iraq by the end of 2011. This was supposed to be accompanied by a Status of Forces Agreement (SOFA) allowing a smaller number of American troops to stay on after 2011, while remaining subject to United States rather than Iraqi law. There were also supposed to be agreements between Baghdad and the regions over oil revenue, territorial demarcation with Kurdistan, reforms to permanently broaden the recruiting base of the police and military (still heavily Shi'a) and a revision of Bremer's de-Ba'athification statute, which Shi'a officials had used as a tool to persecute ordinary Sunnis. None of this happened.

Instead, U.S. forces pulled out completely at the end of 2011 leaving no residual troop presence whatsoever, which in turn meant that civilian assistance programs couldn't be safely carried out, diplomats couldn't get out and engage with Iraqi leaders, and political leverage for U.S. officials quickly plummeted. So, no, the Surge wasn't a victory in any sense. Not for the first (nor, unfortunately, the last) time, the nation proved unable to convert military success into political stability, or to translate achievements on the battlefield into long-term strategic progress.

That doesn't mean the Surge wasn't necessary—it absolutely *was* necessary, on moral grounds, to halt the carnage and restore some normality to a society we should never have invaded in the first place. We owed Iraqis that, not just as an ethical matter but also as a matter of international law. Neither was it a failure, as some claimed later when things went bad, nor proof that counterinsurgency doesn't work.

Counterinsurgency (in fact, warfare generally) is a complex discipline, like medicine or architecture. If your building collapses, it doesn't mean "architecture doesn't work"—it means you built a bad structure. If a patient's fever drops when you apply a particular treatment, and then she gets sick again when the treatment ends, it doesn't suggest that the treatment failed—on the contrary, it suggests that perhaps you should have continued. Similarly, in a conflict like Iraq, if violence drops when you apply counterinsurgency techniques, then returns when you stop (as happened both in Iraq and, later, in Afghanistan) it doesn't mean those techniques don't work: on the contrary, it suggests they *do* work—at least on a temporary basis—and you shouldn't have stopped before figuring out a way to maintain the progress. The reporter Thomas E. Ricks—whose first book on Iraq was rightly titled *Fiasco*—called the Surge a gamble, pointing out in 2009 that "the decisive events of the Iraq War haven't happened yet."[7] To me, that's the best verdict.

As the Obama administration took office, there were signs that the situation was becoming increasingly fragile. One of these was the existence of a small but determined remnant of AQI (now, if you recall, calling itself ISI, the Islamic State of Iraq). Allied with ISI was a cadre—far larger and more influential than many realized at the time—of former Saddam loyalists, intelligence and special operations people, specialists in clandestine warfare, who tended to hang back, direct traffic and treat the jihadists as useful idiots to further their own goals. Another danger sign was the continued existence of Shi'a militias and special groups backed by Iran. Remember that whereas ISI had been all but destroyed, the Shi'a militias had merely accepted a ceasefire, and as long as they retained their organization, weapons and Iranian support, the potential remained for renewed violence.

Ignoring (or perhaps unaware of) these danger signs, President Obama's priority was to deliver on his election promise and leave. The flawed but unifying construct of the Global War on Terrorism was gone, replaced not with a single framework but with many "Overseas Contingency Operations," each treated as a discrete engagement. For someone who'd argued against the over-broad "War on Terror" concept, it was disappointing to see Washington come up with something even worse. Treating each theater as a separate engagement was like trying to run each World War II campaign—Burma, New Guinea, Greece, North Africa, Italy, Normandy—as a stand-alone war in its own right, a recipe for incoherence.

To the extent that a main effort was discernible, in the early days it was Afghanistan. In fact, though, the principal shift was tactical, not strategic, and went unannounced at first: the Obama administration dramatically ramped up the use of drones in Pakistan and Yemen, emphasizing killing-at-a-distance outside declared war zones, mass electronic surveillance, and "surgical" strikes in the form of special forces raids, rather than large-scale commitment of boots on the ground.[8] Indeed, of all drone strikes since 9/11, more than 90 per cent happened during the first six years of the Obama administration, against less than 10 per cent in all eight years under President Bush. This could be described as "light-footprint" counterterrorism—drones, mass surveillance and raids.

On Iraq, President Obama was far less engaged than his predecessor had been—the phone calls to Maliki and videoconferences with the force commander and ambassador ceased abruptly. Obama, like most new American presidents, was putting domestic issues (the global financial crisis and his new health-care law) ahead of foreign policy.[9] He was the opposite of President Bush, which of course was quite appropriate, since that's exactly what he'd been elected to be. But President Obama's aloofness cut Prime Minister Maliki adrift, freeing him to pursue his personal (and his party's sectarian) agenda.

In the comparatively peaceful environment of 2008, with substantial U.S. forces on the ground and American advisers acting as arbiters among Iraqi factions, it had been relatively safe for Maliki to act inclusively towards Kurds and Sunnis, and to take on the Shi'a militias. But as U.S. withdrawal began in earnest in 2010, things became increasingly zero-sum: with a coalition drawdown, deep funding cuts and negligible attention from President Obama, Maliki had to fall back on other sources of support, including his base in the Shi'a-supremacist D'awa Party and the Iranians who, as U.S. influence waned, were increasingly overt players. It's worth recalling that Maliki was close to both the Iranian and Syrian regimes, having spent almost twenty-four years in exile in Tehran and Damascus, and working with Hezbollah and the Quds Force against Saddam. All this pushed him in a Shi'a-supremacist direction, unleashing an authoritarian streak that grew over time—or perhaps merely revealing one that had been there all along.

Rightly wary of a coup, Maliki created structures to cement his control over the military, police and intelligence services.[10] These included the Office of the Commander in Chief (OCINC), a post Maliki set up in his own office. Some within OCINC had track records of sectarian abuse; many were Shi'a supremacists. Maliki created a Counter-Terrorism Service under his own authority to direct Iraqi Special Forces, often against Sunni targets, and replaced competent technocrats with loyal functionaries. Within the military and police, the relatively apolitical and competent leaders appointed at American insistence were gradually purged and replaced with people from Maliki's inner circle or protégés of his personal patronage network. Maliki set up a series of Operations Commands at the province level as a parallel command chain, reporting directly to him via OCINC and creating confusion in the minds of combat commanders who were unsure whom they reported to. Again, this approach was perfectly rational on Maliki's part—it's just that it was optimized for coup-proofing and regime preservation, rather than prosecuting effective operations against the residual insurgent and terrorist threat.[11]

In January 2010 Maliki used his control of the Independent High Electoral Commission—clearly something of a misnomer—to bar more than 500 candidates (mostly Sunnis) from the March elections, claiming they had Ba'athist connections. He cut funding to the Sons of Iraq, arrested hundreds of Awakening Council members, including tribal elders leading the fight against AQI, and restricted the Iraqi press.[12] He also concentrated key cabinet positions in his own hands: from December 2010 he acted as defense minister and interior minister as well as prime minister. By April 2013, Middle East analyst Marisa Sullivan had concluded that "the national unity government that was formed in the wake of the 2010 parliamentary elections has given way to a de facto majoritarian government in which Maliki has a monopoly on the institutions of the state … Maliki's institutional control has enabled him to use de-Ba'athification and accusations of corruption and terrorism as political tools to advance his interests at the expense of his rivals."[13]

Maliki's authoritarianism alienated Sunnis, created grievances that surviving AQI cells could exploit, and eroded the security created by the Surge and the Awakening. This gave Sunni nationalists and Ba'athists an increasingly strong case: "The Americans are leaving, Maliki is a dictator in league with Iran, you need us to defend you." And as American leverage diminished, any idea Sunnis might have had that the United States would continue to protect them evaporated.

This created a domestic version of what international relations theorists call a "security dilemma": as far as he was concerned, Maliki may have been acting defensively, taking what he saw as appropriate measures to protect himself against threats from the military and the Sunnis as American influence waned. But his measures *looked* offensive to Sunnis, who began to protect themselves against the risk of Shi'a oppression. This in turn looked offensive to Maliki, who increased his authoritarianism, further alienating Sunnis, and so on. After 2010 it was hard for Washington to break this cycle, since the drawdown, lack of presidential engagement, spending cuts and—most importantly—failure to agree a SOFA that would have kept forces in Iraq after 2011, progressively reduced Washington's influence. Even if President Obama had wanted to fix these problems, it's unclear whether he would have been able to do so.

By early 2011 I'd been out of government for two years. I had worked for General Stanley McChrystal, the new commander of the International Security Assistance Force, to help set up civil–military counterinsurgency advisory and assistance teams embedded with Afghan and coalition units across Afghanistan, and helped train U.S. government military and civilian advisers for the Afghan effort. I'd also founded a research firm that combined pattern analysis of immense amounts of remote-observation data (now called "big data") with the ability to field indigenous research teams, usually in denied or dangerous environments, to validate that data, understand local conditions in detail and help co-design solutions with local populations. The focus of most of our work was not counterinsurgency, but rather economic development, public safety, renewable energy and urbanization. But our presence in these regions gave me, my data science team, our forward-deployed analysts and our field teams—often drawn from the neighborhoods where they worked—a close-up view of the tsunami that was about to swamp the greater Middle East.

If Iraq was the first factor undermining Disaggregation, the second was this immense wave of change, which was triggered by three events, all of which happened in 2011: the death of bin Laden, the failure of the Arab Spring and the rebirth of ISIS.

6

TSUNAMI

Pakistan, Iraq and the Greater Middle East, 2011–14

Just after 1 a.m. on 2 May 2011, U.S. Navy SEALs attacked a compound close to Pakistan's military academy, near Abbottabad in the country's northeast.[1] Stealthily climbing a staircase to the upper floor, two special warfare operators—Robert O'Neill and Matt Bissonnette—confronted an unkempt man in pyjamas, cowering behind a young woman he was using as a human shield. O'Neill shot him twice in the forehead and once more as he hit the floor. The SEALs recovered a Russian AKSU-74 carbine and a Makarov pistol from near the body, and collected a vast trove of intelligence from the compound. It had taken a decade to find him but, ten years after 9/11, Osama bin Laden was dead. The raiders spent only thirty-eight minutes on the ground.

The bin Laden raid has been described elsewhere, and I don't plan to discuss it in detail here. The operation was a testament to the immense professionalism, commitment, tactical skill—and, frankly, utter ruthlessness—of the SEALs, their sister units in the Special Operations Command, and the U.S. Intelligence Community. But the broader strategic significance of bin Laden's death was also huge, and it lay not so much in the killing of bin Laden, but in the raid's twin effects—on U.S. strategic thinking, and on al-Qaeda's senior leadership—at a pivotal moment of the Arab Spring.[2]

The bin Laden raid let President Obama claim an achievement that had eluded President Bush. He lost no time taking credit for it, announcing the raid immediately, and then boasting about the achievement throughout the 2012 presidential election campaign and beyond.[3] This created unhappiness among some military veterans' groups, who saw the president as exploiting their sacrifice for political gain, but it was scarcely surprising behavior for a highly partisan politician in a divisive re-election battle. The real problem was not the political point-scoring, but the fact that magnifying the raid's significance made people expect a quick end to the War on Terror, or whatever we were now calling the global campaign against al-Qaeda.

The point of Disaggregation, remember, was to render bin Laden irrelevant, so that it literally wouldn't matter whether he lived or died. As early as 2006, this had largely been achieved. Alec Station, the CIA's special unit created in 1996 to track and disrupt Osama bin Laden, was closed in late 2005, as the agency broadened its focus to AQ affiliates and self-radicalized terrorists, in recognition that regional groups and "lone wolves" were now more dangerous than the core leadership.[4]

In line with the Disaggregation strategy, the CIA and the Pentagon maintained pressure on AQ leaders in Pakistan, through a combination of intelligence activity, including repeated attempts to penetrate the organization and place agents in positions where they could access its principals, along with special operations raids and drone strikes. This effort helped find bin Laden, but in some ways the killing of the AQ leader was a secondary goal—the program's main strategic purpose was to keep AQ leaders on the run, unable to communicate freely or catch their breath, and thereby to hamper the AQ core group's ability to aggregate the effects of its regional franchises, and limit its ability to plan or conduct future 9/11-style terrorist attacks on U.S. or allied cities.

For at least six years before he was killed, in fact, bin Laden was effectively marginalized, playing a minor role in operational planning and acting as more of a figurehead and source of inspiration than a day-to-day leader. Indeed, to the extent that he played a role in the strategic direction of AQ's global movement it was that of restraining a newly emerging, more radical and even more hyper-violent generation of hotheads. Thus the U.S. celebration of his death, though understandable, was both premature and a strategic misstep. It over-inflated the man's significance to the movement by creating the impression that he was the key driver of AQ's brutality and operational capability (he no longer was) and that therefore killing him, by definition, must have critically weakened the organization (it didn't—though, as we'll see, it did throw AQ into turmoil for a brief but critical period).

The public presentation of bin Laden's death as a major victory against AQ thus contributed to a complacent mind-set, which made a string of subsequent decisions—withdrawing completely from Iraq in late 2011, re-balancing away from Europe and the Middle East toward the Asia–Pacific in 2012, cutting U.S. military manpower and budgets in 2013, setting a December 2014 deadline for withdrawing combat troops from Afghanistan—seem sensible in the light of a soothing narrative that killing bin Laden had reduced the threat, the nation's wars were ending, and people could get back to normal. None of these things was true.

By 2011, in fact, the main threat came from al-Qaeda in the Arabian Peninsula (AQAP), the AQ franchise that had established a base in the Abyan and Aden districts of southern Yemen, from which it orchestrated numerous high-profile terrorist attacks, including a bombing attempt against a Northwest Airlines flight on Christmas Day, 2009—the first attack inside the United States by an al-Qaeda affiliate since 11 September 2001.[5] As core AQ receded in importance, AQAP widened the scope of its goals and developed global ambitions. But AQAP was just one of several groups expanding into the space vacated by the AQ central leadership. Another was the Pakistani Taliban, which sponsored an attempted bombing in New York's Times Square in May 2010. "Light-footprint" counterterrorism—drones, surveillance and raids—failed to reduce this threat, while the increase in drone strikes under President Obama inflamed anti-American sentiment in Pakistan, creating a more receptive environment for terrorists. Similarly, al-Qaeda in the Islamic Maghreb (AQIM, the AQ franchise in northwest Africa and the Sahel) and al-Shabaab, the Somali AQ affiliate, were expanding their reach. The light footprint was proving no more successful in these places.

Most concerning was the emergence of self-radicalized terrorists—individuals acting alone against targets of opportunity, in self-organized, self-directed acts of violence. For example, the Fort Hood shooting—in which Yemeni–American cleric and AQAP leader Anwar al-Awlaki used email, video and social media to radicalize Nidal Hasan, a U.S. Army psychiatrist, prompting him to kill thirteen and wound thirty-two at an army base in Texas—occurred in November 2009.[6] By the time bin Laden was killed, there was strong evidence that self-radicalization was being replaced by "remote radicalization"—the exploitation of dramatically improved electronic communications systems, social media and increasing access to mobile phones and the Internet by terrorists who were able to spot, assess, develop, recruit and then handle an operational asset from a distance.

Through outlets like Inspire, AQAP's English-language online magazine, terrorist networks could now publish target lists, issue planning advice, share lessons learned, warn supporters about new counterterrorism measures and offer how-to guides to anyone with an Internet connection. Email, YouTube, Facebook and Twitter allowed figures like al-Awlaki to contact recruitable individuals anywhere in the world, offer support and develop attacks without ever meeting them. Jihadists moved their conversations from online message boards and chat rooms into peer-to-peer messaging and social media (especially Twitter). Secure messaging—along with new cryptographic measures and security services like Tor, OTR chat and PGP—made some communications harder to detect, but even messages that were lightly coded or "in the clear" were now increasingly difficult to spot in an ocean of innocuous message traffic. The explosion of electronic connectivity (most pronounced since about the year 2000 in developing-world cities, with Nigeria, Libya, Egypt, Kenya and Syria seeing some of the fastest growth, and diaspora populations worldwide now tapping into home-country networks in real time) had shifted the threat from deliberately planned expeditionary attacks by formal organizations like al-Qaeda toward *ad hoc* networks of radicalized individuals connected on social media. Killing bin Laden did nothing to change any of that.

Thus, the main effect of over-hyping the Abbottabad raid was to obscure the fact that although the first part of Disaggregation (dismantle core AQ) was working, the second (help regional partners defeat the local threat and address its causes) was not. If anything, we'd become addicted to killing terrorist leaders, using drone strikes and unilateral special forces raids, as a tacit recognition that partnerships with local governments were *not* succeeding.

There were three main reasons for the lack of success in building partnerships. The first was the sheer long-term difficulty of such efforts: some partners just couldn't handle local threats and would need years of assistance (and as Condoleezza Rice had insisted in 2005 and Barack Obama had argued after 2009, would have to undertake thoroughgoing anti-corruption and political reforms) before they ever could. The second reason was sequencing: taking down core AQ took much less time than building countermeasures against regional terrorist networks, thus the suppression of the core group left a leadership vacuum, which these franchises and other terrorist groups expanded to fill. The third reason was a self-inflicted loss of trust: local partner governments in the Muslim world hesitated to cooperate because of residual anger among their populations over the invasion and botched occupation of Iraq or, paradoxically, because at the governmental level they perceived our *withdrawal* from Iraq as leaving allies unprotected, proving our unreliability.

Meanwhile, in geopolitical terms, America's great-power rivals Russia and China, which had stood aside from the wars in Iraq and Afghanistan militarily (while both profiting commercially from these conflicts), took advantage of U.S. preoccupation to expand their influence. China, in particular, was increasingly attractive to countries facing internal security challenges but wary of Washington. Beijing offered military equipment, financing, know-how and economic support with few strings attached, while taking a less preachy approach to human rights and the rule of law. As a cabinet official told me during a private meeting in a South Asian country three weeks after the bin Laden raid, "You Americans used human rights as a stick to beat us over the head for years, but we don't need you any more: we have the Chinese now."

But if the effects of the bin Laden raid on U.S. strategic thinking and relations with partners were negative, within the core leadership group of al-Qaeda they were catastrophic. Bin Laden's death catapulted AQ into an immediate succession crisis. Choosing the new leader—bin Laden's deputy Ayman al-Zawahiri—took six weeks, and the selection process was far from unchallenged. Zawahiri (who, as we saw earlier, can come across as pedantic and uninspiring) lacked bin Laden's charisma. Some believed only a native of Arabia was eligible to lead the organization, disqualifying Zawahiri, who was Egyptian. A separate clique didn't care about the ethnic origin of a new leader, but criticized Zawahiri for lack of military expertise: members of this faction favored senior AQ military commander Saif al-Adel (a former special forces colonel, also Egyptian, who'd fought in Somalia in 1993–95, planned the 1998 East African embassy bombings, written AQ's *Al-Battar Military Camp* tactics manual in 2004 and developed a military strategic concept out to 2020) whom they saw as better qualified.

After sharp internal debates, the succession struggle ended in Zawahiri's favor, but it took most of 2011 for his authority to be accepted across the wider AQ network. This meant that al-Qaeda senior leaders were missing in action—inward-looking, consumed with their own internal leadership crisis—during the critical stage of the Arab Spring in mid-to-late 2011.[7]

As a result, AQ was not a major player in the first months of the so-called "Arab Spring" in Egypt, where the principal opposition to the Mubarak regime came from a secular pro-democracy movement and from the Muslim Brotherhood. Likewise in Tunisia, Algeria, Morocco and Jordan, the organization failed to exploit unrest to its own advantage, while in Libya strong jihadist elements quickly emerged in the struggle against Gaddafi but lacked guidance from core AQ, especially after the dictator's death in October left a power vacuum. In Syria, a conflict initially dominated by street protests from a broad-based, civilian-led, secular pro-democracy movement escalated into armed insurgency after a violent regime crackdown in mid-June 2011, and a full-on civil war emerged by the end of the year.

All these countries—especially Libya and Syria—experienced decisive shifts between May and October 2011, exactly when core AQ leaders were consumed with the bin Laden succession, and unable to offer guidance or support to local jihadists. Worse than that: as we've seen, AQ's business model is to exploit and manipulate others' grievances, aggregating their effects into a global whole. AQ senior leaders were entirely failing (for the moment) to infiltrate the Arab Spring, and the grievances they sought to exploit were being resolved peacefully or taken up by non-AQ armed groups— the last thing they wanted. To understand why this mattered so much, we need to backtrack a little.

Founded in August 1988, al-Qaeda is a mash-up of several strains of militant Islam. The first was a movement against secular, authoritarian governments across the Middle East and North Africa that traced its origins to the Muslim Brotherhood in the 1920s and, more recently, to the Egyptian Islamic Jihad (EIJ) and a backlash against Egyptian President Anwar Sadat's U.S.-brokered peace deal with Israel in 1978. Members focused on what they called "apostate regimes": governments in Egypt, Syria, Libya, Algeria, Tunisia, Turkey, Iraq, Iran and Lebanon, which they saw as traitors to Islam and creatures of European colonialism (or American neo-colonialism).

For this school of thought—which included Zawahiri—the decline of Islam as a global power in the eighteenth and nineteenth centuries, the humiliation of European colonialism, the abolition of the caliphate in 1924 after the fall of the Ottoman Empire, the establishment of Israel as a Western outpost in the heart of the Middle East in 1948, successive military defeats at Israeli hands (most humiliatingly, the loss of the West Bank and Gaza to Israel in 1967 and Egypt's defeat in the 1973 Yom Kippur War) were merely surface symptoms of a deeper disease.

The reason for Islam's loss of status was simple: Muslims had lost the true faith and been corrupted by European values (capitalism, secularism, nationalism, socialism and communism). They'd abandoned the comprehensive blueprint for establishing and running a state that was embodied in Islamic law, and had effectively sunk into a state of pre-Islamic ignorance (*jahiliyya*). Egypt's accommodation with Israel in the 1978 Camp David Accords only confirmed the secular regimes' loss of legitimacy, which in turn released devout Muslims from any obligation to obey them—on the contrary, true believers now had a duty to work for the apostates' overthrow.

Like many revolutionary narratives, this school of thought looked back to a presumed golden age to explain present troubles and prescribe a redemptive program of action: Muslims needed to overthrow the secular governments, reintroduce sharia and remake the relationship between the Islamic world and the global order until the two were one and the same.

The Islamist militants weren't the only ones clamoring for change. Secular democrats and nationalists, religious and ethnic minorities, trade unions, students and women's organizations all demanded reform. In the 1970s improvements in public health and education—combined with economic stagnation, and compounded by the failures of state socialism and crony capitalism—created a bubble of educated, articulate youth whose job and marriage prospects were poor, whose expectations had been raised and then dashed, and who rejected the repressive governments that had disappointed them. Authoritarians worried that Islam might become the vanguard for revolution.

The shockingly public murder of President Sadat by radicalized military officers during a parade in October 1981, coming after the Islamic Revolution in Iran and the seizure (and bloody siege) of the Grand Mosque in Mecca in 1979, was followed by an Islamist uprising savagely suppressed by Syrian dictator Hafez al-Assad in early 1982. All this panicked the authoritarian regimes. In Egypt, Zawahiri was swept up in a wave of arrests, spending three years in prison on weapons charges. After his release he made his way to Pakistan, arriving at the height of the Soviet–Afghan War. Here he encountered Osama bin Laden, a Saudi of Yemeni descent and scion of the bin Laden construction dynasty, who'd rejected his own privileged upbringing and journeyed to Afghanistan to support jihad against the Soviets.

Bin Laden had a specifically Saudi critique of the authoritarian regimes: he viewed the House of Saud, with its cozy relationship with the United States and its failure to fully enforce Wahhabi Islam, as a Western puppet unworthy of the Prophet's legacy as guardian of the holy places of Mecca and Medina. Like Zawahiri, the ascetic bin Laden saw Muslim humiliation as a result of compromising values, befriending infidels and succumbing to the lure of luxury and comfort. From this mix something new was born: bin Laden's group (the "Afghan Services Bureau") merged with Zawahiri's EIJ to form a new organization whose name (Qa'idat al-Jihad) means "the base for jihad."[8] Often shortened to al-Qaeda ("the base") it was intended as exactly that—a base upon which to rebuild jihadist movements in the Middle East, propagate global revolution, and use a new clandestine organization, forged in combat against the Soviets, as the vanguard for a new strategy of jihad.

This strategy drew on Zawahiri's hard-won realization—formed in the aftermath of the Sadat assassination and the massive crackdown that followed—that confronting apostates on their own turf, through civil unrest or domestic terrorism, could never work. In

Zawahiri's view, regional states like Egypt were sustained by the United States and could thus draw on functionally unlimited financial, political and military support from their overlords in Washington, who would turn a blind eye to any oppression their protégés inflicted as long as the oil kept flowing, Israel remained secure and the United States retained its pre-eminence. The answer, bin Laden and Zawahiri insisted, was to punch past the "near enemy" to attack the United States directly. Bin Laden argued, "We have to cut [off] the head of the snake."[9] A strike in depth would make America withdraw, or provoke an overreaction that would trigger a mass regional uprising and force it out. Once Washington could no longer protect its puppets, they could be overthrown through direct military action, led (of course) by al-Qaeda. From this emerged the 9/11 attacks, designed—in what the historian Niall Ferguson called "a hideous compliment" to the centrality of Manhattan and the Pentagon to the Western-dominated world—to strike at the sources (financial, military and political) of U.S. power.[10]

By 2011, all this history made the Arab Spring a huge problem for AQ. For twenty years bin Laden and Zawahiri had been telling ordinary people across the Middle East that they could never change their regimes through local (let alone peaceful or democratic) action, that the only solution was global jihadist terrorism against the superpower. In all that time, AQ had only managed to kill a few thousand Americans, while slaughtering a vastly greater number of Muslims and bringing about even stronger U.S. engagement in the region. The Arab Spring thus contradicted AQ's entire narrative.

Ordinary populations, through civil disobedience, peaceful protest and democratic activism, had just overthrown regimes in Tunisia, Egypt, Yemen and Libya, and forced concessions from Algeria, Jordan and Morocco. In less than six months they'd achieved vastly more than AQ had in two decades—"the popular revolts demonstrate[d] to the world the bankruptcy of al-Qaeda's strategy and tactics."[11] People power, not terrorism, looked like the way forward, and far from rushing to defend its protégés as AQ had predicted, Washington seemed to be choosing democracy over stability. President Obama announced in February that "the status quo is unsustainable" and that Egypt's transition to democracy "must begin now."[12] By May he and Secretary of State Hillary Clinton were rallying a coalition to protect anti-Gaddafi rebels in Libya; by

August the president was saying, "The time has come for President Assad to step aside."[13] And with bin Laden dead and Zawahiri mired in the succession struggle, AQ's core leadership group was nowhere to be seen and unable to respond.

Of course, the Arab Spring did not usher in a new age of democracy. This was clearest in Egypt. By November 2011, parliamentary elections forced voters to choose between Egypt's only two organized political blocs: supporters of the former regime of Hosni Mubarak, and the Muslim Brotherhood's Freedom and Justice Party (FJP). The election selected members for a constituent assembly to develop a new constitution. The victory of the FJP, and the subsequent election of the Brotherhood's Mohammed Morsi as president under the new constitution in mid-2012, was in effect a vote for anyone but the old regime. Many Egyptians didn't trust the Brotherhood, believing (like people in many other countries) that the Brothers' doctrines of separatism and gradualism—achieving power by democratic political processes, and then using that power to remake society in an Islamic image—represented a fundamentalist, anti-democratic, authoritarian outlook that would amount to little more than "one person, one vote, one time." But since the alternative was to vote for former regime remnants (*al-fulūl*), people held their noses and voted for the lesser of two evils.

As soon as he was elected, and despite inclusive rhetoric during the election campaign, Morsi began to reveal his underlying religious authoritarianism. In November 2012 he issued an emergency constitutional decree in which, in effect, he granted himself unlimited powers and the authority to rule without parliamentary oversight or judicial review. This confirmed people's worst fears about the Brothers, and was seen as nothing short of an Islamist coup. It prompted mass protests, significant street violence, and a military counter-coup in July 2013 that brought a return to secular authoritarian rule. The Obama administration refused to designate Morsi's overthrow as a coup, though military aid to Egypt was suspended. The Egyptian military was less coy: one officer I spoke with in early August 2013 asked rhetorically "If the German Army had overthrown Hitler after the Reichstag fire [sic], would that have been a coup?"

In any case, by 2015 Egypt's military government confronted ISIS guerrillas in the Sinai and in the country's western desert, civil unrest from Brotherhood supporters and democracy activists in the cities, and a nationwide flood of refugees and foreign fighters associated with the uprising against President Bashar al-Assad's regime in Syria. The government's response—police and military crackdowns, suppression of the media, and military trials in which hundreds of activists received life prison terms and former President Morsi was sentenced to death—represented (for many Egyptians) something even worse than the stable authoritarianism of the Mubarak regime. In a mark of how far things had come since 2011, the U.S. government quietly restored military aid to Egypt at the end of March 2015—to the tune of $1.3bn annually, including advanced aircraft, tank parts and weapons systems—returning Egypt to its status (secure since the 1978 Camp David accords) as the second largest recipient of American military aid in the world, after Israel.

In Libya, Muammar Gaddafi was overthrown and brutally killed on 20 October 2011, but competition among regions and clans severely weakened the transitional government that followed. Having enabled Gaddafi's fall through a light-footprint combination of air power, covert action and limited Special Forces presence on the ground, the international community now stepped back from playing a major role in the country's reconstruction. However hardworking and dedicated, the small UN mission in Libya couldn't make up for lack of funding and continued political engagement by major world and regional powers.

The jihadist element of the anti-Gaddafi uprising, always a significant component of the rebellion, grew apace in these conditions. By September 2012, Islamist militants controlled several Libyan cities and violence had spread to many others. A new network of jihadist groups—*Ansar al-Sharia* (AS)—emerged across North Africa, with especially strong roots in Algeria, Tunisia and the eastern Libyan region of Cyrenaica, including the regional capital, Benghazi. The killing of four Americans in Benghazi that month (including Chris Stevens, the first U.S. ambassador murdered in the line of duty since 1979), in coordinated AS attacks on a U.S. diplomatic facility and a CIA base, underlined the country's descent into violence.[14]

Visiting Libya a few months after the Benghazi attack, I entered the country through an airport controlled by an armed tribal faction. They seemed like perfectly nice people, to be honest, but the airport compound was heavily defended. Driving the streets with a small, discreetly armed escort, I saw extraordinarily gunned-up and well-equipped paramilitary police of the Libyan Shield militia patrolling in heavily armed "technicals"—pickup trucks, mounting heavy weapons and carrying six-to-eight men, moving with the packed traffic on city streets or encamped on street corners manning impromptu checkpoints. For troops who were, in theory, "irregulars," they looked extremely professional, their posture at least as state-like as that of the transitional government's own police service.

Talking to people on the street, and in a series of discussions in cafés and sheesha bars, I heard repeatedly—from both young people and older Libyans—a strong desire for greater international engagement, a sense of embarrassment and shame over Ambassador Stevens' death, and a surprisingly pro-American attitude. But people were frank about their fears that growing violence in Cyrenaica, along with disputes among tribal and political factions, might lead to national disintegration. Government officials I met, including staff in Prime Minister Ali Zeidan's office, seemed well intentioned but overwhelmed, and I left with a strong sense that the country was teetering on the edge of chaos, despite the peaceful aspirations of most Libyans I'd met.

Then in October 2013, a unilateral U.S. special operations raid into Libya's capital, Tripoli, succeeded in capturing former AQ operative Abu Anas al-Libi, wanted for the 1998 U.S. Embassy bombings in East Africa, but fatally undermined Libya's government in the process. Two days afterwards, militants protesting the raid kidnapped Prime Minister Zeidan; he was forced to flee Libya a few months later, his government collapsed, and the country fragmented into warring blocs.

Elsewhere in the region affected by the Arab Spring, a similar pattern emerged. In Bahrain, a Saudi-backed crackdown in 2011 suppressed democracy protests, and in Yemen the fall of Ali Abdullah Saleh's regime in early 2012 plunged the country into a civil war and provoked a regional proxy conflict, which, after festering for several years, dragged in regional powers including Iran, Saudi Arabia and Egypt as it escalated in March 2015. In Mali—regarded until 2012 as a rare instance of democratic stability in the Sahel—an outflow of weapons and fighters from Libya after the fall of Gaddafi prompted a surge of guerrilla activity, enabled Tuareg separatist rebels and AQ's local franchise to seize the northern third of the country, led to a military coup that overthrew the elected government, and prompted a French-led military intervention in 2013. Of all the countries that had experienced regime change during the initial wave of the Arab Spring, only Tunisia seemed—for the time being—to be progressing toward inclusive democracy. In general, judged in terms of its original aspirations, the Arab Spring was a failure.

In the face of this failure, people from the broader movement for change, including both religious radicals who'd temporarily considered a parliamentary route to power and secular democrats who'd backed peaceful protest and civic action, became disillusioned and started returning to the armed struggle. This was a golden opportunity for AQ, or for Zawahiri himself, with his personal history, and eventually AQ did recover, throwing itself into the fray, building close relationships with Ansar al-Sharia and other local Islamist groups, and making significant gains. But at the crucial moment in 2011, AQ was unable to react as fast as its powerful new rival: the Islamic State of Iraq and Syria.

7

REBIRTH

Iraq, Libya and Syria, 2011–14

When it began in March 2011, the Syrian crisis looked much like the Arab Spring uprising in Egypt: a broad-based, secular, largely non-violent movement demanding reform from a repressive regime. But the street protests escalated into full-on urban warfare within weeks, as troops gunned down protestors, government warplanes struck residential areas, and regime death squads (*shabiha*, "spooks," or "ghosts") launched a campaign of kidnapping, torture and murder. According to government officials who later defected to the Syrian Opposition Council, Assad's regime quickly released hundreds of jihadists from its jails, encouraging them to join the uprising so as to ensure the protests would quickly turn violent, creating a pretext for harsh military action to stamp them out. Among those released were senior AQ figures.

The Islamic State of Iraq (ISI, the former AQI), although it had fallen on hard times in Iraq as a result of the Surge and Awakening, maintained an excellent network in Syria. For most of the previous decade the vast majority—somewhere around 85 per cent—of foreign fighters traveling to join AQI had made their final approach through Syria, sometimes simply crossing the country but often remaining in Syria for weeks or months before moving into Iraq. Recruits from across the Middle East, North Africa, Southeast Asia and elsewhere had travelled to Syria to meet facilitators and formally enlist in the insurgency before crossing the frontier, and many native Syrians fought in Iraq for jihadist groups. As a result, by 2011 a dense network of contacts, facilitators, guerrilla alumni, underground cells and auxiliary networks was available to ISI inside Syria. The Syrian intelligence services were well aware of this network—in fact during the American war they had used it to funnel fighters into Iraq themselves. The outbreak of conflict in 2011 gave ISI leaders the opportunity to turn this support network operational, and Syrian intelligence did nothing to stand in their way. On the contrary, they were more than happy to assist.

As it turned out, Syria's dictator, Bashar al-Assad, had learned from watching what happened to the region's other autocrats—Zine el Abidine Ben Ali in Tunisia, Ali Abdullah Saleh in Yemen and Hosni Mubarak in Egypt—and from the catastrophe that was overtaking Muammar Gaddafi in Libya. He had no intention of going quietly; on the contrary, he was determined to crush the uprising as quickly and brutally as possible. Assad also had sponsors—Iran and Russia—who were committed to his survival, and who were there for him in ways the United States no longer was for Mubarak or Saleh, and nobody had ever been for Gaddafi or Ben Ali.

The Iranians, in particular, stepped up quickly to assist Assad.[1] They had been through their own pro-democracy unrest a couple of years before, during the Green Movement—a protest against the rigging of the 2009 Iranian presidential elections against reformist candidate Mir Hossein Mousavi. Mousavi's coalition drew on a very similar base to that later seen during the Arab Spring: a collection of youth, student groups, small business owners, reform activists and middle- and lower-class urban families who felt excluded by the regime's autocratic control of society—and, perhaps even more so in Iran's case, enraged at the corruption and cronyism of the ruling elite and disappointed at President Mahmoud Ahmadinejad's failure to fulfill his election promise to clean it up. When the regime declared that Ahmadinejad had won the 12 June 2009 elections in a landslide, protests erupted on the streets of Iran's major cities. Over a six-month period, the protest rapidly spiraled into large-scale, deadly street demonstrations in a sort of Persian precursor to the Arab Spring. Laura Secor, the insightful and well-informed *New Yorker* writer, noted at the time that the uprising:

> … was the culmination of decades of frustrated hopes and indignities. Among the protesters were those who had placed their trust in the

reform movement, which had promised evolutionary change through legal means; these people were already bitterly disappointed by the end of the [relatively reformist] Khatami years, in 2005, and had, with some difficulty, mustered the will and the optimism to participate in the electoral process once again. What propelled them to the streets was the long, slow burn of accumulated grievance, and there is little reason to believe that their fury has so swiftly expended itself. Iran's broad middle class has entered into open revolt against its government. The reformists, who once sought to triangulate between these forces and the theocracy, have by and large chosen the side of the protesters. This is a confrontation to be measured not in days but in months, or even years.[2]

In the event, the outcome of the protest movement amounted to a soft military takeover of the Iranian state, as civilian instruments of national power were sidelined in the crisis, while the Guardianship Council and IRGC seized the lead in suppressing the democracy movement, which was largely contained by early 2010. Iranian government hardliners—especially those associated with the Revolutionary Guards and its covert action arm, Qassem Soleimani's Quds Force—used the experience of crushing their homegrown revolt to hone the already well-developed tools of repression of their overseas protégés.

When the Arab Spring uprisings hit Syria two years later, the availability of a well-practiced repressive apparatus from Iran was a key addition to Assad's capability. At the same time, military support in the form of arms and advice from Russia, the international focus on Libya (which was at the peak of the anti-Gaddafi uprising in June–July 2011, just as the Syrian revolt was transitioning from street protests to armed insurgency), and the presence of capable home-grown Syrian repressive institutions such as the widely feared Syrian Air Force Intelligence Directorate, may explain why Assad survived the democracy movement when Mubarak and Gaddafi didn't. Disunity among a highly factionalized set of opponents also played a role.[3]

Whatever the reason, under the regime's lethal repression the peaceful protests faded, armed resistance groups organized, secular civilians—including leaders of the democracy movement—were marginalized, and a collection of regime defectors, Islamist militants, Kurdish separatists and secular nationalists arose in their place to lead an armed uprising. And, of course, the inevitable conflict entrepreneurs emerged to exploit the chaos.

As in other uprisings of the Arab Spring, my research team and I had front-row seats to the horrifying spectacle of Syria's descent into madness. By now we had analysts in Cairo and in Iraqi Kurdistan, regularly visiting Turkey and Lebanon and working in Libya, Egypt and Iraq. Through a lucky accident—our senior Middle East analyst had spent years at university in Iraqi Kurdistan, done his post-graduate research on Syrian dissident politics, travelled frequently to Damascus before the war and developed close contacts in the democracy movement—by 2012 we had several field research teams on the ground in Syria, working for two NGOs and an aid agency that was trying to get humanitarian relief supplies to vulnerable civilians. Our task was to monitor where aid shipments were going (including who was stealing and selling them), to understand the scope of the humanitarian, economic and governance crisis, to map zones of control and contested areas, and thereby to evaluate the effectiveness of the aid.

By this stage we were a pretty hardened bunch—working Pakistan, Afghanistan, Somalia, Iraq and Libya in quick succession will do that to you—but the conflict in Syria was so gruesome that even analysts desensitized by long exposure to Iraq and Afghanistan quickly became disheartened and needed frequent sanity breaks. Travelling to the region to meet our field teams, ironically, boosted their morale, as they saw ordinary Syrians striving selflessly under heartbreaking conditions.

Despite President Obama's glib declaration that Assad's days were numbered—an assertion which, as far as most of our researchers could see, was based on little more than wishful thinking—by mid-2012 it was clear that the regime was if anything more entrenched while the opposition was increasingly fractured. And the Syrian conflict was rapidly pulling in outsiders. Lebanese Hezbollah sent advisers to help Assad stand up a paramilitary defense force around the nucleus of the *shabiha*, and by 2013 was fielding whole combat units inside Syria—a commitment that cost the organization much political support within Lebanon, where it had presented itself as supporting Lebanese interests against Israel, rather than (as it now appeared) intervening in a Shi'a–Sunni conflict on behalf of its Iranian masters. The Iranians sent Quds Force operatives, weapons, and economic and humanitarian aid, and offered intelligence support. In Iraq, Prime Minister Maliki (who, remember, had a long history in Iran and Syria during his exile from Saddam's Iraq) opened his country's airspace and borders for the transport of supplies to the Assad regime, allowing Tehran to sustain a vital air bridge of military and humanitarian aid to Damascus. Hadi al-Ameri, the Iraqi transportation minister who was simultaneously the head of the Iranian-sponsored Badr Organisation, helped organize aid shipments and recruit Iraqi Shi'a militias to fight for Assad.

For its part, Russia—which maintained a naval base at Tartus, on Syria's Mediterranean coast, the Russian Federation's only Mediterranean base (indeed, its only military base outside the former Soviet Union and one of only a handful of warm-water naval ports available to it worldwide)—was less overt about its assistance, but soon Moscow began to provide Assad with trainers, advisers and military and humanitarian supplies of its own.

The Russians' main contribution at this early stage, however, was diplomatic: Russia's representatives at the United Nations successfully blocked a draft UN Security Council resolution that might have authorized an international humanitarian intervention in Syria along the same lines as the UN-backed, NATO-led intervention in Libya that had helped topple Gaddafi.

Russian leaders (especially Vladimir Putin, at that time serving as Russian prime minister while his protégé Dmitri Medvedev took a turn as president) regarded the 2011 Libyan intervention as a profound betrayal of trust. UNSCR 1973—the UN Security Council Resolution signed on 17 March 2011, which authorized the Libyan intervention—framed the operation around protection of civilians, in line with the UN's self-declared "responsibility to protect," and explicitly ruled out the use of ground occupation forces.[4] U.S. leaders, including Vice President Biden, Secretary Clinton and Ambassador Susan Rice, had assured Medvedev that the intervention would have a purely humanitarian focus rather than one of regime change. As a result President Medvedev (to Putin's dismay and later criticism) directed Russian representatives to abstain, rather than voting against the resolution in the Security Council.

But in the event, special operators from at least five countries did deploy into Libya, and arms and advisors flowed to the rebels.[5] The operation had originally been conceived as a limited humanitarian no-fly zone, intended to lift regime pressure on the rebel stronghold of Benghazi and avert a massacre of civilians. But once airstrikes had pushed the regime back from Benghazi, opportunism took hold: the United States and other NATO nations (along with regional Arab powers) redirected airpower to support the rebels' advance toward Tripoli, seizing the opportunity to get rid of Gaddafi altogether.

Putin and the Russian foreign ministry, as well as Russian military leaders, were furious at what they saw as a bait-and-switch, a feeling only exacerbated by Secretary Clinton's triumphalism on the death of Gaddafi ("We came, we saw, he died!" she crowed on CBS television when she heard the news) or her subsequent portrayal of the dictator's fall as one of her key foreign policy accomplishments.[6] Secretary Clinton was lauded for "using her mixture of political pragmatism and tenacity to referee spats among NATO partners, secure crucial backing from Arab countries and tutor rebels on the fine points of message management."[7] She told the *Washington Post* "we set into motion a policy that was on the right side of history, on the right side of our values, on the right side of our strategic interests in the region."[8] These comments almost certainly provoked some table slamming in the Kremlin, and Vladimir Putin's feeling that the West had duped Medvedev contributed to Putin's return as president in 2012.

This time around, as the Security Council discussed intervention in Syria, the Russians were having none of it—not that leaders in Washington seemed to have the slightest appetite for getting involved in Syria either, despite the president's off-the-cuff assertion that Assad must go.[9]

On the rebel side, volunteers flooded into Syria from North Africa, the Arabian Peninsula, Central Asia and the former Soviet Union (with many Chechen and Daghestani fighters interested in taking down a Russian ally). Weapons and supplies came from Libya into Syria by sea, and from Arab states by land via Turkey, which left open its long border with Syria, while money flowed in from the Arabian Gulf and from charities and wealthy individuals worldwide. PKK-aligned Kurdish groups and peshmerga from Iraqi Kurdistan joined Syrian Kurds to protect northern and eastern Syria, while tribal forces arose in Hasakah, across Syria's frontier with Anbar. Core AQ, as it recovered in late 2011, directed its unruly Iraqi affiliate, ISI, now led by Abu Bakr al-Baghdadi, to organize a group to fight in Syria.[10]

Baghdadi was not the first to succeed Abu Musab al-Zarqawi as leader of ISI after his death in 2006. Zarqawi's immediate successors were Abu Ayyub al-Masri as military commander, and Hamid Khalil al-Zawi (whose *nom de guerre* was Abu Omar al-Baghdadi) as ideological head. The two men led AQI through its absorption into the Mujahidin Shura Council (Majlis Shura al-Mujahideen fi'l-'Iraq, MSC) an umbrella body for jihadist insurgents, which they established with five other jihadist insurgent factions at Ameriya, Baghdad in September 2006. They then oversaw MSC's absorption of its component groups and its transformation into ISI, only to be killed in April 2010 when U.S. forces located their safe house near Tikrit by tracking two of their three couriers.

The third courier—who, clearly, had been playing much more than a go-between role—took over as ISI leader in May 2010, at which point he assumed the name of Abu Bakr al-Baghdadi. Born near Samarra as Ibrahim Awwad Ibrahim Ali Muhammad al-Badri in 1971, Baghdadi's backstory remains sketchy. What we *think* we know is that he combined strong religious ideology with a close relationship to Saddam's regime. As a young man, he was a local preacher in Samarra, and had several relatives—including two uncles and at least one brother—in Saddam's military or security services. He was educated at the Islamic College of Saddam University in Baghdad which, despite the religious-sounding name, was actually a state-run body established to co-opt Islam in the service of Saddam's regime as part of the Faith Campaign (*al-Hamlah al-Imaniyah*) directed by, among others, Izzat Ibrahim al-Douri. Baghdadi earned a doctorate in Islamic Studies, and later claimed descent from the Prophet Mohammed via his son-in-law Ali. But it's clear that he was also, even at this early stage, closely connected to the Ba'athists.

Like many Iraqis, Baghdadi's life was transformed in 2003: after the U.S.-led invasion, he co-founded one of the dozens of independent resistance groups to emerge after Saddam fell, was arrested near Fallujah in February 2004, held as a civilian detainee at Camp Bucca in southern Iraq until December that year, and then released (according to U.S. records) or escaped (according to his ISIS biography).[11] It's unclear whether U.S. forces knew of Baghdadi's insurgent connections before he was arrested—his status of "civilian detainee" suggests they may not have. In any case, he was held at

Bucca with several future ISI leaders (many of them former Ba'athists or members of Saddam's intelligence and security services), and after being released from his detention he became increasingly active in the Salafi-jihadist wing of the insurgency. Baghdadi's guerrilla group became a founding faction of the Mujahidin Shura Council. Within a few months, the MSC absorbed its constituent groups to become ISI, and Baghdadi became an ISI commander in Diyala and the Baghdad belts before assuming overall leadership in 2010.

Baghdadi took over ISI at its lowest point, when the Surge had massively reduced the group's numbers, supporters and activity. Almost certainly his first goal was simply to keep a low profile and stay alive. But as the U.S. drawdown[12] continued in 2010 and 2011, it became much easier for ISI to plan and run operations.[13] Baghdadi was able to replenish ISI's leadership with former Ba'athist intelligence and special operations personnel, all with experience fighting the occupation, so that by late 2010 former regime officers represented at least a third of ISI's leadership, including its top military commander, Haji Bakr (whose real name was Samir Abd Muhammad al-Khlifawi), an ex-Iraqi Army intelligence colonel who'd been imprisoned with Baghdadi in Bucca. In this way, Baghdadi preserved a core of military experience, and by early 2011 he was able to restart offensive operations.

Like the core AQ leadership group, ISI was hugely affected by bin Laden's death and the failure of the Arab Spring—but for ISI (still at this time a nominal affiliate of AQ, albeit a fractious and often insubordinate one) the impact was positive. As bin Laden's death became known, Baghdadi announced a retaliatory terror campaign. By late 2011, ISI had launched more than 100 operations across Iraq, killing hundreds of Shi'a police, troops and officials.[14] As well as hitting security forces, Baghdadi ran a systematic assassination campaign against Sunni members of Iraq's parliament and against tribal leaders who'd joined the Awakening, and staged dozens of coordinated bombings and attacks. Unlike core AQ, ISI had stable leadership and no succession issues—Baghdadi had been running the group for almost a year by the time bin Laden was killed, and henchmen like Haji Bakr had orchestrated the expulsion or assassination of any potential rivals—so these attacks cemented his position (albeit making him increasingly dependent on former regime loyalists). The ISI attacks also drew little response from U.S. forces (who were in the final stages of pulling out, allies like Australia and the United Kingdom having already left). On 22 December 2011, days after the last American troops left, ISI exploded fifteen bombs across eleven districts of Baghdad, killing sixty-nine and injuring 169.[15] Even Baghdadi must have been surprised at his apparent impunity when these strikes drew no significant response.

His most important move, however, was to send a small band of experienced fighters into Syria in August 2011, followed by a more senior group (led by Haji Bakr) in late 2012. The move, as I mentioned, was initially directed by AQ central leadership, with the purpose of injecting AQ into the Syrian conflict so as to regain some traction in the Arab Spring. For ISI itself, the goal was more straightforward. The cadres had three objectives—preserve ISI's capability to rebuild, create strategic depth by expanding the group's operations into Syria, and exploit the emerging sectarian conflict there, which was starting to mirror the carnage AQI had provoked in Iraq, as resistance to Assad's urban-centered Alawite and Shi'a regime increasingly came from poor, pious, rural Sunnis. In Syria, ISI operatives found a better situation than they'd left in Iraq, for three reasons.

First, unlike the Syrian resistance, which was fragmented into dozens of groups and pulled apart by the interests of competing sponsors, ISI was a much more mature organization. It had evolved through consolidation and unification in 2004–6, learned from its mistakes during the Surge and developed battle-proven tactics. This made it better structured and more effective, helping it absorb other groups. ISI could also draw on the already-existing underground and auxiliary network it had created in Syria during the U.S. occupation to facilitate foreign fighters.[16] Likewise, the organization could draw on the expertise of experienced operatives from Saddam's intelligence service and the clandestine stay-behind network established by al-Douri.

Second, whereas the Syrian resistance in 2011 looked a lot like the Iraqi resistance of 2003—a collection of ex-soldiers, regime defectors and citizens with little battlefield experience—ISI fighters had years of tough combat under their belts. The cadres Baghdadi sent to Syria were survivors of the Surge, hardened veterans who knew exactly how to fight an urban guerrilla war and understood the Assad regime's tactics (which were not dissimilar from Maliki's). This quickly made them the best game in town, and many politically neutral Syrians (and increasing numbers of foreign fighters) joined ISI simply because it seemed the most capable and professional group.[17]

The third reason was subtler but more significant. Early in the war, when things looked grim for his regime, as his wife Asma was frantically emailing friends in the region to try to arrange safe passage for the family out of Syria, Bashar al-Assad began to portray the resistance as composed entirely of jihadists, and himself as the lesser of two evils.[18] This was the motivation behind Assad's release of jihadist prisoners from regime prisons at the start of the conflict, and behind the alleged support his intelligence service offered some jihadist groups. At first Assad's claim that the resistance was made up of jihadists was a barefaced lie, but when ISI turned up—as genuine a bunch of hyper-violent extremists as he could hope for—this dramatically bolstered Assad's narrative. So the regime did little to target ISI, letting it gain control of contested areas and carve out a safe haven in Raqqa province. For its part, ISI avoided confronting the regime, and a de facto truce emerged between the two, which lasted until late 2013. ISI had no need to confront the regime because its goal in Syria (at this stage) was to create a sanctuary where it could recover from its near-death experience in Iraq; by mid-2012, after a year in Syria, the recovery had been so successful that it could turn its operational focus back to Iraq.

But by this time, the relationship between ISI and AQ had also begun to break down irretrievably. The first ISI cadres to go to Syria served under the command of a veteran AQI operative of Syrian descent, Osama al-Absi al-Wahdi, whose *nom de guerre* was Abu Muhammad al-Jolani. Like Baghdadi, Jolani had done time in Bucca and risen through the ranks of AQI to become a regional guerrilla chief (in Jolani's case, heading ISI's cells in the Mosul area of Nineveh province). Like Baghdadi, Jolani had lived through the organization's near-collapse during the Surge and the Awakening, but unlike Baghdadi he'd concluded that the correct lesson from this experience was the need to form alliances with tribes and local communities, create humanitarian, rule-of-law and administrative programs to win the population over, establish coalitions with other armed groups, rein in the practice of *takfir* (excommunicating and killing other rebels who followed different ideologies) and pursue mass uprising rather than sectarian civil war. Jolani began applying this set of lessons—with increasing success—when he arrived in Syria.

This is not to suggest that Jolani was less of a jihadist than Baghdadi—quite the contrary—but in his attempt to create a broad-based uprising against Assad he was following Zawahiri's popular front model, rather than the sectarian provocation-intimidation cycle favored by Zarqawi and later Baghdadi. Within a few months, rifts were emerging between Jolani's group, Jabhat al-Nusra (JN), and Baghdadi, to the extent that both men complained to Zawahiri and sought his mediation.

The rift deepened through the second half of 2012, as JN continued working with secular nationalist rebels including the Western-backed Free Syrian Army, and cooperating with other jihadist (but non-ISI) groups such as Ahrar al-Sham. Haji Bakr's foray into Syria with the second group of ISI cadres in late 2012 was, at least partly, designed to reinforce Baghdadi's control over the increasingly autonomous Syrian faction. But in early April 2013, when Baghdadi demanded that JN formally acknowledge its membership of ISI, Jolani instead announced his direct allegiance to AQ's central leadership in Pakistan, publicly rejecting ISI's claim of control. Baghdadi responded by declaring ISI to be the Islamic State of Iraq and al-Sham (an archaic term for the Levant or, more narrowly, Syria)—otherwise known as ISIS.

When Zawahiri in Pakistan heard the news, he was furious, and expelled Baghdadi and ISIS from AQ—only to have Baghdadi deny that his group had ever been part of AQ, since it had grown from the Mujahidin Shura Council and ISI, rather than solely from Zarqawi's AQI. This hair-splitting did nothing to hide the fact that Zawahiri had irrevocably lost control of his wayward Iraqi franchise, and henceforward AQ and its allies (including the Taliban in Afghanistan and Pakistan, and JN in Syria) would be in open—often violent—conflict with ISIS.

Despite Baghdadi's open break with core AQ, and Jolani's secession in 2013, ISIS still maintained a powerful network and a growing military capability in Syria, and the war in Syria now gave ISIS the same advantage of interior lines that I mentioned earlier for

Iran. As we've seen, Baghdadi sent his cadres to Syria because his network was under pressure in Iraq; once the Americans had left Iraq and the Syria safe haven was established, the group could build up forces for its break back into Iraq, and when (in August 2014) this eventually brought an international response, it could swing back to Syria, where it continued to gain ground against Assad and competing rebel groups, even while losing territory in Iraq. By early 2015, coalition and Iraqi efforts had reduced the group's territorial holdings by as much as 25 per cent in Iraq, but in the same time-frame it had used its interior lines advantage to gain at least the same amount of ground in Syria, and then to mount the counterof-fensive (discussed later) that allowed it to capture Ramadi and Pal-myra in late May 2015.

In July 2012 Baghdadi declared that ISIS would return to its old operational heartland in Anbar, Diyala and the belts, called on Sun-nis to support him against the Shi'a government of Iraq and announced a year-long campaign he called "Breaking the Walls," with the goal of freeing ISI prisoners from Iraqi jails and attacking Shi'a officials and police.[19] An immediate spike in violence followed in Iraq, with bombings, assassinations, prison raids and attacks on government installations all over Iraq, bringing incident numbers to their highest level since 2007. By mid-2013, ISIS posed a significant threat to the Iraqi government, with bases, staging areas and train-ing camps in Anbar.[20] In August, Jessica Lewis of the Institute for the Study of War sounded the alarm:

> As of August 2013, AQI has regrouped, regained capabilities, and expanded into areas from which it was expelled during the Surge. AQI in 2013 is an extremely vigorous, resilient, and capable organization that can operate from Basra to coastal Syria ... The "Breaking the Walls" campaign ... consisted of a series of 24 major vehicle-borne improvised explosive device (VBIED) attacks and eight prison breaks that demon-strate the evolution of AQI's military capability over that time ... Since May 2013, AQI has consistently exceeded the number of VBIED attacks per month that it conducted in June 2007, while sustaining operations in Syria as well. The "Breaking the Walls" campaign ended on July 21, 2013, when al-Qaeda in Iraq successfully breached the prison at Abu Ghraib, leading to the escape of 500 or more prisoners, the majority of whom were detained during the Iraq War for terrorist activities.[21]

That same month, Maliki—who'd been only too happy to see the Americans leave in 2011—changed his tune.[22] He began calling urgently for U.S. drone strikes and renewed counterterrorism assistance, but was repeatedly rebuffed by Washington. Precisely why his requests were rejected remains unclear even now, but was almost certainly a White House decision since President Obama said around this time (in a speech at the National Defense University in May 2013) that he personally approved all drone strikes.[23] In any case, by September 2013 a new crisis had arisen, and it was the mishandling of this, more than anything else, that undermined U.S. leverage as the ISIS threat grew.

On 20 August 2012 President Obama had laid down a "red line" on the Syrian regime's weapons of mass destruction. He told reporters:

> I have, at this point, not ordered military engagement in the situation. But the point that you made about chemical and biological weapons is critical. That's an issue that doesn't just concern Syria; it concerns our close allies in the region, including Israel. It concerns us. We cannot have a situation where chemical or biological weapons are falling into the hands of the wrong people. We have been very clear to the Assad regime, but also to other players on the ground, that a red line for us is [if] we start seeing a whole bunch of chemical weapons moving around or being utilized. That would change my calculus. That would change my equation.[24]

The president's "red line" implied that the United States would consider a military response to Syrian use of chemical weapons, and White House spokespeople reinforced that interpretation in subsequent days.[25] Then in April 2013 the White House told Congress that chemical weapons would constitute a "game-changer."[26] It's possible this was simply a further example of the administration's unfortunate tendency to equate brave talk with effective action, but some Syrians saw a different rationale.[27] Several field sources told our researchers they believed the president was telegraphing a change of policy: "Assad must go" had been replaced by "Assad can stay, as long as he doesn't use chemical weapons." The Syrians' take was that U.S. policy had shifted from regime change to regime *behavior* change, that this was Washington's way of communicating—to Assad, but also to leaders in Tehran, with whom the administration was negotiating on Iran's nuclear program—that leaving Assad in power would be acceptable, provided he drew the line at massacring his own people (or, at least, did the massacring with artillery and barrel bombs rather than chemicals).

If that *was* the message, Assad ignored it. On 21 August 2013 the *New York Times* reported: "The Syrian government pounded rebellious areas east of the capital, Damascus, early Wednesday, and anti-government activists said some rockets included chemical weapons that killed scores of people, and possibly hundreds. Photographs and videos showed rooms full of lifeless bodies laid out in rows, some wrapped in white cloths, others lined up in mass graves. Some showed victims staring and motionless, others twitching uncontrollably."[28] This strike—around Ghouta, in the eastern suburbs of Damascus—was just the latest of several reports of chemical attacks by the regime, launched in response to unprecedented military gains by moderate (i.e. secular nationalist) rebels including the Free Syrian Army.

The White House was trapped by its own rhetoric. The administration temporized at first, questioning the eyewitness accounts, video and photographs of the attack.[29] But evidence for the Ghouta attack—if not proof of who'd done it—was incontrovertible, and as the casualty figures mounted into the thousands there were widespread calls for action. The president demurred, uncharacteristically seeking approval from Congress, while allies, including the UK, pushed for military action, and the White House sought to recast the "red line" in fuzzier terms. The message—to Syrians, allies, Americans and ISIS—was one of vacillating reluctance. Where President Bush was reckless, President Obama seemed feckless, and it was hard to know which was worse.

Compounding the humiliation, the administration was saved from its self-inflicted dilemma by the Russians, of all people. In what *Mother Jones* called a gaffe, "but maybe it's the good kind of gaffe,"[30] Secretary of State John Kerry, during a press conference in Paris, gave an "off-the-cuff response to a reporter who asked if there was anything Bashar al-Assad could do to avoid an American military strike. 'Sure,' Kerry said dismissively, he could turn over his entire arsenal of chemical weapons this week. That would do it. 'But he isn't about to do it,' Kerry said, 'and it can't be done, obviously.'" Russia's foreign minister, Sergey Lavrov—who was meeting with Assad's foreign minister, Walid al-Moallem, at the time— jumped on this to propose a compromise. Syria would hand over its chemical weapons, and in return Washington would take military action off the table. Soon an agreement was reached—and though

Damascus stalled, failed to comply and quietly kept using chemical weapons (at a smaller scale) through 2014 and 2015,[31] the military threat was removed. The relief in Washington was palpable.

Syrians were less relieved: for them, the way the regime was killing them mattered less than the fact that the slaughter went on apace, and that a chance for international action to stop it had been missed. Moreover, the regime's use of nerve gas had been an act of desperation, precisely because it was losing ground to a strong, moderate, non-jihadist coalition: international action against Assad at that point would have immeasurably strengthened the uprising, and moderate factions within it, at the expense of both the regime and the extremists. The failure to act, by contrast, empowered emerging AQ and ISIS factions and permanently weakened the prospects for a moderate post-Assad regime. Not for the first time, Washington's long-term strategic goals had been undercut by short-term tactical timidity.

The meta-message—lost on neither the Kremlin nor ISIS—was that acting against U.S. interests was now essentially risk-free, since no provocation, however severe, would prompt a response. Many subsequent problems in 2014–15 (in Iraq, Syria and Libya, but also, arguably, in Crimea, eastern Ukraine and the Baltic States) flowed from that perception of weakness.

As this played out, ISIS in Syria (which had rebuilt its networks after the defection of Jolani, and was now stronger than ever) was still largely ignoring the Assad regime and going after its rivals in the uprising—secular resistance groups, civil governance councils, and other jihadists, including JN. As our field teams worked to map the conflict in Aleppo in late 2013, we saw ISIS launch armed offensives against JN and others, gobbling up smaller groups, taking territory in the east and northeast, without ever seriously opposing the Syrian military's hold on the city's west. Fighters from the Islamic Front and secular groups who actually *were* on the front-lines told us they were being attacked by Assad from the front and by ISIS from the rear.[32] This gave Assad's military crucial breathing space, which it later used to recapture large parts of the city—and, unsurprisingly, fuelled conspiracy theories among Syrians that the regime (especially Air Force Intelligence, headquartered in northwestern Aleppo) was cooperating with ISIS to the east of the city. By then, ISIS had grown even stronger in Syria, captured all of Raqqa and parts of Idlib, Aleppo and

Deir ez-Zor, created rudimentary governance structures, and acquired funds, weaponry and recruits.

As 2013 reached its sorry end, ISIS made its move in Iraq. As so often in the past, the group applied its trademark strategy of hyper-violent intimidation, manipulating others' grievances, and exploiting sectarian conflict. In this it was abetted by Maliki's government, which had finally and fatally overplayed its hand.

8

COLLAPSE

The Fall of Maliki's Iraq

The Iraqi prime minister wasted no time after U.S. forces left in 2011: within days Maliki issued an arrest warrant against his Sunni vice president, Tariq al-Hashimi, on terrorism charges.[1] Hashimi (who immediately fled to Kurdistan and then to exile in Turkey) was sentenced to death in absentia in September 2012. A few months later Maliki targeted the finance minister, Rafi al-Issawi, arresting 150 of his staff, provoking protests by Sunnis that spiraled when Issawi narrowly survived an assassination attempt (which many Iraqis blamed on Maliki) in early 2013.[2] Demonstrations that had begun across Anbar in early 2012, with hundreds of thousands of Sunnis marching and staging Occupy-style protests, now spread across the country as Sunni grievances—the abuse of de-Ba'athification and anti-terrorism legislation by officials under Ahmad Chalabi, the denial of pensions and jobs to Sunnis based on connections to the old regime or supposed terrorist links, the hostile occupation by a Shi'a-led military and police, illicit seizure of property, and the increasingly powerful role of Iran in Iraqi politics—erupted. Shi'a communities joined these demonstrations in some areas, in Iraq's own version of the Arab Spring, to protest Maliki's increasingly autocratic behavior.

Maliki was now triple-hatted, having appointed himself defense minister and interior minister as well as prime minister, and continuing to centralize authority in his own hands. As mentioned, much of this behavior was just Maliki's reaction to changing incentives, as the U.S. drawdown made Iraqi politics zero-sum (veteran CSIS analyst Anthony Cordesman called it a "blood sport") and increased the relative influence of Iran. But there was a baffling short-sightedness to his approach. He was targeting *moderate* Sunni politicians: those who had rejected the insurgency, chosen to participate in the political process and were peacefully pursuing their interests through Iraq's institutions. Likewise, he was harassing precisely those tribal leaders (in the Awakening Councils) who'd turned *against* AQI and were merely seeking to protect their communities, rather than (like the Ba'athists) to reverse the outcome of 2003 or (like the jihadists) to drown the world in blood. Maliki's actions convinced many Sunnis of something AQI had been unable to persuade them of in 2006: that peaceful politics would never work, that armed struggle was the only route to survival. The new deal for Iraq's Sunnis, which we had pulled together in 2007 after so much chaos, blood and suffering—and which had helped defeat AQI in its first incarnation—had finally fallen apart.

In May 2013 Iraqi police and troops destroyed a protest camp at Hawija, killing dozens of Sunni civilians in a massacre widely broadcast on Iraqi television. The Hawija massacre brought a host of insurgent groups into the fight—including al-Douri's network (the Supreme Command for Jihad and Liberation), an allied Naqshbandi Sufi militia, fighters from the Dulaim tribal confederation under Ali Hatem al-Suleiman, veteran Sunni nationalist insurgents like Abdullah al-Janabi, and of course ISIS. This prompted the Kurdish regional government to deploy peshmerga around Kirkuk—only to be accused of expansionism by Baghdad. Violence spiked massively over just a few weeks in summer and fall 2013: a new uprising against Maliki was in full swing.

In January 2014 ISIS fighters from Syria—well-trained, well-equipped and in huge numbers—surged across the now-illusory border into Anbar in large conventional columns of armed and armored vehicles, joining guerrillas who had already been active in Fallujah and Ramadi, in an offensive that drove the government out of both cities. The initial push left ISIS in complete control of Fallujah, and in partial control of Tikrit (Saddam Hussein's home town and a long-standing center of Sunni insurgency) and Ramadi, capital of Anbar. The offensive was noteworthy in part because of its speed and violence, in part because of ISIS numbers and capabilities, but mainly—to my eyes, anyway—because it telegraphed that ISIS had moved beyond its recovery phase of 2011–12, beyond the renewed insurgency of "Breaking the Walls," into what guerrilla-warfare theorists call a "War of Movement." ISIS was acting more like a conventional army than a guerrilla organization: instead of operating in small, clandestine cells, in plain clothes, by night, with civilian vehicles and light weapons, ISIS was running columns comprising dozens of technicals, trucks, artillery pieces, and captured armored vehicles. It was moving openly, in large groups, by day, in uniform, fielding heavy weapons (mortars, rockets and heavy machine guns). Its tactics combined urban terrorism and clandestine reconnaissance with mobile columns, snipers, roadside bombs, suicide attackers and terrorist cells, showing a level of sophistication well beyond that of AQI in 2006–7. And as it captured territory, it was acquiring tanks, heavy armored vehicles, artillery and vast amounts of funding, and picking up recruits. ISIS was thinking and fighting like a state: it had emerged from the shadows.

Iraqi police and military counterattacks against Fallujah and Ramadi failed in January, and ISIS expanded towards Baghdad, Nineveh and the Kurdish region in March. Further ISIS victories followed in April, and government countermoves failed—because most Sunnis had given up on Baghdad, and because Maliki's politicization of the army and police had left their leadership corrupt, hollow and lacking in skill or commitment.[3] The clincher came in May, when Maliki announced another offensive against ISIS-held towns, but also irrevocably alienated the few Sunnis who might still have been willing to trust his government by framing the fight as a battle between Sunni and Shi'a.[4] The offensive, after some initial successes, had failed by early June. The rotten, hollowed-out edifice of Maliki's military collapsed, Mosul fell, a string of other towns followed, and the ISIS blitzkrieg was rolling.

On 29 June an ISIS Twitter account announced the renaming of ISIS as "Islamic State" and declared a caliphate with Abu Bakr al-Baghdadi at its head. A week later, Baghdadi announced the caliphate before an assembly of worshippers in the Grand Mosque of Mosul, declared himself the Caliph Ibrahim and called on Muslims worldwide to obey him. His next move, however, would be his boldest.

9

RETRIBUTION

War with the Caliphate, 2014–15

I happened to be off-grid when Mosul fell—in the Colombian jungle, of all places, at a combat outpost in the northern Andes ranges, partway through a research trip with two colleagues studying the Colombian government's fight against the FARC guerrillas.[1] As night fell, we flew down from the mountains to the provincial capital, through a tropical rainstorm, and back into cellphone range. The very moment that the big Russian Mi-17 troop-lift helicopter touched down on the military airfield at Montería, its tires still rolling across the rain-slicked tarmac, my phone lit up. Nine text messages and four voicemails: something big was going on.

Yasir Abbas and Dan Trombly, members of our research team who'd spent two years tracking events in Iraq and Syria, wrote one of the first detailed assessments of the fall of Mosul. Their analysis is worth discussing at length, because Mosul was not an aberration: the problems that led to the city's fall were widespread across the Iraqi police and military, and were repeated in battles across the country throughout 2014 and 2015.

The fall of Mosul dragged the world's attention back to Iraq, startling many who had hoped to move on from it—not least, if his West Point speech twelve days earlier was anything to go by, President Obama himself. Observers were shocked by the "stunningly weak performance of the Iraqi Security Forces," especially given the vast amounts of money and effort that Americans and coalition partners had poured into these institutions over the past decade.[2] But as Abbas and Trombly pointed out, the Iraqi military and police didn't collapse overnight: both organizations had been failing, under pressure from a resurgent ISIS, for over a year before Mosul fell. What was new was that the "retreat was voluntary and disorganized rather than forced by heavy fighting. Based on interviews with … active and former Iraqi soldiers, along with civilians living in their area of operations, and supplemented with open-source research,"[3] Abbas and Trombly identified a series of structural weaknesses that left Iraqi units like the Army's Second Division, responsible for Nineveh Province (of which Mosul is the capital), vulnerable to a rout. These weaknesses included corruption among officers and civilian officials, shortfalls in supplies and equipment, and lack of personnel.

Another problem, as I said earlier, was the lack of a clear chain of command. The Second Division, though responsible for countering ISIS across Nineveh, lacked authority over its own operations. In Nineveh as elsewhere, Prime Minister Maliki had established a parallel command structure, reporting directly to him, the Nineveh Operations Command (NOC). This made sense for Maliki from a coup-proofing standpoint, but in military terms it was a disaster waiting to happen. NOC continually interfered with Second Division's planning and operations, and those of the other main combat unit in Nineveh, the Third Division of the constabulary force known as the Iraqi National Police (INP), part of the Ministry of the Interior (also headed by Maliki). But when the main ISIS attack developed in early June 2014, NOC was unable to coordinate the battle and quickly fled. Units gave up their positions without a fight, a chaotic rout of defeated soldiers and police streamed toward Baghdad in a panic, and the Iraqi forces abandoned thousands of weapons, hundreds of vehicles and artillery pieces, several aircraft, billions of dollars worth of Iraqi government funds and much other valuable equipment, all of which was seized by ISIS.

At the tactical level, the design of Mosul's defenses was fundamentally flawed. After being attacked in an escalating series of car bombs, assassinations and suicide attacks since late 2013, NOC decided to lock down the city, setting up vehicle checkpoints and placing guard posts on many intersections, aggressively searching vehicles, and detaining large numbers of people for questioning. This intrusive approach choked Mosul and did much to alienate and irritate the population—one resident described conditions there as like living inside a military base—but it also drew Iraqi forces back from the peri-urban space around Mosul and concentrated them inside the city itself, allowing ISIS to maneuver freely in the city's outskirts and around the Mosul region.

This defensive crouch amounted to ceding both the initiative and the rural environment to ISIS. It tied down soldiers and police in static urban security tasks, in such a way that the Second Division was heavily overcommitted to guard and garrison duties—so that, despite vast numbers of troops deployed in Nineveh province (upwards of 60,000 soldiers, according to some observers), the army could muster too few reserves at the critical place and time to respond as the ISIS main attack developed on 6–7 June. The military and police laydown was designed to protect against small-cell asymmetric attacks—the kinds of threats that AQI and ISIS had conditioned the Iraqis to expect throughout much of 2012 and 2013. But when 800 ISIS fighters turned up simultaneously on the city's outskirts, moving fast in a compact column, with heavy weapons, artillery, armored vehicles and technicals, and launched a conventional-style maneuver assault into the heart of Mosul, the garrison forces were overwhelmed.

In part, poor tactical choices by Second Division's leaders (most of whom, like their troops, were Shi'a) reflected a view of the civilian population as enemies to be guarded against, rather than as actual or potential allies and sources of information. At a political level, this was an inevitable result of the Iraqi government's systematic purging of competent Sunni officers and non-political Shi'a after the coalition's departure, and then garrisoning a mostly Sunni and Kurdish city with Shi'a troops and police led by political cronies of the prime minister, who took their orders from a Shi'a-supremacist government in distant Baghdad. The same problem can also be seen in the extremely poor relationship between Prime Minister Maliki and Atheel al-Nujaifi, the Sunni governor of Nineveh province—who happened to be the brother of Osama al-Nujaifi, one of Maliki's main political opponents. Coordination between city, province and national-level defense plans was virtually non-existent as a result. Provincial and local police loyal to Governor

Nujaifi (drawn from, and thus closer to, the local population) could have played a critical role in protecting the city and giving early warning of the ISIS thrust. But they'd been systematically excluded and marginalized by INP and NOC for years, leaving them alienated and unable to assist—though many stayed at their posts until well after the INP and Army had fled.[4]

In military terms, the choice to focus on static security also reflected the lack of capacity of the Iraqi forces, which had suffered neglect in terms of funding, training and leadership since the U.S. withdrawal. Manning checkpoints was relatively easy for garrison troops like these, but active defense against a fast-moving enemy was beyond them. "Corrupt military and police practices, such as soliciting bribes for the release of detainees or extorting business owners, only compounded this problem," Abbas and Trombly pointed out.[5] On the subject of corruption, their analysis is worth quoting at length:

> Prior to 2012 [i.e. before the departure of American advisers] the 2nd Division commander, Staff General Naser al-Ghanam, tried and failed to enforce military discipline and discourage corruption, much to the chagrin of the rank and file ... In the Iraqi army, leadership at the division level maintains enough sway over logistics and pay to embezzle and extort lower ranks. Many officers see their units as businesses with reliable revenues rather than combat outfits. "You don't earn a [command position]: you buy it," a Captain in the Iraqi army said. The administrative structure of Iraqi forces aggravates this problem. For example, high-ranking officers are supposed to budget food purchases for their soldiers and deduct money for them out of their salaries. In practice, officers pocket most of this money, and establish revenue quotas for subordinates. Soldiers in Mosul often had to purchase their own food and water from civilian markets and cook themselves, adding additional duties onto already undesirably long working hours. Practices such as selling valuable fuel on the civilian black market and the embezzlement of money meant for food reduce readiness and willingness to fight. "[Corruption] takes more than soldiers' food rations. It takes their dignity and self-respect as well," an Iraqi officer explained. These units are left with a command climate where illicit payments are more important than effective operations or combat performance. Although many forms of corruption are detrimental to soldiers, some create mutually beneficial arrangements. Higher-ranking officers often keep absent soldiers on the payroll, offering soldiers the opportunity to leave or never even report for duty in exchange for pocketing a portion of their salaries. Consequently,

many estimates of Iraqi force strength include these absent soldiers, dubbed "aliens," a problem soldiers in 2nd Division attested they were familiar with. Not only do these practices reduce manpower, they also undermine the unit cohesion of soldiers still on the battlefield. Knowing that their fellow soldiers are still receiving some pay after effectively deserting, units lose—or fail to develop—an *esprit de corps* necessary to sustain strenuous operations. In Mosul this was compounded by [ISIS] assassinations of soldiers returning from leave. For many, incentives to desert ... became compelling.

This corrupt and demoralized force collapsed like a rotten outhouse as soon as ISIS gave it a solid shove.

The same pattern emerged elsewhere: as Mosul was being captured, a string of other towns and cities was falling to ISIS. Tikrit fell the day after Mosul, while ISIS pushed into a series of towns west and south of Kirkuk, captured the city of Bayji and besieged its important oil refinery. ISIS fighters and other rebels took control of ten towns and cities across Saladin province in the next week, while a further thrust developed toward Baghdad, creating near panic among some residents. Then, two weeks after Mosul, the Iraqi government lost two critical crossing points on the Iraqi–Syrian frontier, at Waleed and al-Qaim, giving ISIS complete freedom of movement between Iraq and Syria.

As C.J. Chivers—the intrepid, widely travelled war correspondent for the *New York Times*—reported at the time, these crossings collapsed without a serious fight, much as Mosul had. Chivers' assessment was damning: "The account of the Ninth Brigade of Iraq's border guards, confirmed by an official who witnessed many of the events, is a portrait of generals unfit to lead in war and of mismanagement, incompetence and ultimately treachery under the patronage of Prime Minister Nuri Kamal al-Maliki."[6]

The Ninth Brigade was not permanently based in al-Qaim: the unit was part of the Fourth Division of the Iraqi Border Police, stationed on the other side of the country, in the southern Shi'a city of Basra, and drawn from the local Basrawi population. The Brigade's move to al-Qaim was part of a surge of Shi'a units from the south to try to stem the tide of the ISIS advance after the fall of Mosul. "Inspired by the call to arms against Sunni militants by Grand Ayatollah Ali al-Sistani on June 13, they danced with weapons in ceremonies, chanting that they would prevail. Many of the ceremonies were attended by journalists in Basra and Maj. Gen. Ali Waham al-Maliki, the division commander [and a member of the prime minister's tribe]."[7] General Maliki had been dismissed from another command in 2008 for diverting weapons to Shi'a militias targeting Sunnis, but was quietly reinstated once the Americans left.

Ninth Brigade departed for al-Qaim on 14 June, but suffered from lack of food and water, intense desert heat, and a contract-based supply system that was adequate in their home location of Basra, but failed when the Brigade deployed to a war zone where civilian contractors could not accompany it and local communities were hostile. Far from its normal, peacetime environment—guarding the quiet border with Iran, and surrounded by friendly Shi'a population—the Brigade was out of its depth, though its commanders didn't yet realize it.

"By June 17," Chivers reported, "the brigade was in position around Qaim, with hopes of blocking ISIS fighters' free passage to and from Syria. But supplies were so depleted the troops could barely fight. Its members said they were given only a small piece of cake and about 10 ounces of water a day. Morale sank further, brigade members said, because another unit in Qaim had already run out of water and food, prompting the Ninth Brigade to share its meager stores. Moreover, the local people refused to help, police officers said, either because they had sided with ISIS or were afraid, and did not want to risk the militants' wrath."[8]

At this point the Brigade Commander, Brigadier Sadiq Rasheed Abdilal, left al-Qaim, claiming he was going to higher headquarters to complain about the lack of support. He never returned: an officer on his staff claimed he'd left for "business in Baghdad." On 22 June, after only five days in position, the Brigade was ordered to abandon al-Qaim and move to Waleed. During a harrowing desert journey, in which the police took more than eleven hours to cover only 180 miles, a combat group of ISIS fighters mounted in heavily armed technicals appeared suddenly from the flank to ambush and scatter the column of more than sixty soft-skinned police vehicles. Continually harried by flank attacks that would emerge with no warning from the desert, the Brigade lost cohesion, ran out of water, and the withdrawal turned into a rout. General Maliki, accompanied by news cameras, met the survivors at a rally point on the main highway and made an ostentatious show of distributing water, but the police felt like involuntary props in the general's personal action movie, and promptly rebelled:

> After General Maliki's visit, the Ninth Brigade began to disintegrate, with troops loading themselves onto their trucks and leaving pell-mell. General Maliki fled to a position down the road. Many of his troops pursued him there, and demonstrated outside the building he stopped in, firing in the air, according to a border guard who was there. Another contingent chased the head of Iraq's border guards, Lt. Gen. Hussein al-Awadi, to a headquarters used by a commando unit, they said, and briefly cornered him there. "Everyone was cursing him and threatening to kill him," said a non-commissioned officer who participated in the confrontation. That contingent of the brigade's remnants then drove toward Karbala, he said, to discover that General Awadi had told forces defending the city that ISIS had defeated the Ninth Brigade and would attack wearing border-police uniforms. A standoff ensued before the border police convinced the checkpoint that they were not militants.[9]

As these accounts suggest, what happened in Iraq in mid-2014 was more than just a military defeat. It was the collapse of the entire post-Saddam social and political order, a failure of national and organizational cohesion across the board, and a retribution—both for neglect and arrogance on the part of Iraq's political elites, and for complacency on the part of the United States and other coalition partners who had put so much blood and effort into stabilizing the country, only to walk away and ignore both the danger signs and the Iraqis' repeated calls for assistance. It was also a stinging indictment of Western military and police assistance, a critical element of the Disaggregation strategy, which—as in other countries where the formula had failed—had proven simply unable to produce a partner force capable of stabilizing its own country against a terrorist threat.

As well as being an indictment of Disaggregation, the ISIS breakout of 2014 was an indication that the terrorist organization had retained an impressive capacity for rapid tactical adaptation. When I served in Iraq in 2006 and 2007, as I've described already, AQI used classic guerrilla tactics. They wore civilian clothes, drove Toyota pickup trucks or BMWs, moved covertly, operated by night, used light weapons, and carried out bombings, assassinations and kidnappings to intimidate populations and security forces. They never really controlled terrain, nor did they seek to administer or govern populations. Their key weakness at that time—one that almost proved fatal for them during the Awakening—was their failure to win support from local communities or build alliances with other jihadist groups, while their reliance on terror turned tribal and Sunni nationalist fighters against them.

By mid-2014, in contrast, ISIS fighters wore full military uniforms, organized themselves in large units, carried standardized field equipment and weapons, operated openly by day, and applied a consistent set of conventional maneuver tactics. The battles of summer 2014—including the capture of Mosul, Samarra and Tikrit, the capture of al-Qaim and Waleed, fighting against the Kurds near Kirkuk and around the Bayji oil refinery and Mosul dam—were all set-piece "combined arms" assaults that used IEDs, mortars, artillery, infantry, snipers, tanks and other armored vehicles in close coordination. ISIS guerrillas and urban terror cells still operated across Iraq, but their purpose now was as an adjunct to conventional maneuver by the main force. The guerrilla groups operated in advance and on the flanks of fast-moving armored columns, with clandestine cells destabilizing regime-held cities like Mosul, and swarms of technicals scouting ahead of the main armored force. The role of terrorist attacks (especially suicide bombings), at this stage of ISIS's tactical evolution, was primarily to intimidate security forces, push them into a defensive posture, and force them to concentrate on urban areas to protect critical infrastructure, freeing the main ISIS force to maneuver without opposition or detection, and allowing ISIS cadres to organize the local population in rural and peri-urban zones now denuded of government presence.

ISIS was also learning from past political mistakes and taking care to construct broader alliances. By mid-2014 it was just one of fourteen groups fighting the Iraqi government in western Iraq, as part of a political front that included tribal fighters, Ba'athists, al-Douri's Naqshbandi militia, and several smaller militant groups. Beside its newfound political sophistication, ISIS was putting more effort into governance: it was administering territory, appointing governors (tellingly, often former Ba'ath generals from Saddam's regime), building roads, and operating courts, hospitals, and food distribution centers. The organization was levying taxes, and controlling key water, electricity and oil and gas infrastructure. Its capture of government treasuries in Mosul, Fallujah and Tikrit gave it billions of dollars in assets, along with daily revenues of well over US$1.5 million. Despite rejecting Zawahiri and Jolani's hearts-and-minds, governance-heavy approach during their breakup with core AQ, ISIS leaders had nonetheless implemented—in some fashion—many of the same ideas. But the group also had exploitable weaknesses, and as the U.S. government finally began to recover from its initial shock at the end of summer 2014, these began to emerge.

In the first weeks after the fall of Mosul, U.S. policy seemed to be in complete disarray. The day Mosul fell, as ISIS columns were launching their final push to capture Tikrit, White House deputy press secretary Josh Earnest seemed to be dialing in from a different planet, one where the counterterror strategy was still going perfectly well. Responding to criticism of Hillary Clinton's record, Earnest said "In terms of important foreign policy accomplishments for which Secretary Clinton can rightly claim her share of the credit [alongside the president] I would put ending the war in Iraq, responsibly winding down the war in Afghanistan, and decimating and destroying core al-Qaeda—those are a handful of accomplishments that certainly this President and this Commander-in-Chief are proud of, but it's one that … Secretary Clinton can justifiably be proud of as well."[10] To be fair, Earnest was simply repeating the talking points he'd been given, which the U.S. government had not yet had time to update in response to such a rapidly developing catastrophe. But in practice the Pentagon was moving fast in response to the disaster.

By 19 June, the U.S. Navy had established combat air patrol—a continuous stream of fighter aircraft on station over central Iraq to protect key locations and engage targets of opportunity. This created the basis for future offensive strikes, and helped blunt ISIS moves against Kirkuk and into the outskirts of Baghdad. It illustrated the strategic flexibility, poise and speed of action unique to aircraft carriers and naval forces more broadly—but also, of course, highlighted the cost of the earlier decision to remove land-based strike aircraft from the Iraqi theater. Carrier aircraft lacked the endurance to remain on station over Iraq for lengthy periods of time, and while they provided a crucial early response there was a need to back them up with air-to-air refueling and land-based aircraft, as soon as possible.

By the end of June, American troops were at Baghdad International Airport, setting up an airhead through which more U.S. military personnel arrived, soon including a special operations team given the job of helping Iraqi commanders with planning, providing intelligence support, and training and advising Iraqi forces. These were the first U.S. troops based in country since the end of 2011; apart from their formal mission, they also provided a pretext for intervention in "self-defense" if American personnel came under attack. Then in August, after a gradual build-up throughout July, President Obama formally announced U.S. military intervention, framing the operation around humanitarian goals—the same "protection of civilians" language he and Secretary Clinton had used during Libya—and to protect the U.S. forces now deployed in Iraq.

But as the air campaign got underway, most of the initial airstrikes into Iraq were directed on the Kurdish front, first to relieve pressure on Irbil from yet another ISIS thrust that was threatening the city and had encroached on the outskirts of Kirkuk and around the town of Amerli, and then into the Sinjar area where 50,000 men, women and children of the Yazidi religious minority were surrounded by ISIS and faced a threat of genocide. The initial effort came from the U.S. Navy's Carrier Strike Group Two, centered on the aircraft carrier USS *George H.W. Bush*, which had been in the North Arabian Sea supporting operations in Afghanistan, but passed the straits of Hormuz into the Arabian Gulf and began strike operations in Iraq within a few days. Land-based aircraft, including Australian and British planes, joined in after a few weeks, operating from airstrips across the region.

In mid-August, 130 additional U.S. military advisers deployed to northern Iraq to help the Kurds, and President Obama notified Congress that the air campaign would expand to protect infrastructure (including the still-encircled Bayji oil refinery and the Haditha and Mosul dams, all of which had been seized or threatened by ISIS) and to directly target ISIS. Other allies—including the UK, France, Canada and Australia—began conducting airstrikes and deploying advisers as well, and on 14 August the British government acknowledged that Special Air Service troops were in northern Iraq. A week later, U.S. Marines and British special operators landed on Mount Sinjar in small numbers to coordinate the air evacuation of the Yazidis, and combat controllers were inserted by helicopter onto mountaintops in the area, setting up observation posts from which they could designate targets for air strikes to cover the rescue mission. Australian aircraft dropped humanitarian relief supplies to the Yazidis, and a peshmerga offensive broke through the encirclement, allowing many Yazidis to escape into Kurdish-controlled territory. While the rescue was made much of in the international media, as one of the few positive news stories of a terrible month in Iraq, the Sinjar massacre was an utter disaster for the Yazidis as a people: ISIS captured at least 5,000 members of the group on Mount Sinjar, beheaded or shot the men and boys, enslaved the women, and forced girls as young as eight to become sex slaves for their fighters.[11]

Protecting Iraqi civilians like the Yazidis wasn't the only purpose of the intervention, however: it was around this time that ISIS began publicly executing Western hostages, beginning with the beheading of American journalist James Foley on 19 August. U.S. special operators had already launched a raid into Raqqa district in Syria on 4 July in an unsuccessful attempt to rescue Foley. More beheadings followed: on 2 September, ISIS murdered Israeli-American journalist Steven Sotloff, prompting media outrage and driving President Obama to make his clearest statement so far about U.S. strategy against ISIS. Using the U.S. government acronym for the group, the president stated:

> Our objective is clear, and that is to *degrade and destroy ISIL so that it's no longer a threat not just to Iraq but also the region and to the United States.* In order for us to accomplish that, the first phase has been to make sure that we've got an Iraqi government that's in place and that we are blunting the momentum that ISIL was carrying out. And the airstrikes have done that. But now what we need to do is make sure that we've got the regional strategy in place that can support an ongoing effort—not just in the air but on the ground—to move that forward.[12] [Emphasis added.]

The moment of clarity passed: the president immediately offered several caveats and qualifications, emphasizing "it's going to take time for us to be able to roll them back. And it is going to take time for us to be able to form the regional coalition that's going to be required so that we can reach out to Sunni tribes in some of the areas that ISIS has occupied, and make sure that we have allies on the ground in combination with the airstrikes that we've already conducted."[13] He also immediately walked back his stated intent to destroy ISIS: "As we've seen with al Qaeda, there are always going to be remnants that can cause havoc of any of these networks … But what we can do is to make sure that the kind of systemic and broad-based aggression that we've seen out of ISIL [is] degraded to the point where it is no longer the kind of factor that we've seen it being over the last several months."[14]

If the president's goals were unclear in theory, the new "Counter-ISIL Coalition" formed in response was soon clarifying them in practice: on 3 September the U.S. announced the deployment of an extra 350 special operations and intelligence personnel to Baghdad on a "joint assessment mission," bringing U.S. forces in Iraq to 1200. A week later another 500 trainers were deployed, though prohibitions remained against advisers accompanying units in combat or taking direct action against ISIS. For its part, ISIS responded by releasing a video showing the beheading of British aid worker David Haines near Raqqa, upon which the coalition expanded its air operations into Syria. French aircraft struck ISIS positions on 19 September, then on 22 September U.S. and Arab partners (Bahrain, Jordan, Qatar, Saudi Arabia and the United Arab Emirates) launched airstrikes, missile strikes and drone attacks. The air campaign was on: the coalition was at war with the caliphate.

The new, more conventional style of ISIS operations—which had evolved in an environment without much air threat—made the group highly vulnerable to coalition air strikes once they eventually began in earnest across Iraq and Syria in August–September 2015. The introduction of air power into the conflict forced ISIS to take cover in the cities among the civilian population, blunted its lightning advance, and enabled Kurdish ground forces (the now better-armed, better-supported peshmerga) to regain territory and relieve the Yazidis near Sinjar—though not, as we've seen, in time to prevent a massacre.

As the ISIS blitzkrieg stalled, the organization was still deeply unpopular with other insurgent groups—it was involved in violent clashes with other Iraqi rebels near al-Qaim as early as July, and Ba'athist and tribal leaders spoke, at several conferences over the summer, of "cleaning house" against ISIS once their territorial gains against the government had been consolidated. There was also fear and resentment from civilians in Syria and Iraq who had been subjected to the ISIS brand of *sharia*, including regular beheadings, floggings, amputations and crucifixions. The group was also, of course, in open conflict with core AQ, whose leaders continued angrily to denounce it, and ISIS fighters were battling Jolani's JN and its allies in several parts of Syria. And many Islamist groups, in Iraq and the wider Muslim world, were beginning to decry Baghdadi's announcement of the caliphate as arrogant and over-reaching.

Indeed, the situation seemed virtually unprecedented: ISIS now had the United States, the Russians, the Iranians, the Israelis, the Iraqis, the Syrians, the Saudis, the Arab Gulf states (even AQ!) in arms against it. On the surface, at least, it seemed as if this group of rivals and enemies had finally found something in common, in their desire to crush ISIS. Still, as ISIS consolidated its control of Mosul, Fallujah and Tikrit in late 2014 and coalition planners and diplomats met in crisis discussions like the one I attended that November, ISIS was still in a strong central position and it was clear that rolling it back would be immensely difficult. And as 2015 began, things were about to get much, much worse.

10

ROLLBACK?

Iraq and Syria, Winter 2014–15

As planners and policy experts met in late 2014 to consider their options, it seemed that a counter-offensive against ISIS would be tough, but do-able. The difficult question (in conferences like the one I described at the start of this book and, I presume, in classified planning meetings also) was not "can we defeat ISIS" but rather "and then what"? Assuming that military action against ISIS would have international support, and that Western politicians would have the will to carry it out (both of which turned out to be enormously problematic assumptions), it was easy to sketch out how the military campaign outlined by President Obama in September would need to be constructed to have any chance of success.

From the outset, it was clear there would be no Western ground invasion or re-occupation of Iraq. Even if the will to do so had existed among Western leaders (and President Obama, in announcing the air campaign, had very clearly signaled that it didn't) or if Iraqi politicians had been willing to contemplate such an operation (and Iraqis of all political parties were telling us that they weren't) it would have taken months or years to pull such a campaign together, and required logistic, military and political resources that simply weren't available fifteen years after 9/11 and more than a decade after President Bush's initial, horribly ill-judged invasion of Iraq. Instead, a rollback operation would need to look more like the invasion of Afghanistan in 2001, the intervention in Libya in 2011 or perhaps the air campaign (and subsequent ground-based stabilization operation) in the former Yugoslavian enclave of Kosovo in 1999.

Such a war against the Islamic State would need to start with a sustained, intensive air campaign, aiming to destroy the columns of tanks, armored vehicles and artillery ISIS was fielding across Iraq, and which as we've seen had been operating openly in "war of movement" mode since 2013. The ISIS approach had worked against the demoralized Iraqi Army with its structural problems, capability shortfalls and political weaknesses. But as the initial round of airstrikes into Iraq and Syria showed in August 2014, this way of operating also made ISIS vulnerable to air power.

Clearly, airpower alone could not defeat ISIS—although the initial air strikes had blunted the ISIS summer offensive. Instead, coalition planners at this time were examining how to apply Combined Arms, the same technique ISIS had used so effectively in the Mosul fighting. Combined Arms uses disparate forces, closely coordinated, to deliver what amounts to a one-two punch, each force exposing weaknesses the other can target. In a campaign against ISIS, this would take the form of joint air-ground maneuver, in which ground troops would stop enemy units from dispersing into cover, and flush them out, letting aircraft target them. In turn, aircraft would stop the enemy counterattacking or massing in defence, letting ground troops move forward to attack them and maneuver to continue the process.

Done well, as in the opening months of the Afghan war of 2001, this can bring rapid results. In that campaign, U.S. bombers (including massive, Cold War-era B-52s) and strike aircraft did most of the killing using both precision guided munitions and unguided rockets and bombs, enabled by Afghan ground forces that identified targets, forcing the Taliban to maneuver and reveal their positions to the pilots so that they could be destroyed. In turn, the aircraft protected ground troops, helping them seize territory and close with enemy forces, which could not concentrate to defend their positions lest they be targeted from the air.

Within days, airstrikes allowed local anti-Taliban forces to begin advancing from their defensive positions north of the strategic airbase at Bagram; within a fortnight they were on a roll, pushing the Taliban back all across the country's north. On 9 November, just over a month after the beginning of the air campaign, Rashid

Dostum's fighters took Mazar e-Sharif; three days later forces under Ismail Khan seized the western city of Herat, in the fight that wounded Zarqawi and forced him to flee into Iran. The next day Northern Alliance troops captured Kabul, and so on—a series of victories by Afghan ground troops supported by U.S. and coalition airpower and coordinated by tiny teams of U.S. specialists on the ground. The Taliban never came up with a way to counter these tactics—their last stronghold at Kandahar fell on 7 December, only eight weeks after bombing began. On that day there were only about 110 CIA personnel, along with a few hundred military intelligence and special ops people, in Afghanistan—but there were more than 50,000 Afghans fighting the Taliban.

For all its tactical brilliance, though (and noting what I said earlier about how success in Afghanistan turned policy-makers' heads, making them more enamored than the facts justified with light-footprint approaches, "Shock and Awe" and the "New American Way of War"), there were two huge problems in applying this model to Iraq and Syria. The first was political timidity in coalition capitals.

President Obama and others had publicly and repeatedly ruled out deploying Western combat troops against ISIS. But Afghan-style results would, by definition, require putting troops into combat—although not necessarily the deployment of full combat units, a fine distinction with lots of political significance but not much practical meaning on the ground. To make the light-footprint approach work, a combination of special operations teams and Joint Terminal Attack Controllers (JTACs—specialists in controlling airstrikes from forward positions) would need to move into battle with local forces, designating targets, coordinating air support, and offering tactical advice. In the business, this is known as "advise, assist and accompany."

But in the intervention of 2014, coalition support was limited to "advise and assist" only, a posture that permits training and logistics, but not combat advising or the deployment of forward air controllers on the ground. As General Martin Dempsey, Chairman of the Joint Chiefs of Staff, noted in Congressional testimony in September 2014, this could change as things developed, so commanders and planners were keen to keep this option open, even as politicians seemed perplexingly eager pre-emptively to rule it out.

The second problem, also political, was more local. The ground forces with which coalition teams would need to partner—the equivalent of the Northern Alliance in the Afghan example—were in disarray: deeply so in Iraq, near-totally in Syria. The Iraqi Army was losing virtually all its engagements with ISIS at this time, retreating when it could, getting slaughtered when it couldn't. The Sunni National Guard, a belated attempt by Maliki to recreate the local security forces that had grown from the Awakening and the Sons of Iraq, was likely to be stillborn—unless Sunnis could stifle their suspicion of a Baghdad regime that had so badly betrayed them after the Awakening. At the same time, the growing Shi'a militias, though highly motivated, lacked combat capability, and their extreme sectarian anti-Sunni and anti-Western politics made them unwilling to work with Western advisors and unlikely to win the confidence of Sunni communities. On the Kurdish side, the peshmerga, despite a good showing in the counteroffensive at Sinjar and Amerli and in fighting around Kirkuk, lacked the heavy weapons and training to take on enemy tanks, of which ISIS now fielded more than 100. It would take months, at best, to get this motley crew of potential partners to the point where they could roll ISIS back—especially since the Islamic State was now occupying cities, and urban warfare demands a much higher level of skill and equipment, as we ourselves had spent years discovering the hard way.

And that was just on the Iraqi side of the border (which, though non-existent for ISIS, was a real political and legal barrier for the coalition). The Free Syrian Army and its political parent, the Syrian National Coalition, lacked support in Syria, had extraordinarily rudimentary command and control, and had lost ground against ISIS since the Ghouta chemical attacks of August 2013. The largest Syrian nationalist rebel group aside from FSA at this time, Harakat Hazm, had received Western training and weapons including TOW anti-tank missiles, but could field only about 4000 fighters, making it far too small to take on ISIS with any chance of holding terrain or protecting population. Thus, getting ground forces ready to fight—a matter of months in Iraq—could take a year, at best, in Syria, even with a sharply increased level of support for the rebels. And we were starting from below zero: many of the motivated, secular pro-democracy groups that flourished in 2011–12 and took the lead in the early days of the uprising had since been slaughtered or forced into extremism through lack of alternatives.

All this suggested that the most likely coalition plan was a sustained bombing campaign in Syria and Iraq, lasting weeks to months, while advisors (including Australians, Americans, British, Canadians, several European countries and Arab countries like Jordan) gave Iraqi and Syrian forces training and equipment. The expectation was that by late 2014 or early 2015, Iraqi forces would retake cities like Mosul and Tikrit or (more likely) isolate them from outside.

Behind the scenes, and outside the formal umbrella of the Counter-ISIL Coalition, there was also direct action by some nations' special operations forces (notably the British and French). Other operations included a small Quick Reaction Force to help coalition advisors and trainers should they come into danger, and Combat Search And Rescue teams to recover downed aircrew—so that while no combat *units* (such as, for example, Marine expeditionary units, or infantry or armored brigades) were deployed, there was still likely to be plenty of combat *action*. The coalition offered intelligence, targeting and planning support, and deployed specialist teams into Irbil and Baghdad to dispense arms and supplies, while carefully collecting data on those who received them, lest they be used against us later. In Syria, things also began to develop at this time, but more slowly, at a far smaller scale, from a lower base, and with a much lower profile, since civilian agencies (including the CIA) were running a parallel program alongside the military effort.

There clearly would not be anything approaching the nation-building, civilian stabilization or governance efforts we'd engaged in last time around. These efforts—widely recognized as less than the sum of their parts—were part of our obligation as Occupying Powers under international law, after the overthrow of Saddam. But this time, Iraq had a sovereign—if not very stable or inclusive—government, and the coalition's political efforts were focused on finding an accommodation that could begin to reunite Sunni, Shia, Kurdish and ethnic-minority Iraqis into a functioning entity.

Thus, as the disastrous summer of 2014 drew to a close, simultaneously with the air campaign, Western advisers, trainers and technical staff were deploying into Iraq, managing the influx of weapons and supplies for the peshmerga and the Iraqi Army, and undertaking intensive training and planning with both the Kurds and the Iraqi military. The continuing air effort was intended to suppress ISIS, degrade its capabilities, "fix" it in identified locations while the ground offensive was prepared and—most importantly—allow time for reconnaissance, planning and coordination. This could be facilitated by embedded advisers, but would also take significant political coordination, diplomatic effort and, of course, *time*.

A ground campaign, when launched, would focus on cities that had fallen to ISIS—starting with Mosul, Tikrit and Fallujah. As things stood in late 2014, ISIS seemed to lack the forces needed to defend these cities in a conventional way, so Stalingrad-style pitched battles seemed unlikely. More probably, it seemed, ISIS would melt away, drop back to guerrilla warfare mode, hide among the population and mount hit-and-run attacks on Iraqi and Kurdish forces. This would be the longest and bloodiest phase of any campaign, would be locally led, and would rapidly devolve into internal security and counter-guerrilla operations in the cities. But ISIS would still exist, would still control significant population and terrain in Syria, and could still re-emerge in Iraq after an initial Rollback campaign.

And clearly, whatever the ins and outs of a military campaign, it was obvious that this would be the real problem: it was easy to sketch out a Kosovo- or Libya-sized operation to roll back ISIS: but then what? ISIS had expanded in part, as we've seen, because of sectarian and authoritarian behavior by the Baghdad government. Unless Iraq's Sunni communities were to agree to submit once again to that government, the underlying problem would still exist. Indeed, if every ISIS fighter magically disappeared overnight, but the government in Baghdad continued to treat Sunnis with the same disdain it had shown since the U.S. withdrawal, a new ISIS would simply emerge in another year or so. The same behavior by Baghdad—reneging on previous deals, holding back promised resources, and marginalizing minorities—had already prompted Kurds to establish de facto autonomy, and it was exceptionally hard to see how a unified Iraq could re-emerge from the chaos of 2014. As the fall of Mosul made clear, the entire post-Saddam political order had been broken, and it would take far more than foreign air power and special operations forces to put it back together.

By mid-August 2014, there were signs the Iraqi government realized this. By this time, the Shi'a-supremacist administration of Nouri al-Maliki, in power since 2006, had finally been thrown out of office. The veteran Kurdish politician Fuad Masum initiated the change almost as soon as he took office as Iraqi president on 24 July, at the height of the crisis following the fall of Mosul and the ISIS offensive against Irbil, Kirkuk and Sinjar. Masum was a former PUK leader, a close confidant of former Iraqi President Jalal Talabani, and no friend to Maliki—whose lack of inclusivity (toward both Sunnis and Kurds) Masum rightly saw as a major cause of the crisis. Accordingly on 11 August, Masum appointed Haider al-Abadi as Iraq's new prime minister.

Maliki saw this as an illegal act, and fought Abadi's appointment for weeks, refusing to step down, taking the matter to Iraq's supreme court, and appearing for several days to be on the verge of declaring martial law and trying to rule by decree, a step that would almost certainly have resulted in the immediate and complete disintegration of Iraq. Instead, under huge pressure from the United States, the UN and (most importantly) Iran, Maliki finally agreed to step down, assuming a ceremonial role as one of Iraq's three vice presidents, while Abadi took office as prime minister on 14 August.

Abadi, like Maliki, was a leading figure in the D'awa Party. Unlike Maliki, however, he had spent years in exile in the United Kingdom, where he'd become a well-known specialist in transportation systems and rapid transit planning for urban centers, had graduated from the University of Manchester, and had founded and run several businesses. The contrast with Maliki—whose twenty-four years in exile, as described earlier, had been spent in political intrigue, mostly in Syria and Iran—could not have been greater. After the invasion in 2003, Abadi had returned to Iraq where he was elected to parliament twice and played an important role in business and budgetary policy. Abadi thus saw Iraqi politics through a more technocratic and less sectarian lens than Maliki, even though he came from the same general Shi'a background and was subject to many of the same pressures—from the Iranians, from his Shi'a constituents and from the D'awa Party and its organizational hierarchy. Still, at least in the early days, Abadi showed a clear understanding of the immense importance of rebuilding relationships with Iraq's alienated Sunnis and Kurds.

Abadi quickly moved to mend the relationship with Kurdish leaders, working on a new revenue-sharing agreement under which Baghdad committed to pay the Kurdistan Regional Government 50 per cent of all income from Kurdish-controlled oil fields. This agreement, finally approved in December 2014, was a major step toward resolving a long-standing dispute between Baghdad and Irbil, one that had (according to the Kurds) contributed to ISIS gains near Sinjar and Amerli as Kurdish forces ran out of ammunition and funds to purchase combat supplies after Shi'a bureaucrats in Baghdad failed to honour their previous revenue-sharing commitments. The new prime minister also moved to address corruption in the army and police, removing 50,000 "aliens" (the ghost soldiers Abbas and Trombly had identified as a critical problem in the fall of Mosul) from payrolls. This went some way to address institutionalized corruption and hollowness in the armed forces, and to reassure troops and police in the front lines.

But perhaps Abadi's most important early action was to appoint Khaled al-Obeidi as defense minister. Obeidi was a Sunni politician from Mosul, well known as a competent technocrat with a strong military background. Just as importantly, he was a close friend of Atheel al-Nujaifi (the governor of Nineveh whose marginalization by Maliki had been a contributing factor to the fall of Mosul) and of Osama al-Nujaifi, now serving (alongside Maliki and former Prime Minister Ayad Allawi) as vice president. He was also an important Sheikh of the Obeidi confederation, a major Sunni tribal grouping with enormous influence across northern Iraq. Obeidi was—for that moment in the war and in that political environment—the perfect pick as defense minister.

Abadi showed him every sign of support, trust and confidence—yet it was clear that Obeidi would have an uphill battle. Not only was he dealing with the entrenched and politicized Maliki-era defense bureaucracy, he also had to contend with the rising importance of the Hashd al-Shaabi (Popular Mobilization Forces, PMF), a collection of Shi'a militia groups sponsored by the Quds Force and the Badr Organisation, and close to former Prime Minister Maliki, who continued to play a dangerously destabilizing role from the sidelines.

Despite these positive developments, it would be a huge—perhaps impossible—task to reunite Iraqis around common goals in the fight with Baghdadi's new caliphate. And in any case, merely attacking ISIS in Iraq would be pointless without also dealing with its safe havens in Syria, and doing that might simply help the Assad regime—whose atrocities, as we've seen, were the main cause of instability in Syria, and who'd killed far more Syrians (by this stage of the war, roughly eight times more) than ISIS ever had. Strengthening Assad would also bolster his major allies, Iran and Russia.

And if Iraq and Syria were controlled by Iranian clients, a Western campaign against ISIS might simply create a continuous belt of Iranian-controlled territory all the way from western Afghanistan to the Golan Heights. Around this time my former boss, now-retired General Petraeus, who'd been careful to stay out of the political debate to this point, broke his silence and warned publicly of the risk that the United States might become the Shi'a militias' de facto Air Force in a confrontation with the region's Sunnis.[1] After everything that had happened, and all the blood that had been shed, even a spokesman as supremely skilled as Josh Earnest would find it hard to spin *that* as a victory.

Beyond this, Petraeus's comment pointed to a contradiction inherent in the strategy being developed by the United States and its allies, one that didn't affect Moscow or Tehran, or indeed Baghdadi and ISIS. For whereas in Iraq the U.S.-led coalition was fighting in support of the incumbent against insurgents, in Syria the reverse was the case—it was working with insurgents (the FSA and others) against the incumbent. Russia and Iran, on the other hand, supported both incumbents, in both countries, against what they saw as the same set of insurgents, so that their strategy had a logical integrity that was lacking in U.S. policy. Whereas Russia and Iran were consistent in their support for authoritarian stability across the entire region and against any form of uprising, democratic or jihadist, policy-makers in Washington had to make different (often contradictory) choices on either side of a border that since the fall of al-Qaim and Waleed had become wholly imaginary. For the United States, success against one enemy could help other adversaries—victories against ISIS in Iraq, for example could end up helping Iran, while successes in Syria could help Iran and Russia. For their part, Moscow and Tehran (along with Iran's Lebanese client, Hezbollah) knew exactly what they wanted—to preserve, by any means, incumbent regimes favorable to their own geopolitical interests—and could thus treat the whole region as one unified theater of operations. And so, of course, could ISIS, which opposed incumbents throughout the region and refused to recognize the colonial-era national boundaries anyway.

Despite all these problems, I argued at the time,

> it might still be in our interest to strike ISIS now. The group is already the richest, strongest and most dangerous terrorist group in the world, it has an expressed intent to attack the West, and its string of military successes has created a momentum and sense of inevitability that attracts fighters, in huge numbers, from around the world. There could be a sound justification for the kind of campaign outlined here, to set ISIS back and break its spell of invincibility. But we shouldn't kid ourselves—what's happened in Iraq and Syria is a massive, tragic mess, and a military campaign alone won't fix that. Instead, what's needed is a complete rethink of counterterrorism strategy, for a world that looks very different now than it did at the beginning of the summer. That rethink is the real challenge.[2]

But before such a rethink could begin, ISIS demonstrated that its operations and objectives were far from limited to Iraq and Syria, mounting a string of attacks across the planet that emphasized how far it had come since 2011, and how fundamentally the rise of Baghdadi's Islamic State had changed the rules of the game.

II

INTERNATIONALE

The Atomized Threat, 2014–15

A few hours before flying to Abu Dhabi for the conference in November 2014, I had lunch with Kevin Chinnery, opinion editor of the *Australian Financial Review*. We took a quiet table in a back corner of Mosaic restaurant, one of several smart establishments around Martin Place, the ultra-fashionable heart of Sydney's financial district. It was a beautiful Australian late-Spring day.

The night before, I'd delivered a public lecture on ISIS, and Kevin wanted my take on the state of the threat. What were the chances of a terrorist attack in Australia? "Look, I'm sorry to say this," I answered, "but I'm afraid the chance is 100 per cent. There *will* be an attack. The only question is when, how bad it will be, and what we'll do in response."[1] One occupational hazard of doing what I do is that I tend to get this question a lot, so after finishing lunch, I ran for my plane and promptly forgot the discussion. A month later I saw a news bulletin: *Terrorist attack in Martin Place.*

A gunman had seized hostages at the Lindt Café, less than three hundred yards from where Kevin and I had spoken, called for an ISIS flag and demanded a phone call with Prime Minister Tony Abbott. The siege lasted seventeen hours, ending in an assault by police and the death of the gunman along with two of his eighteen hostages.

Martin Place was one of the first of what turned out to be a string of attacks, by people associated with ISIS or inspired by

Baghdadi's declaration of the caliphate. Along with the emergence of Islamic State provinces—*wilayat*—across Europe, the Middle East and North Africa, these attacks showed that ISIS was shifting the forms of terrorism, and that its impact had gone global. ISIS was building a three-level structure: a state-like core entity in Syria–Iraq, external territories in other countries, and an *ad hoc* global network of supporters and sympathizers, which I began calling, around this time, the "ISIS Internationale." And while the Islamic State's influence was expanding abroad, it was holding its own on its home turf in Syria–Iraq. In line with the ISIS motto, *baqiya wa tatamaddad*, it was "remaining and expanding."[2]

The Martin Place gunman, Man Haron Monis, didn't fit the classic profile of a neo-Salafi jihadist terrorist. For a start, he wasn't Sunni or Arab: he was Persian, grew up in Iran, and self-identified as Shi'a until just before the attack. Monis had fled Iran via Malaysia, overstayed his visa while visiting Australia, and then sought asylum, claiming he was wanted for political dissent in Iran. (Tehran countered that Monis was indeed under investigation, but for sexual assault, black market fraud and theft.) After gaining asylum, Monis was involved in a series of public protests against the War on Terrorism, including a hate mail campaign in which he and his girlfriend wrote taunting letters to spouses, parents and children of Australians killed in Afghanistan and Iraq. When the families complained to the police, he was charged and convicted of using the postal service for threats and harassment, and put on a watch list by the Australian Security Intelligence Organisation. After a court battle to overturn his conviction, the High Court (Australia's supreme court) denied his appeal, and Monis launched his attack in Martin Place three days later. Clearly, then, at least part of his motivation was tied up in a sense of religious and ideological grievance.

But Monis wasn't just a political extremist—he was also involved in numerous incidents of straight-up criminality, including membership of an outlaw motorcycle gang and more than forty counts of sexual assault against customers of a "spiritual healing" business he ran in Sydney's western suburbs, and whose offerings (including astrology, numerology and black magic) didn't sound particularly religious. In 2010 Monis was committed for psychiatric assessment after an apparent psychotic episode in a Sydney parking lot, and in 2013 he was charged as an accessory to murder in the death of his ex-wife, who was stabbed multiple times and set on fire in the stairwell of an apartment building.

Evidently, a volatile brew of political activism, violent criminality and psychiatric instability drove Monis. Had he not terrorized and caused the death and wounding of multiple innocent people, he might be seen as a pathetic loser—or as lawyers who represented him at trial called him, a "pest" and a "dickhead."[3] In any case, Monis is not known to have ever belonged to any terrorist group, was only a sporadic attendee at mosque, changed his religion to Sunni via a Facebook status update just one week before the attack, and called for an ISIS flag only after his assault began.

In no sense, then, was Martin Place organized by ISIS, and it's even a stretch to say the group inspired the attack. Rather, the Islamic State had become a brand, an after-the-fact justification, a psychological crutch that let Monis valorize his personal problems, self-dramatize as a martyr, and dignify his crimes and psychiatric struggles with a veneer of political purpose. But attackers like Monis were still dangerous—in fact, as lone unpredictable assailants, their actions were far harder to detect ahead of time than traditional pre-planned attacks by terrorist cells. By giving lone losers like Monis a program of action and a rallying point, ISIS—as a brand, an idea, or a methodology—was having a global impact wholly separate from its organizational structure or agenda.

For those of us who'd worked so hard to "Disaggregate" al-Qaeda, the implication was as obvious as it was uncomfortable: a fully disaggregated terrorist movement, with an ideology insidiously attractive to alienated and damaged people likely to act on it, combined with omnipresent social media and communications tools that hadn't even existed on 9/11, could enable a spread of terrorist violence unconstrained by time, space, money or organizational infrastructure. Add in a do-it-yourself tactical toolkit of improvised weapons and random targets, and we could be looking at an atomized, pervasive threat even harder to counter than the global insurgency it had replaced. Disaggregation, which had seemed like such a smart move at the time, might be backfiring massively: the cure might be worse than the disease.

Six weeks before the Sydney siege, Michael Zehaf-Bibeau launched an attack in Ottawa, shooting dead Corporal Nathan Cirillo, a reservist standing guard at the Canadian national war memorial on Parliament Hill. Zehaf-Bibeau shot Cirillo three times in the back at point-blank range, then ran into a Parliament building where he tried to attack lawmakers before being killed in a fire-fight with police, parliamentary security officers, and the House of Commons Sergeant-at-Arms, Kevin Vickers. If not for the prompt response, Zehaf-Bibeau would likely have attempted a mass shooting inside Parliament. Coming two days after another attack in Quebec, where Martin Couture-Rouleau (an adult convert to Islam who claimed to support ISIS) ran over two Canadian servicemen in a car, killing one, the Parliament Hill attack raised concerns of lone-wolf or self-radicalized terrorism in Canada.

Like Monis, Zehaf-Bibeau had no known terrorist affiliation. Like Monis and Couture-Rouleau, he was a convert to Sunni Islam, and was known to security authorities because of previous statements and acts (albeit, in both cases, non-violent ones). And also like Monis, he had a history of psychiatric issues and a well-tended criminal record that included theft, drug offences and armed robbery. Born in Canada of a Libyan father and French-Canadian mother, he had converted from Catholicism to Islam, travelled to Libya in 2007, participated in the 2011 uprising against Gaddafi, and expressed pro-ISIS sentiments in social media. At the time of his attack he was living in an Ottawa homeless shelter while trying to acquire a Libyan or Canadian passport for travel to Libya or Syria. Despite his desire to join the *jihad*, whether by traveling to war zones or acting in his own country, Zehaf-Bibeau had no known connection with ISIS, and though jihadists celebrated the attack on Twitter, no terrorist group initially took credit for his actions.[4]

But if the attacks in Ottawa and Sydney showed how ISIS was becoming a branding device, with little practical involvement but huge symbolic influence for disturbed, violent individuals who would otherwise have been seen as simply psychotic, then the next attack, three weeks after Martin Place, was of a different order altogether.

On 7 January 2015, two masked gunmen stormed the offices of the French satirical magazine *Charlie Hebdo*. The attackers used military fire-and-maneuver tactics and carried assault rifles, a submachine gun, pistols, and an RPG launcher. They wounded eleven people and killed another eleven, including Ahmed Merabet, a police officer stationed outside the magazine's office, who happened to be a Muslim. Shooting Merabet early in the attack, the gunmen found him lying wounded in the street as they left the building, and executed him in cold blood, even as he raised his hands in supplication. The attackers, Saïd and Chérif Kouachi, were French-born citizens of Algerian descent, who announced they were acting on behalf of al-Qaeda in the Arabian Peninsula, AQ's franchise in Yemen—and AQAP claimed the attack shortly afterwards. Thus, at least at first, *Charlie Hebdo* seemed to have no connection with ISIS; but this was about to change.

After attacking *Charlie Hebdo* the terrorists disappeared, hijacking cars to move through a series of towns in the Paris outskirts. A massive manhunt ensued, with more than 10,000 French troops and specialist counterterrorism police deployed. On 9 January, forty-eight hours after the attack, the brothers were tracked to a town 20 miles northeast of Paris, where they were holed up on an industrial estate. After a nine-hour standoff they were killed in a firefight with police. As the manhunt unfolded, a third gunman—Amedy Coulibaly, a friend of the Kouachi brothers—launched a supporting attack.

On the evening of 7 January Coulibaly shot and wounded a runner on the street in southern Paris. The next day he killed an unarmed police officer and injured a city worker in Montrouge, on the southern edge of the Paris ring road.[5] Then on 9 January, as the Kouachis began their standoff with police, Coulibaly attacked a kosher supermarket at Porte de Vincennes in the city's east, bursting in with an assault rifle, a submachine gun and two pistols. He killed four people and took fifteen others hostage, including a small child. Coulibaly videotaped his assault with a GoPro camera mounted on his chest, using a computer in the supermarket to upload the seven-minute video, which was picked up immediately on social media. He gave an interview to French news channel BFM-TV, claimed allegiance to ISIS, and told police he would kill the hostages if the Kouachi brothers were harmed. Videos, tweets and Facebook postings continued to emerge from his accounts for several days, possibly edited or managed by his wife, Hayat Boumeddiene, who fled to ISIS in Syria as the attack ended.

Coulibaly, born in France of Malian immigrant parents, claimed that his attack was synchronized with the Kouachis' assault on *Charlie Hebdo*. But he also said his goal was to support Baghdadi's caliphate, to protect Muslims from Jews, and to retaliate for Syrian regime brutality, the U.S.-led invasions of Iraq and Afghanistan, and the French intervention in Mali in 2013. After a four-hour siege, police assaulted the building, killed Coulibaly and rescued the hostages (several of whom were wounded). ISIS subsequently claimed the attack.[6]

Unlike the loners Zehaf-Bibeau and Monis, Coulibaly and the Kouachis were active members of a paramilitary underground. All were part of the "Buttes Chaumont network," a group of young people who undertook military-style training in the park of the same name in northeast Paris, and helped recruit and send French fighters to Zarqawi's group in Iraq. They were also known to police: Chérif Kouachi was jailed in 2005 for terrorist offences and convicted in 2008 of recruiting fighters for AQI. Saïd Kouachi travelled to Yemen in 2009 where he allegedly trained with AQAP and met Anwar al-Awlaki and Umar Farouk Abdulmutallab (the "underwear bomber," mentioned earlier, a Nigerian who tried to blow up a Northwest Airlines plane over Detroit on Christmas Day 2009).[7] Coulibaly had racked up several convictions for drug trafficking and violent theft as a teenager, befriended Chérif Kouachi while doing time for bank robbery, and—after an essentially secular early life as a small-time street criminal—converted to radical Islam in prison. After release, he undertook military training and ideological indoctrination with the Buttes Chaumont cell, before being jailed again in 2013 for helping plan a prison breakout for French-Algerian terrorist Smain Aït Ali Belkacem.[8] Coulibaly (with his wife Boumeddiene) played a key supporting role in the *Charlie Hebdo* attack, setting up a safe house, stockpiling weapons and launching his diversionary rampage as the Kouachis made their escape.

The attribution problem for the Paris attacks was a complex one. Whereas the Kouachi brothers claimed membership in AQAP, Coulibaly claimed to have sworn allegiance to ISIS as soon as Baghdadi declared the caliphate in 2014. Given the bad blood between AQ and ISIS this might have seemed odd, but was less contradictory than it appeared: of all AQ franchises, AQAP had been most welcoming of ISIS, its spokesmen offering fraternal greetings to Baghdadi's organization. And both Saïd Kouachi's AQAP connection and Chérif's links with AQI were from the period when AQI was part of the AQ network—affiliations that predated the AQ/ISIS split. Thus, despite the estrangement between the parent organizations, the Paris attacks could almost be considered parallel AQAP-ISIS operations.

With Ottawa, Sydney and Paris happening in quick succession, fears of a follow-on attack roiled Europe and America in early 2015. Police evacuated Belgian newspaper *Le Soir* after a bomb threat, the French Army increased military and police patrols at public sites, and in Germany competing pro- and anti-immigration marchers rallied under heavy security. In the United States, New York City officials raised threat levels after an ISIS-linked Twitter account repeated calls for supporters to "rise up and kill intelligence officers, police, soldiers and civilians" in France, Australia, Canada and the United States. A month after *Charlie Hebdo*, a gunman attacked a free speech event in Copenhagen, murdering film director Finn Nørgaard and Dan Uzan, a security guard at Copenhagen's Grand Synagogue. Like Coulibaly's attack, the Copenhagen attack involved a mobile shooter, moving by car from target to target, engaging police and security personnel and shooting random citizens on the street. The gunman, Omar Abdel Hamid El-Hussein, fit the lone-loser profile of Monis and Zehaf-Bibeau—Danish-born of Palestinian-Jordanian immigrant parents, he had a record of petty crime and gang membership, had been radicalized in prison, was active on social media, and was known to security authorities before the attack. Clearly, a pattern of adaptation was occurring here, part of the co-evolving relationship between terror threats and responses since before 9/11.

It's worth stepping back briefly to set these adaptations in historical context. The AQ attacks of 2001 were what we might call "expeditionary terrorism", an approach dating back to the 1972 Munich massacre. In this approach—one of several models of international terrorism over the last four decades—a terrorist organization recruits, trains and equips a team in one country, then infiltrates it into another to assault a predetermined target. In 1972, for the Munich attack, Palestinian organization Black September drew recruits from refugee camps near Beirut, selected a small team that moved covertly to Libya for training, and then infiltrated eight attackers into Munich. Once in place, the assault team retrieved a weapons cache that had been set up by a separate supporting cell, reconnoitered their target—the Israeli team accommodations in the Olympic Village—and launched their attack. A generation later, as it prepared for 9/11, AQ recruited from Saudi Arabia, Yemen, and from Muslim immigrant communities in Germany, selected an assault group from training camps in Afghanistan, planned the operation in Afghanistan and Malaysia, and infiltrated nineteen people into the United States to attack the World Trade Center and the Pentagon.

Expeditionary terrorist operations of this kind demand a huge investment of time and resources—AQ spent five years and half a million dollars setting up 9/11—and are high-risk, but high-reward. They can bring massive payoffs in public profile through media coverage, in enhanced support for terrorist groups' agenda, and in victim-initiated damage: expensive, counter-productive responses by targets that magnify an attack's effects. The 9/11 attacks prompted a massive response by the United States and its allies, and it was the scale and expense of this response—the initial "aggregation" approach of the War on Terror, as much as the attacks themselves—that catapulted Osama bin Laden and AQ to the global leadership role that remained mostly unchallenged in bin Laden's lifetime.

In the immediate aftermath of 9/11, governments and businesses spent billions of dollars on border surveillance, airline security, hardened cockpits, biometrics, and information sharing, specifically to prevent another attack of the same kind. These measures mostly succeeded—there hasn't been another 9/11, though attempts like that of Richard Reid (the "shoe bomber") and Umar Farouk Abdulmutallab (who trained in Yemen with Saïd Kouachi) still continue. Safety comes at a cost, though: security spending amounts to a "terrorism tax" on air travel and international commerce, while intrusive surveillance endangers the very openness of the free societies it's designed to protect. Perhaps the saddest aspect of all this is how we've adapted, becoming so used to these restrictions that we hardly notice them.

Here's one example: I teach at a NATO school in Rome, and often fly between Fiumicino airport, outside the city, and Washington D.C. I have seen significant adaptation at Fiumicino in the years I've been making the trip. Fiumicino now maintains a separate terminal, solely for U.S.-based airlines and for El Al, the Israeli carrier. This building (Terminal 5) is set back from the road, and surrounded by barriers to block car bombs, in its own self-contained compound a safe distance from the other terminals. Passengers and bags are screened in a section of the building that has blast barriers disguised as partitions, extra security personnel, fire-resistant furnishings, and a roof system designed to pop off and dissipate a bomb blast without collapsing the building or bringing the ceiling down (there is, in fact, no ceiling at all). Chairs and tables are bolted to the bare concrete floor, there's no carpet or drapes—the building is constructed to minimize blast or fire hazard in the event of a bombing. Having been double-screened and checked in this facility, U.S. and Israel-bound passengers then catch a bus to the main terminal.

The system works seamlessly, and few passengers ever notice the security measures built into it—though if you know what to look for, you can see similar adaptations in most major airports, and many public spaces worldwide. These adaptations are designed to protect against proven threats based on analysis of attacks that have already happened. But those are not the only possible attacks—there are ways to attack an airport that would bypass this security adaptation, though I don't propose to discuss them here, for obvious reasons. Less obviously, intelligence cooperation, financial monitoring, surveillance, and terrorism watch lists (which today include tens of thousands of people) have all been put in place since 9/11, and are virtual equivalents of Fiumicino Terminal 5—after-the-fact adaptations to a specific attack, designed to prevent it from recurring, rather than forward-looking designs to prevent attacks of new kinds.

A reactive security dynamic like this imposed a strong evolutionary pressure on terrorist organizations after 9/11, since a technique that worked once was highly unlikely to work again, at least not in the same form. This encouraged constant evolution in techniques, but it also prompted terrorists to go for large, high-payoff attacks using innovative methods (the equivalent of Zero Day exploits in cyber-security) to achieve the biggest bang for the buck before countermeasures could be designed and widely implemented. And this in turn meant that countermeasures, once in place, did little to prevent new *types* of attack: rather, they prevented copycat or follow-on attacks using *existing* techniques. That didn't make them unimportant—on the contrary, plugging identified gaps in security systems was and is critical—but their expense made them another variety of the post-9/11 terrorism tax, and created a ratchet effect whereby an attack anywhere drove up security (and thus limited freedoms and imposed costs) everywhere.

The extraordinarily high payoff for innovative expeditionary terrorism still encouraged some groups to attempt spectacular attacks of this kind—Lashkar-e Tayyiba's 2008 raid on Mumbai, or al-Shabaab's attack on the Westgate Mall in Nairobi in 2013 are examples—and will remain in the repertoire of terrorists and state-sponsored militants for the foreseeable future. But its high risk, like the demands of time, resources and technical skill it imposed, prompted evolved approaches including guerrilla terrorism, urban siege, remote radicalization and leaderless resistance. As ISIS grew in scope and ambition in 2014–15, the group began to employ all these methods.

Guerrilla terrorism is a way of sidestepping the international travel security measures put in place after 9/11, and a prominent early example of this technique was the London 7/7 bombing of 7 July 2005. For the 9/11 attacks, as we've seen, AQ sent nineteen people into the United States. By 2005, with increased airline security, greater scrutiny of visas, and improved border surveillance, this was hugely risky—and in any case, as described earlier, AQ had lost its Afghan base and many of those who planned 9/11 had been killed or captured. So instead of an expeditionary approach—organize in country A, train in country B to infiltrate country C—the group used a guerrilla (or, as the U.S. military terms it, Unconventional Warfare) model, building a team near its objective, outside the target city, but *inside* the international border security system established since 2001.

For the 2005 London bombing, rather than send nineteen people in, AQ brought one man out. Mohammed Sidique Khan, a British citizen of Pakistani descent, travelled to Pakistan's tribal areas for training, then returned to the UK where he recruited a four-man team inside Britain's international border, but outside London—three out of four attackers came from Leeds in the north of England. The team trained, rehearsed, prepared rucksack bombs, and then travelled to London where they blew up three tube trains and a double-decker bus. The attack killed fifty-two people in addition to the four suicide bombers, and injured more than 700. At relatively low cost, AQ had used guerrilla techniques to sidestep enhanced border security.

Preparing the attack inside the UK, but outside London in the north country, helped them stay below the radar—as a counterterrorism police officer pointed out to me at the time, national authorities focus on securing international borders, whereas city-level police focus on threats to the city itself. But police in Leeds weren't looking for a cell planning an attack on London—and even if they were, such a cell wouldn't necessarily generate a detectable signature for local police, because its activity (reconnaissance, surveillance, planning) mostly wasn't happening in their city. So by planning an attack inside the UK but outside the target city, the 7/7 bombers dramatically reduced their chance of detection.[9]

The *Charlie Hebdo* and Porte de Vincennes attacks illustrated a second evolution in terrorist technique: the urban siege. The technique itself wasn't new, but the size and complexity of modern cities, and the interdependent systems they rely on, made siege approaches increasingly effective. A bombing like London, even a spectacular attack like 9/11, was over quickly—the London attack lasted just over an hour, while the elapsed time between the impact of the first and last planes on 9/11 was only one hour and seventeen minutes. By contrast, in Mumbai in November 2008, ten Lashkar e-Tayyiba operatives seized two hotels and a Jewish center, sparking intense gun battles in heavily built-up areas of South Mumbai that lasted sixty hours and massively disrupted the city, while the Somali terrorist group (and AQ ally) al-Shabaab's attack on the Westgate Mall in Nairobi in September 2013 triggered an urban siege of 100 hours.[10] Both attacks generated massive, sustained global publicity, inflicted billions in costs on their targets, and paralysed large urban areas. Sydney, Ottawa, Paris and Copenhagen escaped relatively lightly in the 2014–15 incidents (in terms of urban disruption) but the power of the urban siege—its capacity to create huge impact over a long time for relatively little input—continued to make it attractive to terrorists.

Attackers like Man Haron Monis, Michael Zehaf-Bibeau or Amedy Coulibaly are often described as homegrown or self-radicalized, in that (unlike the 9/11 hijackers, the Mumbai attackers, or the Kouachi brothers) they were not members of terrorist organizations and hadn't undergone formal military training. But they weren't really home grown: rather, they represented what we might call "remote radicalization," the third key evolution in terrorism. Remote radicalization exploited the connectivity explosion of the last fifteen years—the massive expansion in access to smartphones, penetration of the internet into remote areas, the emergence of social media like Twitter, Snapchat and Instagram, and the proliferation of tools such as Google Earth and YouTube that terrorists could repurpose for operational or propaganda purposes.

As recently as 2005, there was an active debate among analysts and operators in the Intelligence Community as to whether a person could be fully operationalized—motivated and indoctrinated from basic awareness through increasing radicalization, organized, trained and equipped for an attack, and launched into action—purely through electronic means. Until then, though there most certainly were instances of people being radicalized online, full operationalization was extremely rare without some form of personal, face-to-face contact. But by 2015, the explosion of electronic connectivity was changing that.

As mentioned earlier, Yemeni–American cleric Anwar al-Awlaki—the AQAP ideologue who allegedly met Saïd Kouachi in Yemen—succeeded in operationalizing Nidal Hassan though email from Yemen, prompting the Fort Hood massacre. Awlaki also inspired the London 7/7 bombers, though he never met them: they watched his sermons on DVD while building their rucksack bombs. He met Umar Farouk Abdulmutallab before his 2009 Christmas bombing attempt, and inspired or directed plots in Toronto in 2006 and Fort Dix in 2007.

AQ (and more recently ISIS) disseminated terrorist tactics and techniques via their online, English-language magazines Inspire and Dabiq, which published articles on homemade explosives, raiding and ambushing techniques, and methods for making pressure-cooker bombs like those that Dzhokhar and Tamerlan Tsarnaev used to bomb the Boston Marathon in 2013—another example of individuals being operationalized without ever contacting or formally joining a terrorist organization. And terrorist groups now regularly claimed credit for attacks that matched their agenda (as AQAP did for *Charlie Hebdo* and ISIS for Porte de Vincennes) without actively planning or conducting them.

Virtually all the perpetrators in the attacks of early 2014 and 2015 were active on social media and already known to police or security services for their extremist views. But that didn't make it possible for authorities to predict or prevent their attacks, and this in turn was a side effect of remote radicalization: it created a bandwidth problem for security agencies, who (because of mass social media) had to track a vastly larger group of potential plotters. This is not to say that guerrilla terrorism or remote radicalization techniques had replaced older approaches. Instead, they now coexisted—Paris, London, Mumbai and the Westgate Mall demonstrated that terrorists still conducted pre-planned attacks. Remote radicalization just meant that large, pre-planned, long lead-time operations could now camouflage themselves within a higher background level of jihadist activity: a Mumbai-style assault team or a Buttes de Chaumont cell was harder to detect when hiding behind a dozen low-grade individuals like a Man Haron Monis or a Michael Zehaf-Bibeau.

If guerrilla and urban siege approaches offered lower-cost, lower-risk ways for terrorists to operate in target societies, then the rise of remote radicalization enabled a fourth evolution: leaderless resistance. Again, this was an old concept, originating among far-right groups in the United States in the 1980s, as a way to operate in surveillance or law enforcement environments where adversaries were constrained by respect for rule of law and human rights, or subject to pressure from public opinion. The technique was later adopted by a wide range of players, from eco-terrorists and non-violent democracy protesters to jihadists, and AQ was heading in this direction (as described earlier) for several years before bin Laden was killed.

In a leaderless resistance movement, symbolic figures (sometimes anonymous, sometimes acting openly but without detectable links to the movement) issue general guidelines for action, which self-recruited, independent groups and individuals act upon without further coordination or communication. A coded language is sometimes used for public statements, allowing specific messages to be passed. Leaderless resistance reduces risk, since there's nothing to compromise—no hierarchical structure, no communications system, no secret plan, and no formal organization. Because the communication is a one-way broadcast rather than a two-way dialogue, it doesn't need to be encrypted, and it's harder to detect (much less prove in court) any connection between the source of the message and those who receive it. Small groups act on their own initiative, following a general methodology and against a broad target, within operational guidelines published online. Members of each cell know only each other, and thus cannot compromise anyone else. Alternatively, individuals can take up the movement's ideology and methodology, acting alone (and thus with even lower risk of compromise) as a one-member cell or "singleton." Symbolic figures can inspire attacks without directly ordering them, protecting themselves from prosecution, and rendering surveillance pointless.[11]

Al-Qaeda at the time of 9/11, as we've seen, was the antithesis of leaderless resistance: it had 25,000 members, organized in a tight hierarchical structure of committees, camps, operational groups and support networks. It sought to preserve itself by maintaining the secrecy of its clandestine network, not by obfuscating or eliminating the network itself. For that reason, once 9/11 triggered the War on Terror, AQ's structure proved vulnerable to direct action—the light-footprint methods of drones and special operations raids, discussed earlier, that enabled CIA and the military to kill or capture individuals. AQ was also vulnerable to surveillance of communications, interdiction of finances and supplies, provocation and entrapment, and intelligence penetration.

So with core AQ's network damaged and its global leadership beginning to be challenged after 2011 by competitors like ISIS, individuals and groups within the wider AQ-allied terrorist environment evolved an advanced version of leaderless resistance, exploiting social media, the deep web, and broadcast journalism to motivate, train and direct loosely affiliated movements. ISIS by early 2015 was the most accomplished practitioner of this approach: its online presence and active social media, high production-value films and gruesome execution videos attracted large numbers of individuals who could then access propaganda, and learn tactics, techniques and procedures online. ISIS spokespeople—characteristically, using social media and online—urged supporters in Western countries to attack targets of opportunity, using materials to hand, without coordinating or informing others.

This was the very definition of leaderless resistance, and it made ISIS much more resilient, and far harder to kill than AQ had been after 9/11. All the adaptations that governments had made, at great expense, since 2001—drones, enhanced special ops, mass surveillance, improved travel security systems, hardened public sites—were of little help against the atomized ISIS approach. The rise of the "Internationale" after Baghdadi's declaration of the caliphate both contributed to and reflected this evolution. But looking beyond the attacks of early 2015, a few things already stood out.

Clearly, the threat would continue to evolve, through adaptations including (but not limited to) guerrilla terrorism, urban sieges, remote radicalization and leaderless resistance. Second, there would be more attacks, most involving very small numbers of attackers and low technical sophistication—though not necessarily a low level of lethality, as shown by the high death toll from incidents like Paris which included mobile active-shooter attacks with small arms. Third, attackers would not necessary fit the classic stereotype: military-aged males, trained members of clandestine organizations, loners, radicals, with specialized training and a pre-determined plan of attack. These people would still exist, and some (like the Paris attackers) would be linked by personal history or social network to conflicts like Iraq, Afghanistan and Syria. But an increasing number would have a different profile—active social media users, connected electronically but with weak social ties, not members of any radical organization though professing radical beliefs, often adult converts to radical Islam, not displaying special skills or training, but already known to security services and having access to sophisticated online planning tools such as Google Earth and an ability to acquire military-style small arms or other simple but effective weaponry. Age, gender and ethnic profiles would diversify, with increasing numbers being women, coming from ethnic, educational, family or religious backgrounds not traditionally associated with terrorism, and from a wider age range, including children in their early- and mid-teens.

This, indeed, matched the profile of the ISIS Internationale as it emerged in 2015.[12] But it was the second layer of the ISIS three-level structure—the *wilayat*—that had the greatest effect.

12

WILAYAT

ISIS Overseas Territories, 2015

By mid-2015, ISIS *wilayat* had been established in Libya (with separate provinces in Barqah, Tripoli, in Gaddafi's home town of Sirte, and in the southern region of Fezzan) as well as in Algeria, Tunisia, Egypt's Sinai desert, Yemen (including Sanaa and Aden-Abyan), Saudi Arabia, Afghanistan–Pakistan (Khorasan), Nigeria, and the Caucasus. (There were also numerous *wilayat* within the core ISIS territory in Syria–Iraq, acting as administrative subdivisions of the Islamic State.)

Despite a superficial similarity to the AQ "franchises" that still existed in some of the same areas, ISIS *wilayat* were different in concept and purpose. AQ's franchises were guerrilla or terror groups operating in their own way, in their own region, furthering their own interests but as part of a global insurgent strategy—a confederation of independent groups, united not by a parent political entity, but by the informal AQ "aggregation" model that Disaggregation was designed to destroy. By contrast, ISIS *wilayat* were more like overseas provinces of an empire, or colonial possessions of a nation state, pursuing the parent state's interest even at the expense of their own agenda.

The term *wilayat* (meaning governorate, province, or authority) was used under the Ottoman Empire and older caliphates to describe provinces, each with a governor (*wali*) exercising day-to-day authority under the suzerainty of the caliph. This isn't the only way the word can be used—*wilayat* also means "authority" in Shi'ism and Sufism, for example—but this is the sense in which ISIS understands it.

ISIS *wilayat* were formal territorial, legal and political entities within the caliphate, with defined borders and populations, administered by governors appointed or approved by Baghdadi, governing in line with ISIS policy, and conducting operations within a well-defined set of strategic guidelines. As of late 2015, the *wilayat* also acted as catchment areas for flows of fighters trying to join ISIS but unable to make it all the way to Syria or Iraq, as rally points for recruits wanting to bring ISIS to their own countries, or for fighters returning from Syria–Iraq.

Most importantly, they were bridgeheads-in-depth—outposts behind enemy lines that distracted ISIS adversaries from the main fight in Syria–Iraq, diverted resources that might otherwise have been used against the caliphate, and mounted attacks to support ISIS offensives or relieve pressure on its defenses. The *wilayat* could also serve as points of attraction for disillusioned members of rival groups. This may have been what happened in the worst ISIS-inspired attack on Western civilians to occur in the first half of 2015—the massacre at Sousse, in Tunisia.

Since the fall of Zine el Abidine Ben Ali's regime at the very outset of the Arab Spring, Tunisia had made huge progress toward democracy, making it a bright spot among the failures of the wider regional protest movements. But there were danger signs: secular democrats weren't the only ones opposed to Ben Ali. As in the other Arab Spring uprisings, Salafi-jihadists had a very different idea of post-revolutionary Tunisia from that of the people power movements. They organized Ansar al-Sharia (AS, "supporters of Islamic law") in April 2011, a loose movement of like-minded groups with chapters in Yemen, Mali, Egypt, Mauritania, Morocco, Syria, Egypt and Libya.[1] AS Tunisia (AST) focused on propaganda (*da'wah*, literally "issuing an invitation") to society at large, as well as vigilantism (*hisbah*, "holding accountable") against individuals whom the group saw as transgressing Islamic norms.[2] In May 2012, AST held a major rally in the town of Kairouan, calling for the Islamisation of all aspects of Tunisian society.[3]

Over the next year, the group ratcheted up the violence—something its leaders (including its founder, Seifallah Ben Hassine) could get away with at first, since they practiced a form of leaderless resistance that let them avoid responsibility for supporters' actions. But this pose—unconvincing from the outset—was impossible to sustain. In September 2012, Ben Hassine led a mob that stormed the U.S. Embassy in Tunis, in a riot that left four dead and forty-six injured. The pretext was a YouTube video, "The Innocence of Muslims", which AS branches exploited to incite similar protests in Egypt, Sudan, Yemen and India, using social media to manipulate public outrage and trigger deadly riots. These also provided background cover for AQIM and AS Libya's pre-planned assault on the U.S. facility in Benghazi.[4] Indeed, the close collaboration (and overlapping networks) between AS in Tunisia and Libya mean that to fully understand one we need to briefly explore the other as well.

The Benghazi attacks were an example of the broader phenomenon I mentioned earlier, where larger numbers of self-radicalized attacks camouflaged more serious, premeditated terrorist plots. Initial field reporting (subsequently very controversial) seems to have suggested that a spontaneous protest in Benghazi had spiraled into lethal violence; later reports showed there was never a spontaneous demonstration in Benghazi and that the incident was a pre-planned AQIM/Ansar al-Sharia Libya attack.[5] As of late 2015, questions remained about when policy-makers in Washington realized Benghazi was a terrorist attack, and why (or whether) they avoided acknowledging that fact. It's certainly possible that administration spin linking the attack to the YouTube video—which continued, based on emails released in October 2015, for at least five days after Secretary Clinton knew that "two of our officers were killed in Benghazi by an al-Queda-like [sic] group"—was part of an operational cover for the existence of a then-unacknowledged CIA facility in Benghazi (where two of the Americans lost in the attack were killed). Critics of the administration, however, saw the YouTube story as part of a broader attempt to maintain the narrative of reduced terrorism threat after bin Laden's death.[6] Benghazi occurred only two months out from a closely fought election in which reducing terrorism and ending the nation's wars were key administration talking points, and in which Libya (and Secretary Clinton's key role in it) was put forward as a foreign policy achievement. In any case, my own government service suggested to me that error was at least as likely an explanation as malice.

On balance, U.S. Government reaction to Benghazi was probably not (or not only) an effect of the ideological bent of particular policy-makers—it was also an artifact of the new environment where larger numbers of spontaneous, self-radicalized attackers raised the background clutter, letting more serious adversaries (AQIM and AS Libya) fly under the radar. This was yet another failure of Disaggregation: the strategy had reduced the size of attacks, but the atomized threat made it extraordinarily hard to predict or track smaller attacks, and—big or small—each plot required roughly the same intelligence effort, so that the proliferation of smaller plots made it more likely that overstretched intelligence services would miss the big ones when they came along. To my mind this (at least as much as ideological bias or political ass-covering) explains Benghazi.

Back in Tunisia, a few months after Benghazi, AST assassinated two politicians in February and July 2013. The Tunisian government banned the group and launched a crackdown, scattering AST operatives—some to Libya to train with Ansar al-Sharia there, others to ISIS in Syria. This deepened links between AST and ISIS: even as the United States, UK, UAE and UN designated AST a terrorist organization, its leaders travelled to Syria and pledged allegiance to Baghdadi, well before his proclamation of the caliphate.[7] When the caliphate *was* announced in July 2014, AST spokesman Seifeddine Rais immediately offered *bayat* to Baghdadi.[8] AST—allied to ISIS but not yet a *wilayat*—then launched a campaign of attacks on tourists and public places.

The first major attack was on 18 March 2015, when three gunmen stormed the Bardo Museum in Tunis, killing twenty-two (including seventeen Western tourists) and injuring fifty. ISIS claimed the attack, though its involvement remains unproven.[9] The attack used tactics—mobile active shooter, urban siege, diversionary assault, supporting propaganda on social media—like those seen in Paris and Copenhagen.[10] It also signaled the formation of an ISIS *wilayat* in Tunisia: after the attack, an organization calling itself "soldiers of the Caliphate in Africa" posted images of weapons and ammunition on Twitter, under a tourism hashtag (#IWillComeToTunisiaThisSummer), as if to say "we'll be waiting for you." The group linked Tunisia to the U.S.-led air campaign against ISIS: "To the Christians planning their summer vacations in Tunisia, we cant accept u in our land while your jets keep killing our Muslim Brothers in Iraq & Sham. But if u insist on coming then beware because we are planning for u something that will make you forget #Bardoattack."[11]

In early May 2015, analysts warned that ISIS was setting up a Tunisian province—Wilayat al-Ifriqiya—noting that this would escalate the competition between ISIS and AQ (whose regional affiliate, AQIM, was already active in Tunisia) and could lead to increased violence as each group sought to outdo the other.[12] Then Seifallah Ben Hassine was killed in a U.S. airstrike in Libya intended for Mokhtar Belmokhtar, the AQIM leader, who'd been flirting with switching allegiance to ISIS.[13]

Two weeks after Ben Hassine's death, on Friday 26 June, Seifeddine Rezgui Yacoubi—a Tunisian educated in the AST stronghold of Kairouan and trained in Libya—attacked the el-Kantaoui beach resort near Sousse, on Tunisia's Mediterranean coast. Disguised as a tourist, Rezgui infiltrated the Imperial Marhaba Hotel, concealing an AK-47 in a beach umbrella.[14] After socializing at the bar, he pulled out the weapon and methodically swept the beachfront, pool and bar area, shooting hotel patrons and calmly reloading three times. He was killed by police, but not before murdering thirty-eight people (thirty of whom were British tourists) and wounding thirty-nine. Sousse was the deadliest terrorist attack in modern Tunisian history. It brought ISIS huge gain for tiny input—at a cost of one attacker, one rifle and four magazines of ammunition, ISIS had established itself in Tunisia, out-competed its rival AQIM, and retaliated against a country (Britain) that was attacking it in Iraq. The low-cost, high-impact method exploited electronic connectivity to achieve a bang-for-the-buck far in excess of either traditional expeditionary terrorism or the evolved guerrilla terrorism of the post-9/11 era.[15]

And Sousse was only one of three ISIS attacks that day, which included a beheading and bombing at a U.S.-owned factory near Lyon in France, and a suicide bombing at a Shi'a mosque in Kuwait that killed twenty-seven and wounded 227. ISIS claimed all three incidents, while supporters crowed about the triple attacks—which they dubbed "Black Friday"—on social media.[16] Coming three days after ISIS spokesman Abu Muhammad al-Adnani had called for worldwide attacks during Ramadan, Black Friday seemed to signal an expansion of ISIS reach, and the extension of its operations and propaganda to the global stage.

What was impressive was not that ISIS could coordinate simultaneous attacks in multiple countries—indeed, there's no evidence that the attacks were formally synchronized or coordinated in that way. Rather, the attacks showed that ISIS had perfected leaderless resistance, remote radicalization and guerrilla-style terrorism to the point where a central organization no longer even needed to coordinate such attacks: the caliphate spokesman could simply issue a public call, and the Internationale and the *wilayat* structure would act without further direction. By September, ISIS had active provinces in eleven countries (the *wilayat* level of its three-tier structure) and had inspired or directed (via the Internationale) seventy-nine successful or attempted terrorist attacks, in twenty-six countries, since the declaration of the caliphate.[17]

But it was at the third, central tier of its structure, and in just three of these countries—Iraq, Syria and Afghanistan—that ISIS would transform the terms of the conflict in 2015.

13

KHILAFAH

Tikrit, Ramadi and Palmyra, March–May 2015

As ISIS expanded its reach in the first half of 2015, the war on the caliphate's home turf in Iraq and Syria was hotting up. Having dropped back to guerrilla mode after the air campaign began in 2014, ISIS leaders soon realized that the level of air bombardment was light enough to be survivable, and came up with a modified approach to manage the threat. This brought them a string of successes (and one major defeat) in a conflict that was increasingly urban, complex, intense, and very, very ugly—and in which ISIS was more than holding its own.

By now ISIS had established territorial control, and begun to introduce effective (albeit often rudimentary and abhorrent) governance across key parts of Iraq and Syria. The organization was running hospitals and courts, collecting taxes, distributing food, maintaining public services, enforcing a strict Islamic code, and conducting intensive—often very violent—propaganda among the population under its control. Media statements such as "ISIS now controls a large block of territory," correctly emphasized the state-building pretensions associated with these efforts.[1] But they also gave the misleading impression that the Islamic State held a contiguous chunk of terrain across Iraq and Syria. In fact, its territory was a network of cities, many only partially controlled by ISIS, linked by narrow strips of territory that followed road and river networks—in essence, a mesh of city-states under tight control of individual ISIS commanders, but under only loose sovereignty of the self-proclaimed caliphate, *al-Khilafah*.

Cities in the network were connected through commerce, transportation, electronic communications, trade, smuggling and organized crime. These links followed the rivers Tigris and Euphrates, the modern highway systems of Iraq and Syria, and a pattern of desert pathways descended from ancient trading and caravan trails. This reflected the reality of terrain, water and demographic conditions in this region, where vast areas are empty desert. Indeed, Iraq (aside from parts of the south and the Kurdish region) has always been more a confederation of urban centers surrounded by desert—an archipelago of settlement in a sea of sand and stone—than a uniformly governed state. The same is true of eastern Syria, and as the war unfolded in 2015 the region's political geography became hugely important, for three reasons.

First, it meant that the campaign involved mostly urban warfare: wars happen where people live, the populations of Iraq and Syria were mainly urban (69 and 57 per cent, respectively, in 2015) and ISIS needed to be dislodged from cities under its control before it could be defeated.[2] Urban operations are among the most difficult and gruesome a military force can undertake.[3] They bog armies down, breaking large units into small groups so that, instead of one big battle, there are dozens of fleeting close-range fights with a few people on either side. Most engagements last only seconds, and are fought at less than 50 yards' range. Threats can come at any moment, from any direction, including overhead or underground, and there are no safe areas. Snipers, roadside bombs, grenades, flame weapons, rockets and mortars are weapons of choice. Training Iraqis for this kind of warfare, as American, British, Canadian and Australian advisers—among others—began doing from September 2014 onward, was hugely demanding and time-consuming.

Secondly, because the theatre of war was a network of linked cities, overlapping fields of influence among those cities became strategically decisive. Obviously enough, cities have fields of political, military, economic and social influence: what happens in one city influences others and affects rural or ex-urban settlements within its orbit, and vice versa. That notion was implicit in a crude sketch map taken from Zarqawi's body when he was killed in June 2006. It showed Baghdad surrounded by the belts.[4] These lay outside

Baghdad's city limits, but were integral to its urban system, because they supplied commodities and workers the city needed, and dominated chokepoints and supply routes connecting it to the outside.

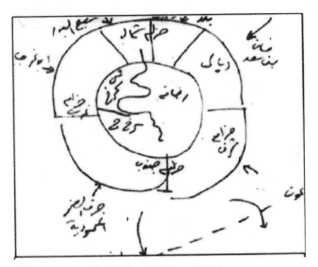

Source: *Long War Journal*, 2014.

Zarqawi's map, in effect, depicted the influence field of Baghdad, and that influence ran in both directions. For example, the counterinsurgency school at Taji, a town in the northern belts where I often worked in 2007, was frequently cut off from Baghdad by ambushes and bombings; one U.S. unit I worked with lost more than thirty people in its daily "commute" running the gauntlet from Taji into Baghdad. AQI leaders (including Abu Suleiman, later the ISIS military chief and probably responsible for the revival of Zarqawi's belts strategy) recognized they had too few fighters to capture Baghdad.[5] Instead, they identified places and populations in the belts that they could target to isolate the city and bring it down without occupying it. AQI used its control of the belts to push Baghdad into an escalating pattern of violence in 2005–6, making the belts a focus of intense combat during the Surge. After the Americans left, ISIS moved back in, and the belts again became a center of enemy activity. ISIS later applied this approach—which we might call "control by interdiction"—across the entire archipelago of Iraqi cities, and against Syrian cities such as Aleppo in 2013–14.[6] Thus in 2015, cities like Baghdad, Fallujah, Mosul, Tikrit and Ramadi were important not only in their own right, but also as nodes in a network that affected a wide area of Iraq and Syria. Whoever owned this network of cities (along with the water, fuel, food and electricity that sustained them) had a good shot at dominating both countries, which was why both sides were intent on controlling it.

Thirdly, this political geography of connected city-states made sequencing the campaign both important and contentious. Many coalition leaders favored a "Mosul first" plan. By far the largest urban center controlled by ISIS, Mosul was the most important in the northern network of Iraqi cities, and second only to Raqqa (the de facto ISIS capital) within the caliphate, giving it huge political significance.

As we've seen, Mosul's capture was the wake-up call that finally made U.S. policymakers and the American people realize things weren't going well, either in Iraq or in the broader campaign against terrorism. It was in Mosul that Baghdadi announced the caliphate, marking its arrival on the world stage. The city's continuing control by ISIS was a daily reminder of President Obama's failure to end the Iraq War, a threat to his legacy as a president who (in Secretary Clinton's words) "had been elected in part because of his opposition to the war in Iraq and his pledge to end it."[7] While ISIS controlled Mosul, no U.S. leader could credibly claim that the group was being "degraded and destroyed so that it's no longer a threat"—President Obama's phrase, from the outset of the air campaign, that constituted the nearest thing available to a coalition war aim. Conversely, if Iraqi and Kurdish forces could retake Mosul with coalition support, this would do massive damage to the Islamic State's ability to control its network of cities, let Washington claim it had degraded ISIS to a level Iraqis could manage, validate President Obama's light-footprint model, and allow him once again to declare victory and leave. Thus U.S. planners pushed for Mosul to become the campaign's first objective.

But Iraqi leaders, including Prime Minister Abadi, Defense Minister Obeidi and senior military officers, saw things differently. For them—in line with Abadi's goal of preserving Iraq as a nation-state—the objective was to restore Baghdad's relationship with Sunnis and regain control over Anbar, the Sunni heartland. Iraqi officials' priority was thus to secure the belts, recapture Tikrit and Fallujah, and regain full control over Ramadi. Mosul was important, but it could wait until after Tikrit. In part this view reflected a clear understanding of the weakness of Iraqi forces—the corruption, leadership and capability issues that had led to the collapse of 2014. Attacking Mosul after other ISIS-held cities had been recaptured would create momentum against weaker ISIS strongholds, generate support for the campaign, and build the confidence of troops unused to urban fighting against a dug-in enemy with tanks and artillery.

But two other factors pushed Iraqi leaders in the direction of a "Mosul later" plan. One was their understanding of how things worked in the urban archipelago of northern and western Iraq. During the Awakening, Sunni tribes first rose against AQI in towns close to the Syrian border, and a chain reaction worked its way down the Euphrates, through the network of cities—to Ramadi, where Sheikh Sattar of the Albu Risha formed the Awakening Council, then Baqubah, 50 miles north of the capital, then Abu Ghraib in the Baghdad belts, then Ameriya in central Baghdad. Abu Abed, the local leader who launched the Ameriya uprising against AQI in June 2007, described the Awakening to me as a wave rushing down the river. Likewise, when ISIS came back in 2014, another wave swept the city-network of central Iraq, with town after town falling to ISIS. Iraqi leaders like Defense Minister Obeidi (who grew up in Mosul) realized that in each case—in the belts in 2005–6, the Awakening in 2007, and the ISIS blitzkrieg of 2014—towns fell in a cascade, each collapse prompting the next. Given all that, attacking Mosul first didn't seem the smartest move.

The second factor for Iraqi officials was the challenge from Shi'a militias, part of the growing alliance around former Prime Minister Maliki, who had been far from idle after his ousting. Maliki quickly emerged as a major opponent of Prime Minister Abadi, undermining Abadi's government at every turn through a political alliance that included the Badr Organisation, led by Hadi al-Ameri, Iraq's transport minister. He built relationships with Badr paramilitaries and with sectarian Shi'a militias sponsored by Iran (somewhat ironically, since Maliki had made his name directing Iraqi troops in a hard-fought urban battle in Basra against the very same militias in

2008). The militias, with Iranian advisers led by Quds Force chief Qasem Soleimani, played a key role in the October 2014 recapture of Jurf as-Sakhr, south of Baghdad, one of few victories at that time. Success gave the militias credibility at a time when the government was suffering a seemingly unbroken series of defeats.

By early 2015 more than forty militia groups had joined the Popular Mobilization Forces (PMF), an umbrella organization under the Ministry of the Interior, which had its own parallel chain of command alongside the military. Whatever their effectiveness against ISIS, the militias were mainly composed of Shi'a-supremacist factions (a few Sunni groups joined, but they were token players). And from the outset, the militias (many of whom had been in the Shi'a death squads of 2005–6) showed a propensity for ethnosectarian cleansing, so that the stronger the PMF's role, the deeper the rift with Sunnis would become. With Maliki's sectarian power base competing with Abadi and the military, it was clear that the government would have just one shot to push ISIS back. A failed attempt at Mosul would give the militias an excuse to break away from government control, inflame tensions, and represent a setback from which Abadi's administration would not recover.

Initially, though, the campaign seemed to go well. Iraqi Army troops, with peshmerga, recaptured ground around Mosul Dam and pushed ISIS back from Kirkuk and Irbil. And in Syria, by the end of January 2015, coalition airpower, and desperate fighting by Kurdish forces had staved off the ISIS capture of Kobani, a town on the Turkish–Syrian border. But as they sought to push ISIS back from the town, the Kurds made excruciatingly slow progress, at high cost in lives and resources, and despite more than 700 coalition airstrikes—while the coalition's focus on Kobani lifted pressure on ISIS elsewhere. And ISIS was already adapting. Fighters no longer moved in large columns vulnerable to air attack, but in smaller, mutually supporting combat groups, making maximum use of cover and of the concealment afforded by night and bad weather, staying mobile, and giving junior commanders wider latitude so as to minimize electronic communications that might attract unwelcome attention.

In late February, the sequencing disagreement leaked into the open when U.S. officials released details of their Mosul plan—a joint assault in April or May, with 25,000 to 40,000 Kurdish and

Iraqi troops, supported by coalition advisers and air power, attacking the city with infantry, tanks, engineers and artillery, and clearing it block by block against expected resistance from between 1,000 and 3,000 fighters out of a total ISIS strength of about 32,000 across the region.[8] As if an urban assault, on a scale unseen so far in the twenty-first century, wasn't hard enough, American officials had helpfully told the enemy exactly what to expect. The most charitable interpretation was that this was a bluff: an effort to convince ISIS to surrender Mosul without a fight and retreat into Syria. If that *was* the intent, it was misguided—ISIS showed every intention of defending the city, its fighters' morale was high, and it was putting Mosul into a state of defense with roadblocks, fortified buildings and a protective berm around the city. And the cover and concealment the city offered (and its sheer scale and complexity) made fighting there safer for ISIS than running into the open to be killed by airstrikes.

The Iraqi government promptly contradicted the U.S. statement on Mosul. Defense Minister Obeidi told Reuters "I don't know where the American official got this information ... they absolutely do not have knowledge on this issue."[9] And in early March, as if to prove who called the shots, the Iraqi Army—with a large contingent of PMF and Quds Force—launched a major offensive against Tikrit.

Tikrit lies 90 miles northwest of Baghdad and about 130 miles southeast of Mosul, just west of the River Tigris. In the city-network of northern Iraq it's about halfway up the string of towns between Baghdad and Mosul. Located south of the oil hub of Bayji, and north of Samarra, Tikrit is linked to both towns via the Mosul–Baghdad road, and east via Highway 24 to Kirkuk (across the only bridge over the Tigris for 40 miles in either direction). Its central location among the overlapping influence fields of these cities makes Tikrit key terrain, and since controlling Tikrit gives you the option to attack in several directions, just holding the city, even in a defensive posture, disrupts others' ability to move through the urban archipelago and is therefore strategically offensive. For these reasons, along with Tikrit's history of support for AQI and the Ba'athists, ISIS went after it early in their 2014 campaign.

An ISIS column, with support from guerrilla cells that had controlled parts of the city since January, captured Tikrit the day after they took Mosul in June 2014. They then committed the worst massacre of Iraqi security forces in the war so far, shooting or beheading at least 1,566 unarmed teenage Air Force cadets at Camp Speicher, a former U.S. outpost west of the city.[10] After the massacre, ISIS held Tikrit against a hasty counterattack by the Iraqi Army in late June 2014, then began fortifying the city, tunneling between buildings, constructing bunkers and fighting positions, pre-registering artillery, building machine-gun nests and laying deep belts of IEDs to channel attackers into killing areas. These defenses helped repel government attacks in July, August and December 2014 and, as the PMF launched their assault on the city, ISIS was waiting. Many of the civilian population had fled, rightly expecting a major battle.

Qasem Soleimani and his Quds Force advisers played a key role in the offensive, which kicked off on 2 March with almost 30,000 PMF and Army troops. Soleimani, accompanied by Hadi al-Ameri and other PMF commanders, moved up to a forward position to control the battle. He initially focused on encircling Tikrit, cutting its external links and capturing outlying strongholds.[11] Progress was slow because of intense sniper fire and huge numbers of IEDs, because ISIS blew the only bridge before Iraqi forces could seize it, and because coalition aircraft were not supporting the attack—in part due to concerns, expressed by newly-appointed U.S. Secretary of Defense Ashton Carter, that the prominent role of Shi'a militias and Iranian advisers would inflame tensions with Sunnis.[12] After advancing along three lines of assault and surrounding the town center, the attack bogged down after the first week.

Only about 1,000 ISIS fighters remained in central Tikrit (the rest having broken out of encirclement) but rather than retreating, these mobile combat groups—independent maneuver teams of twenty-to-forty fighters, three or four vehicles, a mix of light and heavy weapons, and specialist sniper, IED and anti-armor groups—counterattacked, infiltrating past the front lines to attack the flanks and rear of the PMF, causing heavy casualties. By mid-March the offensive was stalled, with Iraqi commanders reporting 6,500 IEDs in downtown Tikrit alone, fierce resistance from encircled defenders, and ISIS counterattacks including multiple suicide bombers.[13]

After a personal request from Prime Minister Abadi, coalition aircraft began supporting the operation on 25 March, striking ISIS positions in the town center and allowing the advance to resume.[14]

Some militias withdrew in protest at U.S. involvement, but Abadi reinforced the attack with Iraqi Army troops, an influx of Iranian weapons helped the PMF regroup, and Tikrit was cleared by the end of the month and secured by mid-April.[15] Combat continued throughout the urban area over the next month, with IEDs and suicide attacks, and ISIS stay-behind fighters emerging to battle Iraqi forces in what remained of the ruined city.

On 7 April, mass graves were uncovered outside Tikrit, containing 1700 bodies—the young cadets killed in the Camp Speicher massacre.[16] In revenge, the PMF allegedly beheaded and mutilated captured ISIS fighters, throwing them from rooftops, dragging them behind vehicles, and torturing prisoners.[17] Earlier in the operation, militias demolished Saddam's mausoleum at al-Awja, flattening the building then covering the site with Shi'a flags and photographs of PMF and Iranian leaders including Soleimani.[18] This alienated local people who were still proud of Saddam, whatever they might think of ISIS: Secretary Carter's fear of a spike in sectarian tension through the militias' involvement in sacking a Sunni town had been well founded. Though ultimately a victory, Tikrit showed how tough an adversary ISIS was going to be. This was no longer just a terrorist group but a state-like enemy applying conventional maneuver, albeit with unconventional means.

Rather than area defense—the checkpoint-heavy laydown that Iraqi forces had used in Mosul, which left them unable to maneuver during the ISIS attack of June 2014—ISIS combat groups in Tikrit maintained a mobile defense. They continually counterattacked, using obstacles and IEDs to channel attackers into killing areas where they could be ambushed. Combat groups frequently shifted positions, aiming to inflict casualties rather than hold terrain. Snipers were placed in depth, behind or above fighting positions, looking for "keyhole" shots against commanders, radio operators and unwary troops behind the front line. ISIS also reinfiltrated from the flanks, using tunnels to move into the rear of fighting positions, or hiding in stay-behind positions to emerge in the rear of advancing Iraqi forces.[19]

Specialist anti-tank teams attacked armored vehicles, and ISIS launched at least one mounted counterattack against an Iraqi headquarters (on 13 March) with fighters in technicals supported by suicide truck bombs. House bombs, suicide IEDs (at least one of which was driven by an American foreign fighter) and enormous armored tanker-truck IEDs served as precision weapons to support these counterattacks, while thick defensive clusters of IEDs, hundreds deep, were used to bog down the Iraqi assault. Once coalition air attacks ramped up and the PMF advance resumed, ISIS dispersed. As the main force melted away, they left snipers, a screen of IEDs and obstacles, and stay-behind groups.[20]

Although it took five long weeks, success at Tikrit seemed to suggest that things were turning the Iraqi government's way. By early April, the Kurds had stabilized their front west of Irbil, and positional warfare—patrolling, trench raids, artillery duels, and occasional assaults across no-man's land—took hold in the north. Even though ISIS was still attacking Bayji, trying to regain the initiative after its loss of Tikrit, coalition leaders again began to speak of an offensive on Mosul in late summer or early autumn. Several ISIS leaders were allegedly killed or wounded around this time: a Shi'a militia group operating in the Hamrin Mountains east of Tikrit claimed to have killed Izzat Ibrahim al-Douri, there were rumors Baghdadi had been killed or wounded in an airstrike, and Abu Alaa al-Afri (his deputy) was also allegedly killed. In an upbeat press briefing on 15 May, Marine Corps Brigadier General Tom Weidley (Chief of Staff of the new U.S. mission in Iraq, Operation Inherent Resolve) claimed: "the strategy to defeat ISIL is working."[21] This turned out to be a spectacularly ill-timed announcement.

The very same day, ISIS captured Ramadi—capital of Anbar, and the third provincial capital (after Mosul and Raqqa) it had seized. Iraqi forces suffered another humiliating collapse, abandoning equipment and positions, and withdrawing ahead of advancing ISIS combat groups who seized weapons, ammunition, fuel and vehicles, overran the Anbar Operations Command (a Corps-level headquarters, Anbar's equivalent to the NOC in Mosul, located on the northern edge of town), forced the elite U.S.-trained Golden Division to withdraw, and besieged the 8th Iraqi Army Brigade base outside the city.[22] By 17 May ISIS fighters were in full control of Ramadi. Around the same time, al-Douri resurfaced with an audio message that referred to current events, disproving claims of his demise, while Baghdadi issued a statement indicating that he remained in command and calling on all Muslims to join the conflict.

As in Mosul, ISIS had been attacking Ramadi for over a year. In January 2014, in the same offensive that captured Fallujah, ISIS briefly took downtown Ramadi, before being pushed to the outskirts by Iraqi forces. Since then, they'd applied the "belts" strategy, mounting attacks to force police and military to concentrate downtown to protect critical infrastructure. This left large parts of Ramadi and its rural zone without any security presence, letting ISIS create base areas in the Albu Faraj and Sijariyah districts southwest of the city, and position forces to assault the government center and the Anbar Operations Command.

As soon as Tikrit fell, Baghdadi issued a written directive to prepare a counterstroke in Ramadi. ISIS displayed impressive operational security by silencing social media and propaganda teams, and covertly bringing in reinforcements in groups of two or three, using civilian cars, from as far afield as Idlib and Aleppo in Syria. From early May, ISIS combat groups infiltrated close to the heavily fortified government center.[23] In a three-day assault beginning on the evening of 12 May, ISIS took advantage of a sandstorm—which obscured the battle area and made it difficult for aircraft to operate—to move close to Iraqi positions, positioning snipers to suppress defenders and keep their heads down.

Then on 14 May, according to a characteristically well-sourced account by Margaret Coker, Middle East correspondent for the *Wall Street Journal*, ISIS began the main attack "by sending a single armored bulldozer to the concrete barriers on the outskirts of the government lines. The bulldozer worked unimpeded for close to an hour, removing concrete walls, Iraqi officials said."[24] While snipers and an ISIS combat group maintained suppressive fire to keep the defenders' heads down, the bulldozer reduced the government center's perimeter fortifications, creating a hundred-foot breach in the concrete barrier. ISIS then launched six simultaneous suicide car bombs, including armored Humvees and an armor-plated dump truck, knocking out guard posts and penetrating deep into the government position through the breach. These car bombs, including one driven by a British suicide bomber, devastated the defenses with giant explosions, which (in at least one case) leveled an entire city block. As the smoke cleared, the defenders—many momentarily knocked out by concussion—regained consciousness to see hand-picked ISIS storm troops (*inghemasiyoun*, "infiltrators") distinguishable by colored head and armbands, picking their way through the rubble to attack their positions.[25] Over the next two days, ISIS launched at least another twenty suicide bombs (roughly one every two hours), combining ground assaults with the sledgehammer-blows of these giant IEDs, and seizing the government center on 15 May.[26]

Car bombs had long been a favorite tactic of ISIS and, before them, of AQI. In the early days, the bombers often weren't volunteers: during the Iraqi elections in 2005, for example, AQI tricked an intellectually disabled teenager into blowing himself up at a polling station, and we saw drivers in 2007 who'd been chained into their cars, their families held hostage until they carried out their one-way mission. But as Ramadi showed, one of the ISIS innovations of 2015 was the coordinated use of multiple suicide bombers, in synchronized attacks on point targets, something that could not have been achieved through coercion or deceit alone. These suicide bombers weren't dupes or psychopaths: rather, they were intelligent, precise, utterly determined members of a sophisticated Combined Arms operation—a horrifically eloquent testimony to Islamic State's ability to motivate and mobilize high quality recruits.

Unlike the AQI bombers who targeted innocent Sunni civilians for political reasons in Baghdad during the sectarian civil war, these ISIS bombers had a tactical purpose: they were attacking, for the most part, military targets rather than civilians. This again was conventional maneuver with unconventional means: ISIS employed suicide bombers (plugged into radio nets so they could coordinate with maneuver commanders, and buttoned up in armored cabs to prevent them being killed before they could reach their targets) exactly as a nation-state military would use precision missiles: to deliver a massive shock effect to a point target, ahead of a ground assault. The closest historical analogy I can think of is the Imperial Japanese *Tokubetsu Kōgekitai* (the program that included *kamikaze* pilots as well as land and sea attacks) of 1944–5—the use of suicide attackers to ensure precision delivery of a tactical weapon in support of conventional forces. The difference was that unlike the Japanese, who were desperately defending their home islands, ISIS was attracting large numbers of Iraqi and foreign volunteers willing to sacrifice their lives in a war of conquest for the self-appointed caliph.

No such motivation existed on the Iraqi government side. Secretary Carter commented: "Iraqi forces just showed no will to fight ... they vastly outnumbered the opposing force, and yet they failed to fight."[27] While strictly accurate, this understates how heavily the Iraqis were overmatched in firepower. Those who withdrew from the government center had fought hard, for months in some cases, repelling numerous ISIS attacks. But at the moment of crisis, they were overwhelmed by a string of massive IEDs, precisely directed by fighters who showed no concern for their own survival, with the first six coming simultaneously, under heavy suppressive fire, in a dust storm that prevented early warning and precluded friendly airstrikes. No wonder they broke—almost any troops in the world would have done so.

At the tactical level, Ramadi said as much about the skills, battle discipline and determination of ISIS (and the logistics and engineering capability they could muster to build so many IEDs and secretly move them into place) as Iraqi morale. ISIS tactics—Suppress, Obscure, Secure, Reduce, Assault—were literally textbook (a set-piece sequence known in the business as a Deliberate Obstacle Breach) except that instead of using artillery to reduce the defenses, they deployed suicide bombers.[28] Again, ISIS was thinking and fighting like a state, applying conventional tactics, but employing unconventional means.

At the campaign level, Ramadi destroyed any momentum that might otherwise have been gained after Tikrit, returned the initiative firmly to ISIS, and was correctly seen as a huge defeat. Al-Asad airbase (50 miles northwest of Ramadi and home to several thousand U.S. advisers) was now isolated by road from the rest of Anbar. Iraqi forces were in disarray along the whole Fallujah–Ramadi corridor, while Haditha was the only major city in government hands along the entire length of the Euphrates west of Baghdad. Towns like Taji, where 300 Australian and 140 New Zealand trainers were now living near the grounds of our old counterinsurgency school, looked increasingly precarious. Assurances that advisers would remain "behind the wire"—safely ensconced in defended bases as part of the light footprint approach—sounded less soothing now that ISIS had seized an entire city, overrunning several such bases, fewer than 60 miles away. Despite calls for an immediate counterattack, there was little prospect of Ramadi being recaptured any time soon; and, as it turned out, Ramadi was only one of two huge ISIS victories in the same week.

Three hundred miles west of Ramadi, in a straight shot across the Syrian Desert, lay Palmyra, in Syria's eastern Homs province.

Famous for its UNESCO World Heritage-listed Greco Roman ruins, Palmyra (and the adjoining modern city, Tadmur) was equally infamous for its enormous arms depot, rumored to contain chemical weapons and ballistic missiles as well as huge ammunition stocks, and its military prison where thousands of Syrians had been jailed and tortured (and where Bashar al-Assad's uncle massacred more than 1000 after a failed escape attempt in June 1980). The nearby airbase was also used by the IRGC as a hub for logistic support to the Assad regime, airlifting supplies, weapons and ammunition from Iran on enormous Russian-made Il-76 transport aircraft, then transporting them by truck to Damascus, 150 miles to the southwest.[29] As in Iraq, control of Syria rests on the ability to hold or influence a network of cities strung out along the country's highway and river systems. And by May 2015 the Assad regime was losing its grip on the northern and eastern part of this network.

The only surviving regime stronghold in the east, Deir ez-Zor on the Euphrates, was encircled and under heavy attack, and Islamic State now controlled almost the entire Euphrates river and road system on both the Iraqi and Syrian sides of the border. The last remaining road from Deir ez-Zor to regime-held territory was the M20 motorway, running through rocky, empty desert to the small town of as-Sukhnah, then to Palmyra: losing Palmyra would isolate the garrison at Deir, so that it would have to be resupplied solely by air, making its fall to the rebels much more likely.

Palmyra was surrounded by gas fields, two of which—al-Hayl and al-'Arak—supplied much of the fuel used to generate electricity for the regime heartland. Loss of these gas fields and power plants would bring hardship to the regime-controlled population (increasing political pressure on Assad) and allow ISIS to cut the flow of petroleum from Iraqi and Syrian oilfields through Syria to the Mediterranean. This would gift ISIS the opportunity to increase its revenues by trading oil and gas on the black market, or selling electricity back to the Assad regime at a profit.

By early May 2015, the regime was extremely hard-pressed. Syrian troops had just captured Moussa Hill, a high-altitude (8,400 foot) artillery firing position in the Qalamoun Mountains near the Syrian–Lebanese border, but needed extensive help from Iran and Hezbollah to do so, losing many casualties in the offensive. Assad's forces had also suffered a string of defeats in the north (in Idlib, at the hands of a rebel alliance that included JN, other jihadists and nationalist groups) and in the south (around Deraa, the birthplace of the Syrian uprising, where it was losing ground to the U.S.-backed Southern Front). On 12 May, the regime pulled troops from Tadmur to reinforce Idlib.

For much of the war to date, Assad's fiercest opponents had been non-ISIS groups—the Southern Front, the FSA, Kurdish groups like the People's Protection Units (YPG), and non-ISIS jihadists such as JN or the Saudi-backed Ahrar al-Sham. ISIS fought other rebels for control of major towns, but generally avoided taking on the regime except in isolated outposts like Deir ez-Zor or areas closer to Raqqa. Now, however, seeing its opportunity as Palmyra was denuded of troops for the Idlib front, ISIS pounced, sending several hundred fighters to Sukhnah, roughly 40 miles up the road from Palmyra. Moving in multiple columns that fanned out over the open desert, they quickly seized the town, sending several thousand civilians fleeing down the M20 to Palmyra, spreading panic.

The authorities threw together a hasty defense. Releasing detainees from Tadmur Prison, they forced them to dig defensive ditches and build berms and obstacles. Those who could escape fled immediately, but within hours ISIS combat groups—using the same tactics and organization as at Tikrit and Ramadi—had seized outlying districts, launched suicide attackers at the airbase, captured the ammunition depot and were pushing into the city's northern and eastern outskirts. Army troops and militias of the National Defense Force (the NDF, successor to Assad's *shabiha* and equivalent to the Iraqi PMF) launched a hasty counterattack before dusk the first day, but ISIS still controlled the M20 corridor and the high ground east of the city. After another day of intense fighting in the northern outskirts and around the airbase, prison and gas fields, the government launched a major counteroffensive. After a massive assault that left much of the city damaged and killed many civilians, the regime had cleared ISIS from most of the Tadmur-Palmyra-Sukhnah area by 19 May, six days into the battle.

But the next day—demonstrating an impressive capacity to reinforce combat units in mid-battle—ISIS launched a fresh attack with more than 700 fighters, heavy weapons, suicide bombers, and both anti-aircraft and anti-armor missiles that enabled them to keep regime helicopters and fighter aircraft at bay. They broke into the city's outskirts for the third time in less than a week, and quickly took the northeast third of the city, leaving the regime hanging on to the prison, the airbase and Air Force Intelligence headquarters west of the city. By nightfall on 20 May these too had been taken, and regime forces were in full retreat, bombing the city as they left with no regard for civilian casualties. As at Ramadi, ISIS immediately advanced beyond the city, down the road to Homs and Damascus, to disrupt any attempt at a counterattack.

Much of this description of the battle of Palmyra comes from reports I received from field sources on the ground in Syria during the fighting, from local citizen journalists, or as unsolicited inputs from people aware of our work. One of the latter captures well the perspective of ordinary Syrian civilians during the battle:

From: [email supplied]
Date: May 24, 2015 at 00:12:10 GMT+10
To: Dave Kilcullen
Subject: Information from inside Palmyra—how ISIS works on the ground

Here is information from someone from Palmyra who is in phone contact with his family there, charting the arrival of ISIS. Apologies for the anonymity, but he is anxious not to give information about his identity or location for fear of reprisals to his family from both sides—Assad forces or ISIS. He is staggered at how much the actions of the Assad regime are helping boost instant reliance and faith in ISIS.

You are probably aware that regime forces destroyed the power and water facilities before leaving Palmyra and blocked and booby-trapped exit routes from the city making it hard for people to leave. This created panic and anger. Army high-ups, well-armed allied militia, local officials and other regime cronies fled in convoys, leaving many local people who had been working and fighting with them stranded and in shock. A lot of cannon fodder army conscripts were also abandoned to become easy prey for ISIS atrocities. Regime-linked "shabiha" who had commandeered local homes fled, leaving them stripped bare, looting further as they left town. The regime is now bombing Palmyra, destroying a school and hospital close to his family and are reported to be even firing mortars into the historic ruins. (There's outrage at why, in contrast, they didn't bomb the ISIS convoys, which could be clearly seen roaring across the open landscape well before they arrived at Palmyra).

His family were terrified, hiding for days in a crowded basement. They emerged to dig wells in the street to get water, but suddenly found ISIS had restored the power and water, and were coming to every street delivering food and modest Islamic garments for the women. There is relief and a sense [that] things could be getting back to normal. ISIS are also reported to be offering assurances that they will not destroy the old city and ruins (psychologically important as the main source of local employment with the tourism industry). People are being told if they need medical services and other things they can go to Raqqa, with the road there open and safe.

So ironically, they are now feeling 'rescued' by ISIS, and their families outside find to their shock that they are sharing this view. Syrians there feel outrage at the betrayal by the Government and its indifference to their welfare, and bewildered fury at Assad's determination to now bomb the city, hitting civilian targets.

The worst is probably yet to come under ISIS, but the people of Palmyra have been slammed by the realization they have no friend in the Syrian government, instead what's proved to be a more ruthless enemy than ISIS. Keep up your good work.

[name withheld]

My contact was right—as the summer campaign of 2015 came to a climax, the worst was indeed yet to come.

14

TRANSFORMATION

Syria and Iraq, Summer 2015

As ISIS settled into its new territory in Ramadi and Palmyra, its situation was generally good. Between its emerging overseas *wilayat*, the Black Friday attacks, and its conquests in Syria and Iraq, Baghdadi's caliphate was an increasingly important player in regional and international affairs. But as summer stretched into autumn, these very successes would yet again transform the conflict.

Several developments, all within just a few weeks of each other, triggered this transformation: government defeats in Iraq and Syria; the Iranian nuclear deal in mid-July; Turkey's entry into the war in August; the European refugee crisis, which spiked dramatically in early September; and a major setback in Afghanistan (including the first coordinated ISIS attacks on the Afghan government) in late September.

Making sense of these events is crucial to understanding the conflict, so I will address each in turn. But these things didn't happen in a clean sequence that would allow policy-makers to handle them one by one. Rather, they occurred near-simultaneously, exceeding the bandwidth of leaders across Europe, the Middle East and North America, creating what aviators call a "task saturation" effect that made it virtually impossible to craft an effective response.

In Iraq and Syria, Baghdadi's caliphate now held 50 per cent of Syrian territory and almost the same proportion of Iraq. The population under its control—roughly 6.5 million people—was smaller than its territory would suggest, but still larger than many nation-states. In Palmyra and Ramadi, ISIS cadres were working to subjugate this population, and put their newly captured cities into a state of defence. In Mosul and Fallujah, which they had occupied for some time, ISIS had already established an effective (though not unchallenged) system of control.

In Palmyra, almost immediately, ISIS began seizing antiquities to trade on the black market. Abu Walid, a Syrian refugee in Gaziantep, told reporters that ISIS was "making tens of millions of dollars through the illegal trade. The group issues licenses to looters to dig in their territory. 'If you find an artifact, you take 80 per cent and ISIS takes 20 per cent,' he said. Or, if the equipment used to unearth the treasure belongs to ISIS, they take a 40–50 per cent cut instead."[1] Despite the population's hope that the ruins would be spared—and ISIS leaders' promise to preserve them—the organization quickly began demolishing structures it considered un-Islamic (which, needless to say, was quite a few in a city predating Islam by five centuries). ISIS cadres blew up temples, defaced images, and searched for treasures they rightly suspected had been moved or hidden. They captured, then spent most of June and July torturing, eighty-three-year-old Khaled al-Asaad, Palmyra's Director of Antiquities and a noted archaeologist who'd spent his life protecting the site, before beheading him in a public square in Palmyra on 18 August.[2] The old man's killers strung up his body by its wrists from a column, with his head, still wearing spectacles, on the ground between his feet. He had told his captors nothing.[3]

Tribal opponents of ISIS met their fate more quickly, and with far less coverage in the international press. Ever since the Awakening, Abu Bakr al-Baghdadi had been extremely wary of tribal leaders, winning them over when feasible, and intimidating them through exemplary violence when necessary.[4] Now ISIS attacked the Sheitat, a tribe that had sided with JN against Assad but been alienated by ISIS attempts to shut down its cigarette- and alcohol-smuggling business and seize the oil wells it controlled astride the border. At least one Sheitat clan sided with ISIS, but most turned to the Syrian government and fought ISIS near Deir ez-Zor, until in November 2014 ISIS fighters captured and beheaded more than 800 Sheitat men and boys and enslaved many women and girls, forcing the survivors to flee. Hundreds escaped to Palmyra, where the men joined Syrian paramilitary training programs to fight back at ISIS and take revenge for the massacre and rape of their families. They were among the local allies the regime abandoned when it quit Palmyra on 20 May, and ISIS cadres proceeded to massacre all the Sheitat survivors they could find, with beheadings and shootings going on for days in the blood-soaked sand of the old city.[5] Syrian contacts estimated that between 400 and 450 people were executed.

Likewise, in Ramadi, mass killings immediately followed the ISIS takeover, as in virtually every city the group had ever captured. One Iraqi official estimated that 500 civilians were killed and 25,000 fled the city within forty-eight hours of its fall (on top of another 114,000 who had left before the battle).[6] ISIS combat groups quickly dug in around the government center and AOC headquarters, built checkpoints on the main access roads into the city, constructed defensive positions, set up sniper hides, laid defensive belts of IEDs and began building a new berm. Simultaneously they searched house-to-house for regime supporters. Those found—or suspected—to have government ties were shot or beheaded on the spot, their bodies left in the street to rot, or dumped into the Euphrates to drift downstream into government-controlled territory.[7] It was a neat reversal of 2007, when tribes in the Awakening—including clans from Ramadi—dumped AQI bodies in the same river, and the headless corpses would turn up, bloated and festering in the irrigation canals, every morning.[8]

Again following a familiar pattern, after their massacre and purge of the city, ISIS cadres worked fast to restore essential services and establish basic governance. They repaired water, electricity and road infrastructure, set up fuel distribution points, established food price controls, reopened bakeries, set up a system to manage the reconstruction of houses damaged in the fighting, reopened hospitals and mosques (under an ISIS-controlled committee of supervision), enforced a strict Islamic dress code, set up internal security and police forces, established sharia courts, and re-opened the prison. Meanwhile the beheadings, crucifixions, amputations and floggings continued.[9]

The model was simple but effective—exemplary violence first, to intimidate the population into cooperation, then essential services and governance to show that cooperation brought material benefits, and propaganda to persuade the population to side with its new rulers. This system, which I've described elsewhere as "competitive control," is common to insurgents and criminal gangs (indeed, to many states) and, rudimentary as it was, represented a significant advance over AQI's old coercion-only methods of 2005–6.[10] Some in Ramadi, living under Islamic State control for the first time, began to see the ISIS cadres as returning the city to normality. "They are acting like the permanent government here," one local man told reporters, "So of course people have joined them. They have the upper hand."[11]

Outside Ramadi, ISIS combat groups maneuvered aggressively to keep the PMF and Iraqi Army off balance and hamper attempts to retake the city. In early June, they seized Ramadi dam and cut the water to Khalidiyah and Habbaniyah, the last two government-controlled towns in the area which took water from it, making it harder for government forces to maintain bases there.[12] In mid-July they attacked a sports stadium 10 miles west of the city, killed many PMF and blew up the stadium. Elsewhere, they continued their assault at Bayji, mounted offensives around Fallujah, Hit and Haditha, raided the Kurdish front, and launched suicide bombings and raids into Baghdad.

Their strategy here was, in part, a repeat of their game plan from Mosul and Tikrit—use terrorist attacks to threaten critical infrastructure (dams, power plants, oil refineries, government offices), forcing police and military to concentrate and defend these areas, which in turn denuded other areas, creating space for maneuver. In part, it was an attempt to flood the government's bandwidth, giving it so many simultaneous problems, in so many places, that it could never mass enough force to recapture the ISIS-held cities. If this worked, ISIS could delay any government attempt against Mosul, Fallujah and Ramadi indefinitely.

The loss of Ramadi showed the Iraqi army was still struggling to remedy the problems of 2014, and was incapable of holding (much less recapturing) ground. At the same time, Iranian advisers like Qasem Soleimani were increasingly visible and dominant: he was photographed many times on the front lines with militia, meeting officials in Baghdad and Irbil, visiting captured areas and celebrating with militias. And the Iranian-backed PMF, now supported by a larger contingent of Iranian advisers and an influx of weapons and resources from Iran, was getting stronger and more capable—

enough to challenge the Iraqi Army, yet politically unacceptable to recapture a Sunni city of 400,000 people like Ramadi.

Coalition commanders pushed for a division of labor: the PMF and its Iranian sponsors would focus on Fallujah and Bayji, the Iraqi Army and its coalition advisers would handle Ramadi, the Kurds would secure their front and push ISIS back where feasible, and coalition aircraft would support all three as needed. The plan to recapture Mosul was quietly and indefinitely shelved. Tactically, this made perfect sense. But strategically, it was very much a second-best option, in that it sought to make most efficient use of fundamentally insufficient resources. Not for the first time, reality fell far short of rhetoric: the assets Washington assigned were utterly inadequate for its stated objectives.

The fall of Ramadi triggered a change in U.S. policy, albeit a minor one. In June an additional 450 trainers were deployed, restrictions on movement and operations were lifted slightly for the advisers, and the U.S. began an effort to train and assist Sunni tribal militias directly, though still funneling most assistance (and virtually all lethal aid) via the Baghdad government. Despite this shift, it was eminently clear that the light-footprint formula—trainers behind the wire, limited air strikes on ISIS battlefield targets—simply wasn't working.

One illustration of this was the way that coalition air strikes failed to save Ramadi. At the start of the battle, the sandstorm stopped pilots identifying targets. By the time the storm cleared, after the first huge wave of IEDs had breached the perimeter and ISIS assaulters were inside the government center, Iraqi forces were intermingled house-to-house with ISIS so that, without combat controllers on the ground to identify friendly troops or designate targets, it was impossible for aircraft commanders to tell who was who from the air. Likewise, on the Kurdish front, though the peshmerga held the line, they too were unable to recapture ground without coalition air support. The same could be said of the Iranian advisers and Shi'a militias—in every place where they'd succeeded, from Jurf as-Sakhr in October to Tikrit in March, the PMF had only been able to do so with help from coalition airstrikes.

Beyond these military concerns, the loss of Ramadi triggered a political crisis in Iraq at least as profound as that caused by the fall of Mosul eleven months earlier. As ISIS had cranked up pressure on Ramadi over the last weeks of April and the first half of May, Iraqi political leaders—including Maliki—pushed to send PMF to defend the city, but U.S. leaders urged them not to. The hope was that the Iraqi army, the police, the Golden Division and a tribal force from the Albu Fahd would suffice to defend the city, and thus avoid the political problems associated with bringing Iranian advisers and Shi'a fighters into the Sunni heartland of Anbar. This plan failed—obviously enough—and after Secretary Carter's disparaging remarks about the troops' will to fight, Iraqi leaders were furious, blaming the coalition and determined to recover Ramadi by any means, even at the risk of heightened Sunni–Shi'a conflict and alienation. All this made the conflict increasingly sectarian.

Since assuming power in August 2014, Prime Minister Abadi had made genuine efforts to act in a more inclusive manner, to curb corruption, and to win back Sunni and Kurdish support. But the fall of Ramadi weakened him with his own Shi'a base and strengthened Maliki and the PMF who were pushing an openly sectarian, anti-Sunni line, and calling for greater Iranian involvement in the conflict. Abadi put forward a comprehensive reform agenda in early August 2015 after nationwide protests, but despite some successes, Maliki ultimately blocked key parts of his program. Ramadi's loss, and the continued inability to recapture the city, reinforced Maliki's disruptive role on the sidelines (and the implied threat to Abadi's leadership), and undermined Baghdad's credibility as it negotiated with Kurdish and Sunni leaders. At the same time, Sunni communities and tribal leaders who'd previously—if tentatively—backed Baghdad, saw less and less reason to do so.

Iraq, indeed, looked increasingly like Humpty Dumpty. Efforts to put the country back together as a unified political entity were fading, leaders were speaking of a soft partition into Shi'a, Sunni and Kurdish regions, and some on the edge of the political debate were beginning to argue for what amounted to ethnic cleansing—driving Sunni communities out of major cities, repopulating whole regions with Shi'a settlers, and permanently restructuring the human geography of Iraq. A look at what Shi'a militias had done in the places they'd already captured—places like Jurf as-Sakhr or Tikrit, both now depopulated areas under Shi'a military occupation—showed that this was more than mere rhetoric. A comment by the International Crisis Group at the height of the battle in Tikrit rang even truer now: Shi'a militias in Sunni Iraq, to the extent that they filled the vacuum left by an ineffective central government, were "defeating the Iraqi state, one victory at a time."[13]

The Kurds, for their part, behind their relatively stable front, were increasingly being treated as fully independent of Iraq in terms of weapons supplies and international trainers, and were stockpiling weapons and equipment. While (in theory) the purpose of this was to enable the peshmerga to participate in a joint effort to liberate Mosul, it was hard to see why Kurdish leaders would be willing to waste their new capabilities, or lose Kurdish lives, recapturing a mostly Arab city for politicians in Baghdad for whom they had little love and less respect.

And the influx of international assistance was disrupting the balance among competing Kurdish groups included the ruling KDP, its bitter rival the PUK, and an increasingly influential militia (the YPG) linked to the PKK's Syrian affiliate. As weapons and support flowed in, each group became better armed and more capable, but increasingly suspicious of others, and the factions' spheres of control were increasingly contested. A family member of one Kurdish leader, for example, approached arms dealers in Cyprus and Eastern Europe at this time with a shopping list of military equipment he described as essential to fight ISIS. But a look at the list—high-end night vision goggles, MP-5 submachine guns, advanced sniper optics, crypto radios—told a different story. It was the blueprint for a gunned-up personal bodyguard or a SWAT team, not a combat unit, indicating that at least some Kurds saw the most immediate threat as internal.[14]

In early May, visiting Washington D.C., Masoud Barzani, leader of the the KDP, was treated by Congress and the White House like the head of an independent state, and took the opportunity—amid increasingly frayed relations with Baghdad—to announce that once ISIS was defeated, Kurdistan would hold a referendum on formal independence from Iraq. "I cannot say if it will be in the next year, or when, but certainly the independent Kurdistan is coming," he said.[15] But when Barzani's term as KRG president ended in August, he sought to extend it indefinitely, citing the war situation, and tensions with his rivals spiked. It seemed that the ultimate outcome might be a better armed, less united, less peaceful, but independent Kurdish state with regional ambitions—with huge geopolitical implications for the entire region, given Kurdish populations in Iraq, Syria, Turkey and Iran.

If things in Iraq looked increasingly like a sectarian stalemate, in Syria the Assad regime's situation was far worse, and it deteriorated further over the summer. As I explained above, the influence of moderate (i.e. non-jihadist) rebels peaked in mid-2013, when they advanced into the outskirts of Damascus, challenging the regime's hold on the capital and triggering the large-scale use of nerve gas. The Ghouta gas attack was a major miscalculation that could have been fatal to Assad, had President Obama only acted on his own red line. Indeed, contacts close to the regime told us Assad was furious at his generals' use of gas without his personal authorization, given the risk of U.S. retaliation.[16] In the event, of course, no intervention occurred and the moderates were severely weakened as a result.

Over the next year, Abu Muhammad al-Jolani and the newly invigorated Jabhat al-Nusra expanded into the vacuum left by the decline of the moderates, assuming leadership of the whole northern zone of the uprising. In part this was due to JN fighters' superior military skill, in part it was because they were taking the fight to the regime—JN was certainly doing far more than ISIS at that time. But it was also due to Jolani's remarkable political savvy. JN made extremely selective use of suicide bombers, focused almost exclusively on military and regime-supportive targets and (unlike ISIS *or* the regime) avoided antagonizing or brutalizing ordinary civilians.

In May, Jolani told Al Jazeera, "We are only here to accomplish one mission, to fight the regime and its agents on the ground, including Hezbollah and others." Once the war was over and the regime was gone, he said, all factions would be consulted before anyone considered establishing an Islamic State, and sectarian retribution would be off the table: "Our war is not a matter of revenge against the Alawites despite the fact that in Islam, they are considered to be heretics."[17] Remembering Jolani's background as a companion of Zarqawi and as AQI's Nineveh operations chief, I recall thinking "Who are you, and what have you done with the *real* AQI?" Whatever else was happening, we were clearly dealing with a new and "better" class of terrorist here: JN was displaying all the combat capability of an AQI, but with the political sophistication and governance aspirations of a Hezbollah.

And Jolani's rhetoric (sincere or not) was working, because unlike AQI in the past—or ISIS, which insisted all rebels swear *bayat* to Baghdadi or face annihilation—he was following Zawahiri's popular front strategy, building relations with all rebel factions other than those directly backed by the United States, promoting unity of effort, but not (at least, not yet) expecting others to sign onto the broader AQ agenda. Whereas Baghdadi and ISIS peremptorily demanded allegiance, Jolani understood that in a diverse and fractious movement like the Syrian uprising, leadership had to be earned, not just asserted. From late 2014, this approach began to pay huge dividends for JN, with the formation of "operations rooms"—command centers where different rebel groups came together in informal coalitions to plan and coordinate joint operations.

In late March 2015, a JN-led operations room (the Army of Conquest, Jaysh al-Fatah, JF) seized Idlib city in Syria's northwest, then expelled government forces from the rest of Idlib province, seized the town of Jisr al-Shugour, and then moved against Aleppo and Latakia. This was hugely threatening to the regime, which (apart from its outposts at Hasakah and Deir ez-Zor, both of which were now entirely cut off) controlled only three regions of the country: Damascus and its environs, the Alawite heartland (the coastal provinces of Latakia and Tartus, and the mountains overlooking them) and the corridor from Damascus to Homs connecting the two.

While JF was making progress in the north and center of the country, the Southern Front (Jabhat al-Janubiya, another "operations room" comprising fifty-eight groups including the FSA southern command, supported and advised by a U.S. Military Operations Center out of Jordan) seized positions in Quneitra province, captured one of the regime's most important military bases near the southern city of Deraa, and attempted to cut the Deraa–Damascus road. Faced with a critical manpower shortage despite harsh conscription programs, Assad was forced to rely on Iranian-backed militias, Hezbollah fighters in the Qalamoun region near the Syrian–Lebanese border, and thousands of "volunteers" from the Iranian Revolutionary Guards Corps. This weakened Assad's control over his own campaign, even as his grip on territory slipped.

Then in July a regime countermove against Palmyra failed to retake the city, and cost Assad further troops and resources, even as JF (in concert with the local FSA front) continued their offensive toward Latakia, where they captured key villages and threatened the regime's central Damascus–Homs corridor. At the same time, rebel advances in the al-Ghaab plain—Syria's breadbasket—and the ISIS capture of al-Qaryatayn threatened the same corridor from the north and east, while simultaneously targeting the regime's food supply and a key transport hub. ISIS also attacked a pumping station and airbase 60 miles from Palmyra, continued its attacks on Deir ez-Zor and Hasakah, and threatened Homs in Syria's center, even as JF moved on Aleppo in the north. By late summer, Assad had suffered huge losses of manpower, economic resources and territorial control—his regime was in full-on crisis mode and more dependent on its only allies, Iran and Russia, than ever before.

As it happened, at that moment, 1400 miles from Damascus and a universe away from the Syrian battlefront, Iranian negotiators were meeting in the opulent Palais Coburg Hotel in Vienna with diplomats from the EU, Russia, China, France, the UK, the United States and Germany, finalizing a nuclear deal—formally, the Joint Comprehensive Plan Of Action (JCPOA). The agreement, signed on 14 July, emerged from talks that had been running openly since November 2013 and secretly since July 2012. It was billed as President Obama's signature foreign policy achievement, and a landmark accomplishment for Secretary of State John Kerry: the president called it "the strongest non-proliferation agreement ever negotiated."[18] The Iranian nuclear deal was the second transformational event of the summer and, leaving aside its merits as a counter-proliferation measure (which, frankly, I wasn't qualified to judge) it had clearly observable effects on the ground in both Syria and Iraq.

Despite the long history of Iranian–American enmity some U.S. leaders—including the president and Secretary Kerry—saw the deal as an opportunity for broader rapprochement, opening the door to constructive engagement on shared U.S.–Iranian interests such as defeating ISIS and stabilizing Syria, Iraq and Afghanistan.[19] Former Secretary Clinton argued that the JCPOA must be part of a broad strategy covering all points of conflict between Iran and the United States.[20] Some Iranian leaders, notably President Hassan Rouhani (a former nuclear negotiator himself, elected president in August 2013 on a pledge to resolve the nuclear issue and lift crippling sanctions from Iran's economy) and former President Akbar Hashemi Rafsanjani, hinted they felt the same way. On the other hand, the Supreme Leader, Ayatollah Ali Khamenei—whose decisions trump those of Iran's president on matters of national security, and who controls the IRGC—publicly rejected a broader rapprochement, or even the notion of bilateral talks beyond the specifics of the JCPOA.

In the event, U.S. officials told me later, they avoided engaging Iranian delegates on the issue of Syria and Iraq, lest this give Iran leverage to delay a deal on the nuclear issue.[21] The negotiations thus focused narrowly on the nuclear deal, though Secretary Kerry and others apparently still hoped the momentum might carry through into cooperation on other issues after it was implemented. In this version of events, Washington sought to convince Tehran to cooperate on nukes without offering concessions on Syria in return.

An alternative version—advanced by Middle East analyst and former Bush Pentagon and White House official Michael Doran, among others—was that Washington appeased Tehran, turning a blind eye to Iran's support for Assad in Syria and its encroachment in Iraq, and that President Obama "treated Syria as an Iranian sphere of interest all along in order to secure the nuclear agreement."[22] Doran's argument was bolstered by media reports claiming President Obama had written to Supreme Leader Khamenei in October 2014, describing "a shared interest in fighting Islamic State militants in Iraq and Syria" and offering to cooperate on ISIS if Iran could reach "a comprehensive agreement with global powers on the future of Tehran's nuclear program ... Mr. Obama's letter also sought to assuage Iran's concerns about the future of [Assad, stating] that the U.S.'s military operations inside Syria aren't targeted at Mr. Assad or his security forces."[23] The president's motivation—to appease Iran on Syria in order to secure a nuclear deal, or (conversely) to offer the nuclear deal in return for Iranian help in Syrian and Iraq—has been hotly debated, and some of the criticism of his motivation was clearly little more than point scoring by his political opponents. But the effects of the JCPOA on the conflict were both clear and profound.

Within days of the agreement, defying a UN travel ban that was still in effect, Qasem Soleimani flew to Moscow and met with Russian defense minister Sergey Shoygu to discuss "bilateral and regional issues" and the sale of Russian S-300 anti-aircraft systems to Iran.[24] Foreign minister Javad Zarif visited a week later for discussions with Russian foreign minister Lavrov on joint Iranian–Russian efforts to "overcome the crisis in Syria."[25] These meetings were seen at the time as indicators that Russia and Iran might put forward a peace plan for Syria at the UN General Assembly meeting in New York at the end of September. In the event they presaged something entirely different.

Regional players—particularly the Israelis, the Saudis and the Arab Gulf States—reacted negatively to the nuclear deal. Israel's Prime Minister Benjamin Netanyahu furiously denounced the agreement as a "historic mistake," said that Israel would not be bound by it, and warned of "negative repercussions in a region already riven with rivalries and armed conflict."[26] Saudi officials were politely noncommittal in public, saying only that they were studying the agreement, but in private they expressed concerns that America was "giving everything to Iran" and hinted they would ramp up efforts to counter Iran's regional subversion.[27] Prince Bandar bin Sultan, former ambassador to Washington and chief of Saudi intelligence, wrote that "the strategic foreign policy analysis, the national intelligence information, and America's allies in the region's intelligence all predict not only the same outcome of the [Clinton administration's failed 1994] North Korean nuclear deal but worse—with the billions of dollars that Iran will have access to."[28] Two weeks later, Saudi Arabia and Egypt announced the formation of a joint military force to counter Iranian sponsorship of Houthi rebels in Yemen (against which the two countries, with several others, had launched an operation in March) and as a broader regional counterbalance to Iran.[29] The Gulf states shared the Saudis' concerns.[30]

On the ground in Syria, the rebels saw the nuclear deal as de facto acceptance by Washington that it was powerless to force Assad out. Jihadist groups portrayed the deal as proof of a U.S.–Iranian war on Sunni Islam—the Crusaders and Jews in league with the *Rafidah* ("rejecters") of Iran, pursuing a condominium over Syria–Iraq for their own purposes. Though this might have sounded, to our ears, like a completely implausible conspiracy theory, given the long history of Iranian–American conflict, in fact it was a very effective propaganda theme that had long resonated with poor, pious Sunnis in Iraq and Syria. For their part, moderate rebels understood the agreement to indicate that, while U.S. resources would still be available to fight ISIS, overthrowing Assad—the goal for which they'd joined the uprising in the first place—was no longer on the cards. Instead, unwilling to commit to another conflict in the Middle East, Washington was outsourcing the anti-ISIS fight to the Iranians, and thus by extension to Tehran's protégé Assad.

Whether these perceptions were accurate is beside the point—their effect on the ground was to empower JN and ISIS, suck even more oxygen from the secular rebel groups, and doom to failure the U.S. military's effort to train moderate rebels (delayed and under-resourced as it already was) since the Americans were now effectively asking Syrians to fight someone other than the regime they'd signed up to overthrow, a regime which at this point in the war had killed at least eight times as many Syrians as had ISIS. As someone with long experience of irregular troops, it seemed to me that the program's collapse (announced publicly in October 2015 but long foreshadowed) resulted partly from policy-makers in Washington forgetting a key rule of unconventional warfare: as an outsider you can arm, organize, train and support guerrillas all you want, but you can only *lead* them where they already want to go.

The other key regional player, of course, was Turkey. Ankara's reaction to the JCPOA was muted, but the broader issue of Iranian involvement in Syria was deeply threatening to Turkey, which saw Assad, his Iranian backers and his Kurdish opposition as more of a threat than ISIS. For Turkey, the question was primarily geopolitical, with Iran's increasingly dominant role in Iraq and Syria (and, in particular, the direct intervention of thousands of Iranian volunteers in Syria and the soft takeover of Assad's regime in summer 2015) representing an intolerable encroachment into what Ankara perceived as its sphere of influence. Turkish leaders saw Iranian encroachment as undermining Turkey's role in the region, and encouraging separatist unrest among local populations, not least the Kurds. Until July, Turkey had declined to allow U.S. or coalition aircraft to operate against ISIS from its territory; it had also refused to intervene against ISIS unless it could also strike Assad's positions and those of his Iranian-backed allies, and stood by as the Kurds battled ISIS in Kobani.

From October 2014 until February 2015, as the battle raged only a few hundred yards away, Turkish troops and tanks literally sat and watched: deployed on the open hills overlooking Kobani from across the border, they passively observed the battle through weapon sights and tank optics, as Kurdish troops fought ISIS house-to-house. I could imagine Turkish commanders channeling Henry Kissinger's comment on the Iran–Iraq War—"It's a pity they can't *both* lose."

By midsummer, however, spooked by Assad's loss of territory (which increased the likelihood that the Syrian Kurdish Democratic Union Party, PYD, might carve out its own state in northern Syria, ally with Iraqi Kurds and attract Kurds in Turkey) the Turkish government—with American support—began quietly putting forward a plan to establish a humanitarian safe zone in northern Syria, 70 miles wide and 40 deep, and to create three "safe settlements" to house Syrians displaced by the fighting. The safe zone, a rough rectangle stretching from the Turkish border opposite the city of Gaziantep to the Syrian town of al-Bab, and from Aleppo city on the west to the Euphrates on the east, would be under military protection, supported by aircraft operating out of the airbase at İncirlik, and defended by coalition-supported moderate rebel forces. It would push ISIS back from the border almost to the outskirts of Aleppo city, enable refugees in camps near Gaziantep to return to Syria, and perhaps create a staging area for rebels to move against both ISIS and the regime.

Aside from any humanitarian intent, the Turks were conscious that they were running out of resources to support Syrian refugees in Turkey, and that if they did not fill the vacuum left by the regime's losses, it might be filled by ISIS or by Kurdish separatists—either of which would be equally unacceptable. They were also facing the prospect that PYD and its newly declared statelet (known as Rojava) would dominate the entire Turkish–Syrian border. The nuclear deal, with its imminent prospect of a richer, stronger Iran freed of restrictions and able to extend subversive tentacles into the Turkish sphere of influence, only hastened Ankara's desire to act quickly. Like many regional powers, Turkey's concerns over the JCPOA were not so much about the nuclear aspect of the deal, but about the potential for conventional weapons exports and subversive activity by the Iranian regime—especially Soleimani's Quds Force—and the effect this would have on an increasingly hot proxy war between Sunni powers and Shi'a Iran that was being fought out in Syria and Iraq.

TRANSFORMATION

In July, Turkey opened the airbases at İncirlik and Diyarbakır to the coalition, publicly proposed the safe zone, and began airstrikes against ISIS. At the same time, Turkish aircraft struck Kurdish positions (primarily PKK-linked forces) across Syria and northern Iraq. And the Turks, like the Israelis, continued to oppose any accommodation with Assad or the Iranians. Turkey's entry into the war was the third transformative event of the summer.

For a time in July and August—with Turkey as part of the coalition (albeit using its participation to go after the Kurds as well as ISIS), Assad losing ground in critical parts of Syria, Russia and Iran discussing options to "overcome" the crisis, the possibility of a humanitarian safe zone in northern Syria, and the potential for broader U.S.–Iranian cooperation on the back of the nuclear deal—it seemed the way might be clearing for a resumption of talks toward a negotiated settlement.

I, like others, saw this as generally a positive trend despite its complications—it was certainly the closest we'd been to a peace process (though that wasn't saying much) since the collapse of the last round of talks in Geneva. These UN-led talks had been stalled for eighteen months, since late 2013, over the question of whether Assad could preside over a transitional or provisional regime as part of a peace process, or whether he must step down first. Syrian peace activists talked at this time about making a distinction between Assad the man—who, they said, would need to leave before any settlement could occur—and the Syrian state, which they believed would have to play a role in any provisional or transitional government. There was a sense of expectation that the UN General Assembly would bring a significant, perhaps positive, shift in the conflict. This turned out to be half-correct—the shift came, all right, but it was in the opposite direction.

15

SPILLOVER

In the first weeks of September, as the UN General Assembly neared, the number of refugees reaching Western Europe spiked dramatically. The European refugee crisis was the fourth transformative development of 2015, one that finally brought home to Western countries the consequences of continued inaction on the Syria–Iraq crisis—in the form of a literal, human spillover.

The number of refugees and asylum-seekers reaching Europe had been climbing steadily since 2011, driven by Syria and Iraq, the war in Afghanistan, the Libyan civil war, conflicts in Darfur, Somalia, Niger and the Congo, and repression in Eritrea. There was also a secondary wave where countries like Syria (which had absorbed more than a million Iraqi refugees during the U.S. occupation) and Libya—a popular destination for African migrants until the upheavals of 2013—became increasingly unsafe themselves, forcing refugees who'd already fled once to move again. The number of asylum-seekers and undocumented migrants reached record levels in 2014, straining EU frontier agencies and police forces in countries such as Greece, Italy and Hungary, who carried most of the burden of border enforcement.

Economic motivations played a part, of course: families fleeing war were drawn by the prospect of prosperity, not just the absence of violence. And even in the depths of the Great Recession and the Eurozone financial crisis, Europe's relative wealth, its educational and employment opportunities, and its generous welfare policies—including government housing, health care and unemployment benefits—made EU countries extremely attractive for those who could make it there. Vetting asylum-seekers, essential to distinguish economic migrants from those fleeing conflict, and from terrorists or criminals, was a huge burden for countries on the EU's external borders, as well as for destination countries including Germany, Sweden, Italy, France, Hungary and the UK.[1]

Then in summer 2015, the number of refugees and asylum-seekers suddenly shot up, way beyond the already unprecedented totals of 2014. Almost all the increase was due to events in Syria, including the regime's continued targeting of civilians, and people fleeing ISIS territorial gains. Assad's desperation for manpower—and his commanders' willingness, in places like Palmyra, to abandon conscripts to ISIS beheading—prompted large numbers of military-aged men to flee, rather than face yet another round of conscription. At the same time, the Syrian government changed its emigration rules, making it easier to obtain passports and exit visas, as losses of territory, economic and agricultural resources, electricity and water prompted the regime to encourage extra mouths to leave.

Simultaneously, the countries that had absorbed the bulk of refugees—Turkey with 1.9 million as of mid-2015, Lebanon with 1.2, Jordan with 650,000—were running out of resources to keep supporting the huge numbers of displaced Syrians on their territory. Despite calls for international assistance, these regional states had shouldered much of the financial, security and logistic burden of the refugee crisis since 2011, and some were being forced to cut support, prompting many refugees to move on to Europe instead of waiting for things to improve in the region. Changes in European policies over the summer—in Greece, which in the midst of its own financial crisis could no longer secure its enormous coastline or process asylum-seekers, and Macedonia, which created a new temporary transit permit letting refugees travel through the country to other EU destinations and so opened up a new Balkans land route—prompted many more refugees to make the short sea crossing from Turkey to Greece, then by land through Serbia, Croatia and Slovenia to Hungary, Austria and Germany.

Whatever the cause, by the end of June 2015, more than 124,000 refugees had arrived in Greece, a 750 per cent increase over the total for all of 2014, leaving the Greek authorities "in total chaos" and unable to cope, according to the UN refugee agency UNHCR.[2] In August, Germany announced that it expected 800,000 people to apply for asylum by the end of 2015—more than for the whole EU the previous year.[3] By the end of September the number of migrants crossing into Hungary was ten times as many per week as at the start of May, prompting unrest, border closures, and accusations of police brutality.

Demonstrators supporting the refugees protested police use of water-cannons and the construction of border fences, as well as what they saw as lack of Christian charity toward undocumented migrants, while counter-protesters demonstrated against an influx of thousands of unemployed military-age males from Syria, Iraq, Afghanistan and parts of Africa, worrying about terrorist infiltration of the refugee stream, the "Islamisation" of Europe and the burden on an already strained welfare system. Both groups saw themselves as acting in support of traditional European, Christian values—a polarization of perception that foreshadowed conflicts to come.

In the first days of September, images of a still, small body, face down in the surf on a Turkish beach—three-year-old Alan Kurdi, who had drowned when his family's rubber dinghy capsized as they fled from the Turkish town of Bodrum to the Greek island of Kos—prompted a moral outcry and calls for increased humanitarian assistance. Europe agreed to absorb another 160,000 Syrian refugees, while Canada committed itself to taking 25,000, Australia said it would accept another 12,000 and the United States announced it would admit 10,000. Finally, a crisis that had been going on in the shadows for years had broken through to the public—and therefore to policy-makers—but whether this would result in a change of policy toward Syria was a different matter. Distant countries (like Canada, the United States and Australia) tended to focus on problems of migrant handling, asylum processing and humanitarian assistance. Countries closer to the problem—including many in Western Europe, experiencing public unrest due to an unprecedented influx of foreigners into societies already stressed by the financial crisis—tended to look more closely at the supply side: addressing instability in Iraq and Syria at source. But nobody had any good solution to offer, and many policy-makers were looking to the United States for leadership.

Any dead child, on a beach or anywhere else, is a tragedy. But the statistics told an even sadder story: by the time little Alan drowned, thousands of others had been killed fleeing Syria—more than 1,200 died in a single sinking incident off the coast of Italy in April, for example. At the same time, by mid-2015 more than 10,000 children had been killed in Syria, along with 240,000 adults. For comparison, this was almost twice as many, in just four years, as died in the twelve years since the U.S.-led invasion of Iraq in 2003, and out of a population only two-thirds the size (Syria had 22 million people against Iraq's 33 million). The humanitarian impact of such heavy losses, in such a short time, was staggering.

Many of those killed in Syria were civilians hit by regime shelling of schools, hospitals and bread lines, dismembered by barrel bombs—44-gallon drums filled with explosives and scrap metal, dropped from helicopters, that made an eerie, rhythmic whooshing sound as they tumbled in the air, shook the ground when they went off, and could collapse an entire apartment block—or slaughtered in raids by Iranian-backed *shabiha* paramilitaries. ISIS, of course, as we've seen, murdered many others. An entire generation of Syrians, renowned as one of the best-educated, most politically and culturally sophisticated populations in the Arab world, had missed out on even a basic education. Syria's economy was in ruins, unemployment was through the roof, and half of Syrians now relied on humanitarian assistance to survive. And the misery on Europe's southeastern borders—a direct result of world inaction on Syria—showed no sign of subsiding.

For three decades before Syrians became the world's majority refugee population in 2014, the largest number of displaced people in the world had come from Afghanistan. And it was in Afghanistan, also in September, just as the European refugee crisis was peaking, that another spillover took place.

NATO's combat mission in Afghanistan had formally ended in December 2014, leaving a smaller NATO mission, Operation Resolute Support, to train, advise and assist the Afghan National Security Forces (ANSF, the Afghan army and police). In practical terms, ANSF had been carrying the main combat burden for almost two years by this time, and had performed surprisingly well against a very resilient and capable enemy.

In summer 2013, for example, the Taliban struck hard in Afghanistan's south, east and northeast, in three separate offensives designed to cow ANSF, intimidate civilians, and destroy confidence ahead of NATO's withdrawal. But after initial success, each thrust was defeated with heavy insurgent losses. ANSF recaptured almost all the lost ground, the police re-established government presence, and civilian officials returned. By the end of 2013, every coalition Provincial Reconstruction Team (PRT) had been closed for at least a year, not a dollar of military stabilization funds had been spent in two years, and the cities had been under Afghan civil police authority for more than three. Coalition airstrikes, along with maintenance and medical support, were a huge help to ANSF in the 2013 campaign, but some units suffered heavily even with these enablers. ANSF had shown it could hold the Taliban with virtually no NATO combat troops engaged, and few embedded advisors—but it was heavily dependent on U.S. air power, and there were questions about how many fighting seasons it could sustain at this loss rate.

The 2014 fighting season was even tougher, with significant Taliban offensives in many of the same areas as 2013, and terrorist attacks by the Pakistan-linked Haqqani Network, cells from AQ (which was re-establishing itself in some parts of the east and southwest of the country) and several smaller groups. Again, Afghan forces carried the main combat burden with very little NATO engagement other than Special Operations Forces. Still recovering from their own losses of the previous year, in April 2014 the Taliban failed significantly to disrupt the first round of presidential elections, which saw high turnout and less violence than expected, and which observers assessed as mostly free and fair. After second-round elections in mid-June, Afghanistan completed the first democratic transition of power in its history, from Hamid Karzai to Ashraf Ghani as president and Abdullah Abdullah as chief executive. Again, ANSF held the line, and fighting ability—so far, at any rate—was not the problem. Instead, the concern was with factionalism and power sharing among Afghan elites, and the formation of an effective cabinet.

For ANSF, the key questions remained long-term sustainability, including high casualty rates, absenteeism, equipment maintenance and logistics issues, financial viability, and the institutional health of the Afghan Army, police and civil service. In other words, the problems facing Afghans at the end of 2014 were similar in nature (though in some ways less severe) than those facing Iraqis at the end of 2011.

In one way the Afghan situation was far better: unlike the "zero option" in Iraq, where coalition troops pulled out completely and left Iraqis to their own devices, substantial NATO and U.S. forces remained in Afghanistan after the formal end of the drawdown on 31 December 2014. By early 2015, International Security Assistance Force (ISAF) Regional Commands—division-level headquarters that once disposed of many NATO maneuver units—had converted to Train, Advise and Assist Commands (TAACs) under Resolute Support, each with a few hundred advisers and support troops, based at Kabul, Kandahar, Jalalabad, Mazar-e Sharif and Herat.[4] Beside the TAACs, which were multinational NATO-led organizations, the United States maintained its own Regional Command East at Bagram Airbase north of Kabul, pursuing a separate counterterrorism mission under a bilateral U.S.–Afghan agreement, focused against AQ and high-value Taliban targets, and operating alongside Afghan Special Operations Forces. All up, as of February 2015, Resolute Support included 13,300 troops from forty-two countries.[5] U.S. forces included roughly 6,300 in Operation Resolute Support, plus 3,200 on counterterrorism tasks. U.S. Air Force and Navy strike aircraft and drones provided cover to NATO and the U.S. counterterrorism mission, and were on call to help ANSF as needed.

Thus, between U.S. counterterrorism forces and support from NATO, Afghanistan had an ongoing international commitment. This was a mixed blessing—the continued presence of infidel foreigners infuriated jihadist and nationalist groups, but also meant troop-contributing nations and the world in general couldn't just forget Afghanistan and (because they still had people and assets in harm's way) troop-contributing nations could be expected to come to Afghanistan's aid *in extremis*. In this sense Afghanistan in 2015 was in a stronger position than Iraq in 2012.

Politically, President Ghani was a technocratic reformer who'd been a successful finance minister in Hamid Karzai's first administration, and followed more constructive and inclusive policies than had Maliki in Iraq. Likewise, Chief Executive Abdullah had agreed to partner with Ghani in a national unity government, and former President Karzai played a more responsible and less destabilizing role than Maliki had in Iraq. But in two respects, the Afghan government faced a very dangerous situation: the Taliban safe haven in Pakistan, and the siphoning-off of U.S. support after the rise of ISIS.

Despite significant losses during the ISAF surge of 2010–12, the Taliban had one great advantage that AQI lacked during the Iraq surge of 2007–9, namely its cross-border sanctuary in Pakistan. Whereas AQI mostly had to wait for the Syrian war and the U.S. departure in 2011 before it could rebuild, Taliban leadership, recruiting, training, financial and support systems were located in Pakistan, out of reach of ISAF throughout the conflict. Despite frequent U.S. drone strikes and occasional raids, the light-footprint approach was no more effective in dealing with Taliban bases in Pakistan than it had been anywhere else.

And after the 2010 Lisbon Summit, when NATO leaders very helpfully told the Taliban exactly how long they needed to wait until the withdrawal would be complete, Taliban leaders were able to pursue an "economy of force" strategy, maintaining their infrastructure and main forces in Pakistan, doing enough in Afghanistan to remain relevant, but essentially waiting out the drawdown. Thus, going into the 2015 fighting season, the Afghan Taliban still fielded 8–10,000 full-time fighters, a significant shadow governance infrastructure, another 20–25,000 part-time fighters, and several times as many members of sympathizer or auxiliary networks. The Haqqani Network, AQ and several smaller groups (all of which could also access sanctuary areas in Pakistan, while some had close and supportive relationships with individuals in the Pakistani intelligence services) fielded capable forces as well.

Secondly, as mentioned earlier, USS *George H.W. Bush* and Carrier Strike Group Two were partway through a deployment supporting ANSF in June 2014 when the fall of Mosul prompted their redeployment to support operations in Iraq. By definition, this meant the aircraft weren't available for Afghanistan, though they were backfilled with drones and piloted aircraft. Over the next year, with more nations joining the coalition air campaign and deploying land-based aircraft over Iraq and Syria, air assets available to assist ANSF increased somewhat—and the Afghan National Air Force grew in capability, though from a low base and with few close air support aircraft.[6]

But now that Afghanistan was no longer the only game in town, the level of international support Afghan troops and police enjoyed in 2013–14 (and which was critical in holding the line) would no longer be available. Likewise, the implied promise of *in extremis* assistance from troop contributing nations in Operation Resolute Support was weaker now that several nations with large contingents in Afghanistan (the United States, Australia and the UK) were also committed to Iraq. And with its losses of 2013–14, ANSF lacked the capacity to conduct maneuver operations in multiple provinces simultaneously, tying it more to fixed locations than in the past.

Unsurprisingly, then, the 2015 campaign was much rougher for ANSF—and more successful for the Taliban—than the previous two had been. By mid-October, after offensives in the east, north and southwest of the country, independent analysts at the *Long War Journal* concluded that the Taliban controlled (that is, permanently held and openly administered) thirty-five of Afghanistan's roughly 400 districts, and contested another thirty-five (i.e. controlled the countryside and population but did not permanently occupy the district center).[7] Given the scale of Taliban auxiliary and underground networks, these figures suggested that 20 to 50 per cent of the country was Taliban-influenced by the end of summer 2015. The one bright spot—which both the Kabul government and old Afghan hands tended to take for granted, because it had never come into question throughout the entire course of the war to date—was that all major cities remained in government hands.

On 28 September, just as world leaders were concluding the first day of the UN General Assembly's plenary debate in New York, three Taliban columns converged on the provincial capital of Kunduz in northeastern Afghanistan. The city had been under heavy attack since the beginning of the northern fighting season in mid-April, part of a general Taliban offensive across the north that targeted the provinces of Badakhshan, Baghlan, Kunduz and Takhar, an area known as the "Pashtun belt," where security had been progressively deteriorating since 2009. Fighting surged around Kunduz, a city of 270,000—at times spilling into the outskirts, with the Taliban briefly occupying one neighborhood in April—but several thousand government troops pushed the guerrillas back.

As in Iraq, the ANSF laydown in northern Afghanistan tended toward area defense: government forces occupied urban centers and guarded critical infrastructure, while rural districts increasingly fell under the sway of the insurgents, and over summer the Taliban again encroached on the city. As in Iraq, terrorist attacks on urban centers proved effective in forcing the military to concentrate in the cities to assist the police (who had primary responsibility for urban security) and thus left rural districts more vulnerable to guerrilla action.

Unlike Iraq, however, the Kabul government recognized that static defenses wouldn't suffice to secure major cities, and, alarmed by the Taliban's penetration of the Kunduz outskirts in April, began to recruit local militias to secure areas outside the city and on its outskirts. Paid, and under loose supervision, by the Afghan intelligence service (the National Directorate of Security, NDS), the militias were mainly former mujahideen, loyal to local warlords rather than the central government. This was a strategy fraught with risk, but one that officials in Kabul saw as the best of a bad set of options, given ANSF's inability to secure the whole country or maneuver in multiple provinces simultaneously.[8]

Throughout the conflict Afghanistan's cities had been relatively safe. There had been bombings, riots and assassinations in urban areas, of course, and a few districts in most major towns had been no-go areas, with Taliban networks, urban terror cells, or bandit activity. But in the whole history of the conflict since 2001, no insurgent group had ever successfully seized a city for any length of time. The received wisdom was that ANSF would struggle to prevent Taliban activity in many rural areas after the NATO drawdown, but that, with militia allies and the support of local police, they could hold the cities and secure the ring road, the critical highway connecting the country's urban centers.

Across the frontier in Pakistan, the Taliban's Peshawar Shura had taken on the responsibility for planning the 2015 campaign in northeast Afghanistan.[9] Qari Baryal—a famous commander from the north who had good relations both with AQ and the Pakistani intelligence service, and long combat experience fighting the French Chasseurs Alpins and Foreign Legion in Kapisa in 2009–11—now headed the Peshawar Shura's military commission.[10] Baryal planned to raid Kunduz but, according to commanders involved in the plan, didn't initially think the chances of seizing the town were particularly good. As Baryal and his commanders saw it, their key problem in the campaign would be logistics and troop numbers, so in the early spring of 2015, as the snow began to clear from the passes, a series of mule trains packed ammunition, medical supplies, explosives, food and water across a network of mountain trails from Pakistan into northeast Afghanistan, gradually stockpiling resources close to Kunduz.[11] At the same time, Qari Baryal and Mullah Abdul Salam (his military commander for Kunduz) mobilized their entire regional network of allies for the offensive, including fighters from the Islamic Movement of Uzbekistan, the Pakistani Taliban, the Quetta Shura, Lashkar-e Tayyiba (the Pakistani terrorist group responsible for the 2008 Mumbai attack), and even commanders aligned with ISIS.[12]

Baryal was engaging in the classic guerrilla diplomacy that normally precedes any important attack in Afghanistan, working hard to build relationships with the new overall leader of the Taliban, Mullah Akhtar Mohammed Mansoor, to rally autonomous commanders for a joint effort, and convince local guerrilla bands to support the offensive despite the likely backlash on their base areas. Baryal took the unusual step of combining forces with the Quetta Shura (a separate, often rival power center within the Taliban command structure) to create a unified command, with Mullah Salam acting both as military commander under the Peshawar Shura's authority, and as the Taliban's civil governor for Kunduz under the authority of Quetta.[13] This joint civil-military appointment gave Mullah Salam the authority he needed to rally a large and capable guerrilla coalition for the campaign.

By the end of the April–May fighting around Kunduz, ANSF had pushed the guerrillas back from most of the city's zone of influence, but Mullah Salam's fighters still held a foothold in Gor Tepa district, 9 miles from the center of Kunduz on the town's northern outskirts, and in several urban districts in the city's southwest, which allowed them to maintain guerrilla cells and weapons caches inside the city. They also held forward bases in districts that were outside the city itself, but close enough (less than one night's march away, the critical distance in Afghan guerrilla warfare) to serve as jumping-off points when the time was right.

The opportunity presented itself in late September, when the Eid ul-Adha festival brought thousands into Kunduz from surrounding districts. Mullah Salam's men joined the stream of visitors, entered the city, linked up with the urban-based guerrillas, received a final target briefing from the auxiliary cells who were monitoring ANSF and tracking events in the city, and recovered their weapons from the caches established at the beginning of summer. Then, in a series of safe houses on the city's outskirts, guarded by their underground networks, they slept.

As the Taliban infiltrated the city, much of the ANSF garrison was on leave, visiting family for the holiday, and troops and police were in barracks celebrating. When Eid ended on 27 September, some prepared to return home, while others slept off the festivities.[14] The provincial governor, Umar Safi, was in Tajikistan. Safi was a British-educated Pashtun who had worked as a security advisor for the UN in Mazar-e Sharif, and was a strong political backer of President Ashraf Ghani. By all accounts a well-intentioned technocrat, he'd struggled as governor in the eight months since his appointment—his long-serving deputy Hamdullah Daneshi disagreed with his desire to disarm militias in the province, and had partnered with police chief General Abdul Sabur Nasrati (a Tajik from the Panjshir, loyal to Chief Executive Abdullah) to block him.[15] So the ANSF and civil government command structure in the city was disunited, and marred by personal distrust.

In the cold early hours of 28 September, the Taliban sprang the trap. Moving by the light of a full moon, 500 Taliban shook themselves out of their lying-up areas in the districts around Kunduz, and advanced on the city. They were dispersed in combat groups of roughly forty fighters each, divided into three columns under the overall command of Mullah Salam. The assault columns approached from the southeast (out of the Khanabad farming district), from Chardara, a hilly region west of the city, from the southwest along the Aliabad Road, and from the northern districts of Gor Tepa, Imam Sahib and Dasht-e Archi (Mullah Salam's home district).

These were main force Taliban—professional full-time fighters, put through rigorous training by experienced instructors in the camps in Pakistan, with uniforms, vehicles, heavy weapons, encrypted radios, and a formal command structure. They lacked the tanks, armored vehicles and artillery seen in Iraq, but were seasoned fighters, could call on technicals (captured Ford pickup trucks and Humvees) for mobility and had heavy machine guns, mortars, sniper teams and anti-armor missiles for fire support. They had a well-proven tactical system for operating in the farmland, mountains and villages of northern Afghanistan. Of 7,000 fighters Baryal and Salam had assembled for the attack, and who were in Kunduz at this time, only a tiny minority—less than 1000—belonged to this main force group. But they provided a hard core, a nucleus around which irregulars—lightly equipped, locally recruited guerrillas who fought part-time but knew the city intimately and could blend into its population—coalesced. Many of these local guerrillas, as throughout the war, were very young (some were boys in their mid-teens) but by this point the main force were hard-bitten veterans with many years of campaigning—while Baryal, Salam and the column commanders had decades of experience between them. About 3:00a.m., from a position on the Kunduz outskirts, Salam gave the order to attack.

Pushing into the city in small combat groups guided by local guerrillas, the main force columns moved directly, as fast as they could, to key locations in the city center—the governor's office, police station, prison, UN compound, Seh Darak Hospital in the city's south, NDS headquarters, and the main traffic circle in the north. As the main force pushed in from outside, guerrillas already in the town attacked ANSF garrison and headquarters positions from the rear, massively disrupting the defensive effort.[16] General Nasrati's police (responsible for securing the city) retreated to join the remnants of the military garrison at Kunduz airport, south of town, and succeeded in holding a perimeter there, but Kunduz itself fell to the Taliban by early morning, with government buildings burning and the movement's white silk *shahada* flag hoisted on the absent governor's residence and at the traffic circle by 7:00a.m., just over an hour after sunrise.

Taliban fighters spent the rest of the day clearing and securing the city, and were extremely active on social media, posting photographs of themselves in government buildings, live-tweeting a continuous stream of updates, and issuing decrees to the population. Taliban spokesman Zabiullah Mujahid announced the city's fall that morning.[17] For his part, Governor Safi—no doubt realizing he'd be held to account for the city's loss—fled from Tajikistan to Uzbekistan, then on to Turkey and Europe. Afghan sources claimed he was in London within two days.[18]

This was a major crisis—not just because of the size of Kunduz and its central location astride the ring road, but because of the symbolic impact of losing an entire city, for the first time in the war, to the Taliban. There was also a historical echo, from August 1988, when Kunduz was the first Afghan city to fall to the mujahideen during the Soviet withdrawal. The government responded quickly, airlifting 200 ANSF commandos with their U.S. advisers (approximately fifty operators from the 3rd Special Forces Group) into Kunduz airport to reinforce the remnants of the city's garrison. Simultaneously, a *kandak*, or battalion-sized unit—which, in Afghanistan at this point in the war, translated to roughly 300 troops—was ordered from Baghlan province south of Kunduz, and directed to move by road to Kunduz and link up with the troops at the airport. The relief force was ambushed en route—Mullah Salam having anticipated this move and placed a guerrilla group in position to block it—and the troops were bogged down, surrounded almost immediately, and failed to reach the city. Meanwhile the commandos and U.S. advisers at the airport launched a counterattack, accompanied by police and troops from the Kunduz city garrison, with the advisers calling in multiple U.S. airstrikes. They made progress initially, but were pushed back within hours by an aggressive Taliban mobile defense.

For the next three days, as the relief force slowly fought its way toward the city and troops from the airport continued pushing into town, intense fighting developed both inside Kunduz and in surrounding districts. By 5 October, a week after the initial attack, the Afghan government claimed it had recaptured the whole city, but security operations—with significant fighting against stay-behind groups and local guerrillas—continued until mid-October.[19] Lacking the heavy weapons, IEDs and other assets seen in Iraq, and without much time to dig in or create fortified positions, the Taliban fought a mobile defense from house to house, inflicting significant losses on ANSF before melting away. The government later claimed it had killed 400 Taliban in the battle; the Taliban admitted to ninety-five, claimed they'd killed 200 ANSF, announced that they had "welcomed 300 defectors" from the government side, and claimed that they still had more than 1,200 fighters in the city as late as 12 October.[20] Mullah Salam's fighters seized significant amounts of money, weapons and other equipment from government buildings during their occupation of the city, and although (notably) no ISIS-style mass killing of civilians occurred, at least thirty townspeople were killed in the fighting and another 340 were treated for wounds in local hospitals. But it was at another medical facility—the Médecins Sans Frontières (MSF) trauma hospital in the center-west of downtown Kunduz—that the largest loss of civilian life in the battle would occur.

MSF had established a fifty-five-bed surgical hospital in Kunduz in October 2011, the only facility of its kind in this part of the country.[21] Known for their impartiality in conflict environments, MSF teams treated casualties from all sides and were generally unmolested. They claim to have provided detailed coordinates for the hospital to both the Afghan government and NATO, as recently as 29 September, and to have informed the Taliban of the hospital's location.[22] The hospital was full of wounded, including two Taliban casualties whom MSF staff thought must be important since they had been escorted into the center by several Taliban fighters, and Taliban commanders made regular inquiries about their progress.[23]

In the early morning hours of 3 October, as Afghan and U.S. forces were clearing the town, the hospital was attacked repeatedly by a U.S. Air Force AC-130 gunship, a close air support aircraft derived from the C-130 cargo plane. The hospital, occupied by 180 MSF staff and patients at the time of the attack, was almost totally destroyed.[24] At least thirty people were killed and another thirty-three remained missing five days after the attack.

The circumstances of the attack remain unclear—several investigations were launched into the incident but none have yet reached any firm conclusions as to exactly what happened. U.S. and Afghan government accounts shifted several times after the incident, from statements that the hospital was attacked in self-defense by U.S. forces who came under fire from Taliban using it as cover, to a claim that Afghan forces targeted the hospital because Taliban were being treated there, to an assertion that the whole thing was a tragic accident.[25]

Whatever the circumstances, this was yet another example of the light footprint failing to work as advertised: even with specialist observers, the fact that the forces were non-local—i.e. not permanently based in the Kunduz area—meant ground troops failed to distinguish legitimate targets, and even with the excellent sensors carried by the AC-130, aircrew couldn't be certain what they were shooting at. Mistakes, very unfortunately, do often happen in war, but even if the MSF hospital attack *was* a genuine mistake (something that remains unconfirmed) the promise of the light footprint—going back to Rumsfeld and Transformation, and continued and expanded by President Obama during his long drawdown—was precisely that those mistakes could now be avoided, that remote surveillance and overhead sensors could provide "information dominance" ensuring precision without permanent presence. Increasingly, by 2016, this looked like fantasy: the greater the standoff range, the fewer boots on the ground, and the less intimately familiar with the environment were those directing a given strike, the less precise the engagement. President Obama was forced to issue a public apology to MSF, in what must be the rather unusual circumstance of one Nobel Peace Prize winner apologizing to another for bombing it.[26]

Kunduz was the highest-profile Afghan defeat during the September/October Taliban offensive, in its own way equivalent to the loss of Ramadi in Iraq—although it's worth noting that in Afghanistan, unlike Iraq, the government did recapture the city within two weeks. But Kunduz was far from the only loss: from late September onward the Taliban took control of more than fifteen other districts in the north and west of Afghanistan, mounted major offensives in the south, southeast and center of the country, and launched several terrorist attacks within the outskirts of Kabul. While (as of December 2015) the Afghan government was still holding all major cities, more districts were falling by the day, and we were looking at a very substantial Taliban success in the fighting season of 2015, with more likely to come in 2016. And to top off a terrible year, within twenty-four hours of the Kunduz attack, ISIS fighters mounted a major attack against police posts in Afghanistan's far eastern province of Nangarhar.

Across the frontier from Nangarhar, and separate from the Afghan Taliban, an indigenous Taliban movement, Tehrik-e Taliban Pakistan (TTP) had grown inside Pakistan. Since 2004, it had fought the Pakistani government in the tribal areas along the Afghan border, and in North-West Frontier Province (known after 2010 as Khyber Pakhtunkhwa, KPK) in a conflict estimated to have cost 50,000 Pakistani lives. It was from TTP that the new ISIS province, Wilayat Khorasan, emerged.

Even before Baghdadi's announcement of the caliphate, ISIS sent representatives to Pakistan and Afghanistan in the spring of 2014, seeking recruits from disgruntled factions of AQ, TTP and the

Afghan Taliban. They were aided by dissatisfaction at the junior levels of the Afghan Taliban (whose field commanders had been isolated from the Quetta Shura by intensive targeting in 2011–12, and who hadn't heard from Mullah Omar for years) and by a succession dispute in TTP that had left several regional commanders unhappy with the movement's new chief. By mid-2014 the ISIS envoys had made progress in winning over splinter groups of TTP, and once the caliphate was announced local groups and individuals began to offer *bayat* to Baghdadi. ISIS leaders did not welcome all these pledges of allegiance, but did accept *bayat* from a group of six TTP emirs who controlled central districts in the tribal areas, stretching from the outskirts of Peshawar in KPK to the Khyber Pass, directly across the frontier from Nangarhar. In January 2015 Abu Muhammad al-Adnani, the Islamic State spokesman, announced the formation of Wilayat Khorasan, appointing former Orakzai area TTP leader Hafez Saeed Khan as *wali* of the new province.

In the December 2014 edition of the ISIS magazine Dabiq, an ISIS writer calling himself Abū Jarīr ash-Shamālī, and claiming to have worked in Pakistan with AQ, strongly condemned both AQ and the Afghan Taliban, including Mullah Omar, for favoring local custom over *sharia*, failing to target heretics (i.e. Shia and other minorities), treating Afghanistan and Pakistan as separate countries and preaching a Pashtunised version of Islam. Shamālī also critiqued the Taliban for failing to seize and hold ground as ISIS was doing in Syria–Iraq, and for taking orders from Pakistani intelligence. Shamālī also repeated rumors suggesting that Mullah Omar might in fact have been dead for some time.[27] His article signaled the beginning of a deadly conflict between ISIS and the Taliban.

By spring 2015, Afghan sources were reporting sightings of ISIS flags, propaganda leaflets and groups claiming to be associated with ISIS in several provinces. ISIS itself claimed a presence in several northeastern provinces, and in the south and west of Afghanistan. Over the summer increasing numbers of reports mentioned ISIS fighters battling Taliban and other insurgents in Nangarhar. Several groups of Afghan Taliban joined ISIS during this period, alienated from the Taliban leadership by the announcement on 29 July that Mullah Omar had indeed died of illness more than two years before, in April 2013, and that his deputy (now successor) Mullah

Akhtar Mansour had been governing in his name without admitting Mullah Omar's death.

On several occasions, ISIS claimed to have beheaded Taliban spies or defectors, or to have killed captured Taliban fighters. ISIS also allegedly assassinated the Taliban shadow governor of Nangarhar, and established a presence in nine of Nangarhar's twenty-two districts, with more than 4,200 fighters (mostly former TTP and Afghan Taliban) now fighting for the group in Nangarhar alone.[28] As in Syria, ISIS seemed to be following a strategy of initially attacking other rebel groups, avoiding taking on the government until it was strong enough to capture and hold territory. Then on 27 September the group broke cover: more than 300 ISIS fighters, some on foot and others mounted in technicals, operating in eight combat groups, attacked police posts across Nangarhar. This was their first attack against government forces in Afghanistan, and it marked the emergence from the shadows of yet another ISIS *wilayat* in Afghanistan–Pakistan.

The 2015 Taliban offensive and the emergence of ISIS in Afghanistan, along with the other transformative events—the European refugee crisis, Turkish entry into the war, the Iranian nuclear deal, and the ISIS victories in Syria and Iraq—contributed to a massive shift in the strategic environment, within just a few weeks, over the summer of 2015. But all these events paled in comparison to what was about to happen in Syria.

16

MASKIROVKA

Enter the Russians

"We all know that after the end of the Cold War—everyone is aware of that—a single center of domination emerged in the world, and then those who found themselves at the top of the pyramid were tempted to think that if they were so strong and exceptional, they knew better and they did not have to reckon with the UN."[1] It was Monday morning, 28 September 2015, and Vladimir Putin had just begun his much-awaited speech at the United Nations General Assembly in New York.

"We also remember," Putin continued, "certain episodes from the history of the Soviet Union. 'Social experiments' for export, attempts to push for changes within other countries based on ideological preferences, often led to tragic consequences and to degradation rather than progress."

> It seems, however, that far from learning from others' mistakes, everyone just keeps repeating them, and so the export of revolutions, this time of so-called "democratic" ones, continues ... I cannot help asking those who have caused the situation, do you realize now what you've done? ... Tens of thousands of militants are fighting under the banners of the so-called "Islamic State". Its ranks include former Iraqi servicemen who were thrown out into the street after the invasion of Iraq in 2003. Many recruits also come from Libya, a country whose statehood was destroyed as a result of a gross violation of the U.N. Security Council Resolution 1973. And now, the ranks of radicals are being joined by the members

of the so-called "moderate" Syrian opposition supported by the Western countries. First, they are armed and trained, and then they defect to the Islamic State.[2]

The last time President Putin had addressed the UN General Assembly, in 2005, George W. Bush was still president of the United States and the occupation of Iraq was less than three years old. Today, a decade later, he was blaming the rise of ISIS on both the Bush and Obama administrations, critiquing not only the unilateralism and exceptionalism that had driven President Bush to invade Iraq and upend the Middle East, but also the Obama administration's languid support for the Arab Spring, Secretary Clinton's bait-and-switch (as Putin saw it) of the Libyan intervention, and President Obama's ineffectual approach to Syria.

Watching the speech, I had to acknowledge that, much as I hated to admit it, Putin had a point—though I was surprised he could stand there with a straight face and criticize the unilateral export of revolutions when, at that very moment, on the street outside UN headquarters, hundreds of demonstrators were denouncing his unilateral annexation of Crimea, and his undeclared proxy war in Ukraine. Putin's words made perfect sense—as long as you ignored his actions. I believe the Russian word for "chutzpah" is *naglost'*.

Back in the General Assembly, President Putin insisted that the only way the international community could deal with ISIS was to come together under UN auspices and support the legitimate (i.e. incumbent) government of Syria. Arguing that it was "an enormous mistake to refuse to cooperate with the Syrian Government and its Armed Forces, who are valiantly fighting terrorism face-to-face," he announced that Russia was providing military assistance to Syria and Iraq. You can accuse President Putin of many things; on this occasion, at any rate, empty rhetoric wasn't one of them. As he spoke, the armed forces of the Russian Federation were launching their own intervention in Syria. It had been ramping up since July, within days of the signing of the JCPOA and the visits of Qasem Soleimani and Javad Zarif to Moscow.

On 21 July two Russian-made (and probably Russian-operated) UAVs—a 3D mapping and battlespace control platform, and a smaller photo-reconnaissance drone—crashed in rebel-held territory in northern Latakia province.[3] By early August Russian advisers, planners and intelligence officers, long in country, were operating more openly in Damascus and elsewhere, and on 20 August the landing ship RFS *Nikolay Filchenkov* of the Russian Black Sea Fleet, home-ported in Crimea, landed at the Syrian port of Latakia and disembarked trucks, BTR-82A armored personnel carriers (APCs) and Russian marines.[4] This marked the onset of a sustained sealift over the next several weeks, with landing ships shuttling between Russia's Black Sea naval base at Sevastopol in Crimea, past Istanbul and through the Bosporus under the close watch of the Turkish Navy, then to Latakia and the Russian base at Tartus, bringing T-90 tanks, more APCs, artillery, and construction supplies. The marines now landing at Latakia almost certainly came from the 810th Independent Naval Infantry Brigade, one of three rapid intervention units involved in the seizure of the Crimea in March 2014, with long experience of counter-guerrilla operations in Chechnya and elsewhere.[5] Three days after the marines disembarked, Syrian militia uploaded footage of Russian-speaking personnel using the same advanced APCs, engaged in combat against rebels northeast of Latakia, not far from where the drones had gone down a month earlier.[6]

Within days of the deployment, enormous Antonov An-124 cargo aircraft began landing defensive materials, prefabricated housing for another 2,000 troops, a portable air traffic control tower, air defense systems, and other military materiel at the Basel al-Assad airport outside Jableh, 20 miles south of Latakia by the coast road. Russian and Syrian engineers began extending the airstrip, Naval Infantry deployed to protect the new base, and Russian helicopters, fighter-bombers and more armored vehicles arrived. Around the same time, Russian Air Force Sukhoi-24 and Su-25 strike aircraft—forty-eight planes in all—began landing at Basel al-Assad, having staged through the Iranian airbase at Hamadan en route from Russia. They'd flown in tight formation below the big Antonovs, transponders off, using the huge cargo planes' radar signature for cover.[7] Simultaneously, offshore, warships from the Black Sea Fleet began exercises designed to last several weeks, which incidentally brought them in range to support the entry operation and deter interference with it.

At the same time as it launched its intervention in Syria, Russia deployed a small intelligence and liaison team, headed by a three-star general, to Baghdad. The team's task was to establish a joint Russian–Iranian–Iraqi–Syrian operations room, facilitate intelligence sharing and coordinate operations against ISIS.[8] The Russian move into Iraq was tiny in terms of personnel, but geopolitically it represented a seismic shift: Russia, Syria and Iran were essentially offering Iraq an alternative to the light-footprint approach that had been failing for the last year. Russian forces were moving into what had been a de facto U.S. military sphere of influence for over a decade, and this, as we'll see, prompted a noticeable change of thinking in Iraq.

Russian officials later claimed they had invited the United States to participate in the intelligence-sharing arrangement and send representatives to the operations room, but American officials had declined. Whatever the truth of that, the deeper Russian message was clear: the U.S.-led coalition had had its chance, Obama had failed to deal with ISIS, and now Russia was stepping in; the Americans could get on board or step aside. In any case, by the time Putin rose to address the General Assembly, the deployment was well underway in Syria, the intelligence-sharing hub was up and running in Iraq, and Russia's move was widely reported.[9]

On 30 September, the day the General Assembly closed, Russia's representative at the Baghdad joint operations room arrived at the U.S. Embassy to deliver a written *demarche* announcing that Russia was about to commence operations in Syria at the request of the Syrian government, and demanding that all U.S. and coalition forces immediately clear the airspace.[10] One hour later, the first twenty Russian airstrikes went in, hitting eight targets—mostly from the non-ISIS opposition—in the Homs–Hama corridor and the al-Ghaab plain (the areas most threatened by recent rebel advances).[11] Not only was this the first direct Russian engagement in the conflict, it was the first overt Russian combat action of any kind outside the borders of the former Soviet Union since 1989, and the first in the Middle East since the British–Soviet invasion of Iran in 1941. To say that this was a game-changer would be putting it mildly.

Two things immediately stood out about the Russian air campaign: its targeting philosophy, and its scale. Despite media reports suggesting Russian aircraft were targeting moderate rebels rather than ISIS, in fact the strikes (which included cruise missiles launched from Russian ships in the Caspian Sea) did target ISIS also, though only about 10 per cent of the time. The initial focus was on Chechen groups, the FSA, JN's Jaish al-Fatah coalition, and other rebels encroaching on the regime heartland in the Homs–

Idlib–Latakia area. As we've noted already, this was not a major area of operations for ISIS, which in any case tended to hang back from confrontation with the regime, preferring to target other rebel groups. So, unsurprisingly, non-ISIS groups—those most threatening to the regime—were targeted first. Within a week, Russian strikes did go in against ISIS, but the focus continued to be on relieving pressure on the regime. ISIS positions were not being struck for their own sake, but only if destroying them would help the regime consolidate its territory and prepare for a counterstroke. Russian intervention thus had a fundamentally different philosophy from that of the U.S.-led coalition in Syria: whereas we were intervening *against* ISIS, the Russians were intervening *in support of* Assad.

Russian forces took less care to avoid civilian casualties than the coalition had done, killing and injuring more civilians (according to Syrian contacts) in the first three weeks of their operation than the coalition had done in its entire campaign to date. This may have had something to do with lack of practice, but in part it was probably because they were operating in support of Assad, who regarded the civil population in rebel-held areas as part of the problem—hence his willingness to barrel-bomb them—rather than treating them (as coalition forces tended to do) like innocent bystanders to be protected. In part it was because the Russians were targeting the rebels as a conventional maneuver force rather than a terrorist organization, and striking a broader range of sites than the coalition's precision, high-value targeting approach allowed. Mostly, though, it was because of the campaign's scale—twenty-to-thirty strikes per day at first, rising after the first week to forty-to-sixty strike sorties per day, with Russian aircraft mounting eighty-eight strikes on 13 October alone.[12] (For comparison, coalition strike sorties per day, across Iraq and Syria, had averaged only about ten-to-fifteen per day for most of the preceding year, with occasional spikes for specific battles).

It was also quickly obvious that the Russians were not the only foreign force now intervening directly in Syria in support of Assad. The Iranians had also significantly increased their effort, with additional Quds Force and Iranian Revolutionary Guards Corps (IRGC) units, extra materiel and ammunition, and an influx of both individual volunteers and combat units from Iran. A heavy recruiting effort among Iraqi Shi'a also brought large numbers of volunteers from Iraqi militias to fight under Iranian leadership—indicating that Iranian commanders saw the situation in Syria as even more critical than that in Iraq.[13] The new IRGC units, with the Russian Naval Infantry, established security checkpoints and defensive positions in regime-controlled or contested areas of Tartus and Latakia provinces, freeing Syrian Army, militia, Quds Force and Hezbollah units from defensive tasks, allowing them to prepare a ground offensive to roll back the rebel advances of the summer.[14] That offensive commenced somewhat tentatively on 7 October 2015, and then ramped up significantly the following week.

The ground assault incorporated five main forces—Iranian, Russian and Syrian government troops, Iranian-backed militia from both Syria and Iraq, and Hezbollah. My impression, watching the offensive develop, was that we were watching a new coalition finding its feet. It seemed Russia was taking the lead in coordinating air operations, with Syrian aircraft operating under Russian tasking and using Russian-supplied intelligence, while Iranian commanders were coordinating the ground offensive. Initially, the ground forces focused on the same Homs–Hama area targeted in the first round of Russian airstrikes, but they soon extended their reach to the al-Ghaab plain and began a concerted effort to recapture rebel-held villages in Idlib, Hama and Latakia across about a 120-mile front.

The ground offensive succeeded by mid-October in taking more than a dozen villages and towns including the important centers of Kafr an-Naboudeh and Mansoura. There were persistent but unconfirmed reports from the rebel side that small numbers of Russian troops (including specialists, armored vehicle crews and others) were engaging in direct combat. More overtly, Russian ground troops provided fire support to the offensive, using artillery and BM-30 multiple-launch rocket systems.[15]

As I write, Russian and Syrian forces, in concert with Syrian militia and IRGC, and with Qasem Soleimani and Russian officers directing the offensive, have launched a second major push on three main axes of advance, in the Azzan mountains south of Aleppo city, moving to recapture rebel-held areas in southern Aleppo province and on the eastern side of Aleppo city, and to secure outlying villages and hills dominating the city's links to the rest of regime-held Syria. This is certain to be a large-scale battle and almost equally certain to be horrifically costly in civilian lives. In keeping with their already-demonstrated willingness to inflict collateral damage in support of

Assad, Russian forces have been documented using cluster munitions (specifically, the SPBE-D air-delivered cluster bomb) against settlements near the city.[16] Given Aleppo's status as Syria's second city, the Aleppo offensive is roughly equivalent to the long-mooted (and long-delayed) coalition offensive against Mosul in Iraq. Supporting offensives are also occurring in the south around Quneitra and Deraa against the FSA southern front, and in the center of the country against ISIS-controlled al-Qaryatayn and Palmyra.

It's far too early to say how the Russian–Iranian intervention in Syria will develop—or whether it will extend to airstrikes or possibly ground operations in Iraq also, as some Iraqi politicians (including Prime Minister Abadi) have suggested they would welcome.[17] The initial results appear to be mixed, at best, suggesting that the operation will be longer, more costly and less decisive than Russian, Iranian and Syrian leaders hope.[18] For anyone with any experience of warfare at all, that's just a statement of the obvious: war is always uncertain and chaotic, with consequences far beyond those that policy-makers can foresee. But strategically and politically, the intervention marks a huge shift.

At one level, Russian motivations for intervention in Syria and Iraq are simple: as I mentioned above, Russia has a major naval base at Tartus—its only Mediterranean base, and its only one outside the former Soviet Union—giving it strong reasons to maintain its foothold. Moscow has also, don't forget, backed the Syrian regime for more than a generation, so that (whatever Vladimir Putin's personal view of Bashar al-Assad) the risk of regime collapse prompted genuine alarm in Moscow as it became increasingly imminent over the summer of 2015. Likewise, as President Putin has repeatedly said, Moscow perceives the rise of ISIS, with its destabilizing effect on the Caucasus and among Russia's large Muslim population, as extremely dangerous: large numbers of Chechens, Daghestanis, and Russian-speaking Circassians are fighting alongside the Syrian rebels, and the risk of them returning to Russia or attacking Russian interests in what Moscow calls its "near abroad" is very real.

At the same time, with Washington telegraphing weakness and vacillation on Iraq and Syria (remember the 2013 chemical weapons fiasco, for example, in which only Russian intervention saved President Obama from his own red line), Moscow saw an opportunity to expand its influence in both countries. Washington—no doubt to the surprise of precisely nobody in Moscow—complained (President Obama claimed Putin was acting "out of weakness" and would become "stuck in a quagmire") but did nothing to contest the Russian intervention, seemingly proving Putin's thesis that opposing U.S. interests was now essentially risk-free.[19]

But behind these proximate causes of Russian engagement in Syria, and possible intervention in Iraq, lies a broader set of issues, implied by President Putin's opening remarks at the General Assembly, where he referred with a bitter smirk to the post-Cold War world in which the U.S. emerged as the sole superpower. Eleven months before New York (and seven months after Crimea), in October 2014, Putin laid out his worldview at a meeting of the Valdai International Discussion Club at Sochi, the resort (and Olympic venue) on Russia's Black Sea coast. Putin's Valdai speech was his most comprehensive, assertive foreign policy speech to date.

It caused a stir in Russia, being described as "the most important political speech since Churchill's 'Iron Curtain' address of 5 March 1946."[20] The speech is wide-ranging, but its clearest theme is a desire to revise the outcome of the Cold War, including the collapse of the Soviet Union, which Putin described elsewhere as the greatest tragedy of the twentieth century.[21] It is worth quoting at length:

> The United States, having declared itself the winner of the Cold War, saw no need for [an accommodation with the former Soviet Union]. Instead of establishing a new balance of power, essential for maintaining order and stability, they took steps that threw the system into sharp and deep imbalance. The Cold War ended, but it did not end with the signing of a peace treaty with clear and transparent agreements on respecting existing rules or creating new rules and standards. This created the impression that the so-called "victors" in the Cold War had decided to pressure events and reshape the world to suit their own needs and interests ... In a situation where you had domination by one country and its allies, or its satellites rather, the search for global solutions often turned into an attempt to impose their own universal recipes. This group's ambitions grew so big that they started presenting the policies they put together in their corridors of power as the view of the entire international community. But this is not the case. The very notion of "national sovereignty" became a relative value for most countries. In essence, what was being proposed was the formula: the greater the loyalty towards the world's sole power center, the greater this or that ruling regime's legitimacy.[22]

Putin rejected the legitimacy of a presumed post-Cold War consensus around Western democratic, capitalist values, suggesting that Russia planned to work toward a new global order that would include the United States, but on the same terms as every other country:

> Colleagues, Russia [has] made its choice. Our priorities are further improving our democratic and open economy institutions, accelerated internal development, taking into account all the positive modern trends in the world, and consolidating society based on traditional values and patriotism. We have an integration-oriented, positive, peaceful agenda; we are working actively with our colleagues in the Eurasian Economic Union, the Shanghai Cooperation Organisation, BRICS and other partners. This agenda is aimed at developing ties between governments, not dissociating. We are not planning to cobble together any blocs or get involved in an exchange of blows. The allegations and statements that Russia is trying to establish some sort of empire, encroaching on the sovereignty of its neighbors, are groundless. Russia does not need any kind of special, exclusive place in the world—I want to emphasize this. While respecting the interests of others, we simply want for our own interests to be taken into account and for our position to be respected.[23]

Putin was putting forward a clear, coherent narrative, and issuing a call for action. More importantly, Russia's military actions were telegraphing a degree of commitment and resolve that gave his words great force. Perhaps the clearest evaluation of Putin's line came from Dmitri Trenin, head of the Carnegie Moscow Center and a former Soviet and Russian army officer.

Writing two months after the Valdai speech, Trenin argued that Putin had begun his first term in 2000 "trying to restore and upgrade Russian-Western relations. In his first few weeks in the Kremlin, Putin reached out to Lord George Robertson, then NATO secretary general, and to then U.S. President George W. Bush, who was starting his own first term." President Putin sought an alliance with the United States, before and after 9/11, "including membership in NATO and integration into Europe in the name of Russia's European Choice. In 2001, Putin ordered immediate, massive, and highly valuable support to the U.S. operation to defeat al-Qaeda and the Taliban in Afghanistan. From 2003 onward, however, Putin has felt increasingly alienated by the West. The U.S. invasion of Iraq that year distracted Washington from seeking closer engagement with Russia. Putin's hopes of an alliance with Washington were dashed."[24]

After the Obama administration's election, and Secretary Clinton's attempted "reset" with Russia during President Medvedev's term, any desire for cooperation was undercut through what Putin saw as Clinton's betrayal over Libya and U.S. interference in Russia's near abroad. President Obama's deer-in-the-headlights response to the rise of ISIS and the Syrian conflict only sealed the deal: ditching any idea of cooperation within parameters defined by American primacy, Putin sought instead to re-establish an independent, co-equal sphere of action for Moscow, founded on expanded sovereignty and leadership of a putative "Russian world." As Trenin argues:

> This sovereignty bid, in practical terms, represents Moscow's clear breakout from the international system as it has been widely, if informally, understood since the end of the Cold War. It challenges the unipolar world order both by erecting barriers to U.S. democracy promotion and by refusing to submit to the norms and practices laid down, policed, and arbitrated by the West.[25]

Of course, Putin's words resonated in the United States precisely because they gave each side in U.S. politics the opportunity to critique the other—Democrats could criticize President Bush for his recklessness in invading Iraq and alienating the international community, while Republicans could condemn President Obama's fecklessness in abandoning Iraq, or his strategic paralysis once things fell apart there and his insouciance in the face of a rising ISIS and catastrophe in Syria. As I've shown, there was more than a grain of truth in all these criticisms. Indeed, there's more than enough blame to go around, on all sides of politics (and not just in the United States). But American politicians, in taking the bait, risked getting played by Moscow. Being drawn into Putin's logic was to be distracted from Russia's actions by his words, to be captured by what his old colleagues in the KGB called "active measures" and Soviet military theorists developed into the art of *maskirovka*, "deception"—a carefully crafted information operation designed to distract Western leaders from thinking about what to do by encouraging them to focus on what they liked best: who to blame.

The truth is that what President Putin was saying, however logical and accurate it may have been on its face, was a red herring—a verbal distraction, misdirecting attention away from his actions. Whether his critique was valid or not, focusing on it amounted to ignoring what Russia had actually been doing: that is, flouting the very set of norms (sovereign independence, mutual respect among countries, economic freedom, the rule of international law) that its president was purporting to defend as an alternative to American primacy. Being taken in by this *maskirovka* was akin to sitting back in a comfortable chair, nodding along to Putin's speech in the UN headquarters, while failing to notice the enormous protest outside the building, the body bags of Russian "volunteers" coming home from the Ukraine, or the fighter jets covertly crossing the border from Iranian to Syrian airspace.

Russia's invasion of Georgia in 2008, and Putin's seizure of Crimea and covert invasion and sponsorship of conflict in Ukraine in 2014 were cases in point. So were Russian encroachment into the airspace and seaspace of countries across Europe, cyber-warfare against the Baltic states, kidnapping of an Estonian official, economic pressure (including the weaponising of oil and gas supplies) against Europe, the shooting down of a civilian airliner by Russian-backed rebels with a Russian-supplied anti-aircraft missile, Russian territorial expansion in the Arctic, the assassination and imprisonment of dissidents and troublesome journalists, and so on.

For Americans or for America's allies, getting into a debate about whether what had happened in the Middle East was mostly President Bush's fault or President Obama's fault was to miss the obvious fact that what Russia was doing was entirely Putin's fault. For Russians, changing the subject from Crimea, Ukraine and the Baltic to Syria, ISIS and Iraq might have muddied the waters, but it didn't change the underlying reality of demographic decline and economic dependency on non-renewable, volatile commodities like oil and gas. Indeed, the gap between rhetoric and reality (on both the Russian and the American side) may have been the most important risk arising from Russia's joint intervention with Iran in the Middle East, because the risk of great-power conflict becomes greatest when armed forces are intermingled or in close proximity to each other—as they now were—and when political leaders lack the strategic vision to understand each others' motives and actions.

I mentioned earlier that both Russia and Iran benefited from a single unified strategic vision with regard to ISIS, in that both favored incumbents anywhere against insurgents everywhere, regardless of human rights or the treatment of civilian populations. This meant that there was no logical contradiction for Moscow or Tehran in supporting both the democratically elected government of Iraq and the dictatorship of President Assad. This, in turn, created a strategic unity of thought and action in the Russian–Iranian approach that was very clear from Russia's intervention in Syria and Iraq—but lacking, for very good reasons, in our own. There was another level, though, at which Russian strategic thinking was unified by comparison to that of the West, and which emerged even more clearly from Russian actions than from the high-minded sentiments of President Putin's speeches.

This was that, unlike the United States and its allies—who (since ditching the problematic but unifying concept of a "War on Terrorism") had treated each problem as a stand-alone crisis requiring its own response—Russia was treating Syria, Iraq, Crimea, Ukraine, the Baltic States and the Arctic simply as different facets of one strategic issue set. Achieving that kind of strategic unity and clarity would have been a worthy goal, as Western leaders considered where things stood, and what to do next.

17

AGE OF CONFLICT

Rethinking Counterterrorism

As I write, Western countries (several, particularly the United States, now with severely reduced international credibility) face a larger, more unified, capable, experienced and savage enemy, in a less stable, more fragmented region, with a far higher level of geo-political competition, and a much more severe risk of great-power conflict, than at any time since 9/11.

It isn't just ISIS—AQ has emerged from its eclipse and is back in the game in Afghanistan, Pakistan, India, Syria, Somalia and Yemen. We're dealing with not one, but two global terrorist organizations, each with its own regional branches, plus a vastly larger radicalized population at home, and a flow of foreign terrorist fighters ten to twelve times the size of anything seen before. Likewise, the Taliban resurgence of 2015 shows that as bad as things seem now, they could get much worse if the Afghan drawdown creates the same opportunity for ISIS in 2017 as the Iraqi drawdown created in 2012.

And with Russia's intervention in Syria—more broadly, with what Dmitri Trenin called Putin's "breakout from the international system since the end of the Cold War"—we're facing a revival of great-power military competition in the Middle East, the Mediterranean, the Pacific and Europe that vastly complicates our options. Far from being coincidental, this too is a direct result of the way our failures in Iraq, in Afghanistan and in the broader War on Terrorism since 2001 have telegraphed the limits of Western power and showed adversaries exactly how to fight us.

In the Middle East, we're watching an escalating Sunni–Shi'a proxy conflict—once a cold war, but getting hotter by the day—in Yemen, Syria, Libya, Iraq and increasingly Turkey, a conflict that's drawing battle lines between Iran and its allies on the one hand, and a fractious coalition of Sunni states, led by Egypt and Saudi Arabia, on the other. We're facing an unprecedented number of asylum-seekers and displaced persons, prompting a mass migration crisis on a scale not seen since the end of the Second World War. Beside the immediate humanitarian impact of that crisis, its long-term effects on the political complexion (and hence on the security environment) of Western Europe and elsewhere are hard to predict, but very unlikely to be positive.

As journalist James Traub put it, writing about the Saudi–Egyptian intervention in Yemen, "America has abdicated its guiding role in the Middle East to a sectarian Arab military force—what could [possibly] go wrong?"[1] You could say the same about Iraq and Syria, except that the sectarian force that has moved into a leadership role is Shi'a Iran, freed from the restrictions of a punishing sanctions regime, allied with a newly aggressive, revisionist Russia, and increasingly able to call the shots in Iraq and Syria. In any case, whether or not we think it's feasible (or proper, or sustainable) for the United States to assume a "guiding role" after Russian military intervention and the Iranian nuclear deal have so fundamentally changed the facts on the ground, today's Western leaders (in the United States, and elsewhere) have proven that they have little appetite for any role at all in the Middle East, let alone for more conflict.

Almost fifteen years after 9/11, people are tired of war—I know I am. What they want most of all is for the conflict to be over, which of course is far from an ideal position in which to be facing such a wide range of resurgent threats. Where do we go from here?

The first step is to admit that this really is, every bit, the strategic failure it seems to be. For the hard truth is that the events of 2014–16, including the "Blood Year" that started with the fall of Mosul, represent nothing less than the collapse of Western counterterrorism strategy as we've known it since 2001. After fourteen years, thousands of lives and hundreds of billions of dollars, we're worse off today than before 9/11, with a stronger, more motivated, more dangerous enemy than ever. So much is happening, simultaneously, in so many places, that leaders are struggling to decide what to do and in what order. The twin dangers are (on the one hand) that policy-makers will engage in knee-jerk responses, rather than taking time to consider what an effective strategy looks like, or on the other that they will freeze, paralysed by analysis, and be unable to respond effectively at all. We've seen both these pathologies since 9/11.

The Bush administration's large-footprint approach, invading and occupying Iraq and Afghanistan, then committing to rebuild those countries from scratch at vast cost in time, troops, money and blood—amounted to what Maajid Nawaz, the former Islamist radical who now heads the London-based anti-radicalisation Quilliam Foundation, describes as "spreading democracy at the barrel of a gun." Iraq, in particular, was an almost indescribably massive strategic error, which bogged the United States and its allies down in a decade-plus counterinsurgency fight that demanded immense sacrifices from our troops, cost us our strategic freedom of action and eroded the legitimacy of a cause that, at the outset, enjoyed huge global support. There's nothing particularly controversial or original about that judgment, by the way—President Bush's brother Jeb, running for president himself, said in May 2015: "Knowing what we know now, I would not have engaged. I would not have gone into Iraq."[2] This framing, of course, misses the obvious fact that policy isn't made with the benefit of hindsight—the real question is "knowing what you knew *then*, what would you have done?"

On the other hand, the Obama administration's strategy of retrenchment—conflating leaving the war with ending it, and mistaking rhetorical poses for effective policies—led to a series of withdrawals, climb-downs and half-measures that pulled the rug out from underneath whatever progress had been made in stabilizing Iraq and Afghanistan, rendering those sacrifices useless, and making a bad situation even worse. It was an equal and opposite error: President Obama's inaction in the face of crises in Egypt and Libya, failure to support democracy movements in Syria and Iran, and reliance on unilateral drone strikes, raids and targeted killings—to use Nawaz's words again, "getting rid of the democracy, but keeping the gun"—signalled weakness to Iran and Russia, midwifed the rebirth of ISIS from the ashes of AQI in Iraq, precipitated a horrific human tragedy in Syria, and ultimately failed just as badly.

Again, there isn't—or shouldn't be—anything politically partisan or controversial about this assessment, which I often hear in private (though not, in an election year, in public) from people close to the administration, including in the National Security Council. If President Bush's administration was a study in the perils of over-reaction and maximalist foreign policy, then President Obama's has been a lesson in the risks of passivity and under-reaction.

America's allies—including Australia, the United Kingdom and virtually all of NATO—went along with both these flawed approaches out of solidarity, while corrupt, non-inclusive governments in Iraq, Afghanistan and elsewhere were just as responsible as anyone for the dire outcomes in their own countries. Nobody's in the clear: this is a bipartisan, multinational, equal-opportunity screw-up. By far the best comment on this comes from General Jack Keane, former Vice Chief of the U.S. Army, who critiqued the decision to invade in 2003, was a key architect of the Surge, and was critical of the "Zero Option" in 2011 (which is to say, he made the right call on every Iraq decision of the last decade). Testifying before Congress in May 2015, Keane said: "We need to get past our political psychosis on Iraq. While [both invading and withdrawing completely] were crucial policy decisions, and there's much to learn about them, we have to get past it. ISIS is much more than Iraq."[3] Keane, yet again, is absolutely right: we *must* focus on the reality of today, because whatever the merits of those decisions, in the here and now there's a war on, and we're not winning it.

The second step is to realize that this war truly is, as many have argued, a Long War. There's no magic bullet, no instant solution, let alone some carefully calibrated combination of firepower, diplomacy and technology that can quickly put the genie back in the bottle. Many ISIS fighters are the sons of Iraqis imprisoned by occupation forces more than a decade ago; many Shabaab fighters in Somalia, Ansar al-Sharia militants in Libya and Boko Haram guerrillas in Nigeria are teenagers. As the Kunduz battle shows, today's Taliban are younger, more radical, more battle-hardened, and better trained than those we fought in 2001—they have plenty of energy, and all the time in the world.

Even as of early 2016, there are still more than 35,000 fighters in ISIS, and roughly as many in the Taliban and other extremist movements. The rise of ISIS, the stimulating effect of its rivalry with al-Qaeda, the Taliban resurgence and, above all, Baghdadi's declaration of the caliphate, is breathing new life into a global movement that seemed to be fading—proving that the ideology, like the movements defined by it, is tough and resilient. This conflict will not be going away any time soon, and it certainly won't end quickly or cleanly. On the contrary: this is, and will be, a multi-generational struggle against an implacable enemy, and the violence we're dealing with in the Middle East and Africa is not some unfortunate aberration—it's the new normal.

Nor can we pull up the drawbridge, disengage from the world, and somehow avoid the fight. For one thing, there *is* no drawbridge now: we live in interdependent, connected societies whose prosperity and success rely on trade, travel and free intercourse with the world. Particularly for Australians, North Americans and Europeans, citizens of multicultural nations, plugged into the global economy, key players in regional and world events, opting out just isn't feasible. For another, if we fail to face the threat where it is today—primarily in the Middle East and North Africa—we'll suffer the consequences at home. I'm not just talking about the massive spillover that Western countries are now experiencing because of our failure to deal with Syria, though that's certainly part of it.

While ever there's an entity, whether it be ISIS, al-Qaeda, or any other group, that can attract and motivate disaffected young people in our societies, preying on their idealism and alienation, drawing them into what the late, great *Time* magazine Baghdad correspondent Jim Frederick called a "hyperviolent, nihilistic band of exterminators", the threat will remain. But as we've sought to disaggregate the threat, the rise of ISIS has exposed the weakness of a strategic approach which, for too long, focused just on neutralizing terrorist plots and killing or capturing senior terrorist leaders. This strategy looked, and often felt, as if it was proactive—"taking the fight to the enemy." But in reality, as the defeats of 2014–15 have shown, Disaggregation was too narrowly focused to succeed.

In short, what we've been doing has failed: we need a complete rethink. That rethink, I would suggest, needs to start with a threat analysis. What, exactly, is the threat we're facing, and how can we address it in ways that are cheap enough, effective enough, and non-intrusive enough to be sustainable over the long term, without undermining the openness, democracy and prosperity that make our societies worth defending in the first place?

It seems to me that there are four main categories of threat arising from the collapse of 2014–15. These include terrorism in our own societies, the flow (and potential return) of foreign fighters, the effect of the rise of ISIS on global terrorism, and the catastrophic (and largely conventional) conflict that is afflicting the Middle East and spilling over into other regions. Let's consider each in turn.

The first threat is what some call *home grown terrorism*—the insider threat that arises from the presence, in our own societies, of individuals and networks motivated by extremist ideology and willing to use violence to further it. As I've tried to explain, this threat is better described as remote radicalization—a process by which terrorists exploit electronic means to project violence into our societies by mobilizing vulnerable individuals. Nidal Hasan, the Fort Hood shooter of 2009, is just one among a much larger group: we discussed many others in Chapter 11. These people were radicalized through social networks, including both face-to-face contact and online social media, which gave them personalized access to Salafi-jihadist ideas, and the tactics to put those ideas into practice. Each case is different, but the similarities are striking: many had a history of petty criminality; several were adult converts to Islam; many were known to police for previous extremism; several attacked Jewish or free speech events or military targets; all had active social media accounts; most acted alone, or in a group of no more than two; many attacked symbolic or institutional targets, but selected individual victims at random; and (obviously enough) all were military-aged males, mostly of Arab descent, with Muslim names.

At the same time, though, it's worth noting that the total death toll from these incidents, over the six years from 2009 to 2015, was only about fifty—fifty-four, counting perpetrators—while the number of wounded was 319. This is utterly tragic for the individuals killed and maimed, and for their families, but it's not a strategic-level threat to their countries. If you compare the toll over the past six years to that of the 9/11 attacks (2,996 killed, more than 6,000 wounded) or the Bali, Madrid and London bombings (together, 449 killed and more than 3,000 wounded) in less than four years, it's clear that the domestic counterterrorism effort since 9/11, including the adaptations I described earlier, has significantly reduced the scale of this threat. The disaggregated, atomized terrorist cells and radicalized individuals of today can mount a larger number of smaller, less sophisticated, and far less damaging attacks than the centrally organized AQ of 2001. If that were the only outcome, you'd have to call the past fifteen years a resounding success.

But, of course, that would be foolish. When you add the loss of life in Afghanistan and Iraq, consider the massive destabilization, cost and disruption created, and think about the rise of ISIS as a direct outcome of the ill-judged invasion of (and equally ill-judged withdrawal from) Iraq, it's a much worse picture. It's worse again if you count Yemeni, Syrian, Libyan, Nigerian, Malian, Somali, Kenyan, Pakistani and other lives lost in the War on Terror. Obviously, claims that "ISIS is not an existential threat to Western societies" are accurate if we focus solely on individual acts of terrorism—but, again, it's foolish to frame the threat so narrowly, since the growth of ISIS has triggered an escalating conflict whose consequences are indeed existential for many regional states, and whose global effects could be hugely damaging.

Equally obviously, radicalized individuals—including, but not limited to, members of the ISIS Internationale—operating alone, without complex support networks, using low-tech weapons, have a much lower profile than traditional insurgents or terrorist cells. Thus, as I explained in Chapter 11, detecting them before they strike is extraordinarily difficult, unless (perhaps even if) we're prepared to accept massive intrusion by security agencies into every aspect of our daily lives, including our online activity and social networks. That means we have a choice: learn to live with a higher background threat, or decide how much freedom we're prepared to trade for security against it. This is likely to be a constantly shifting balance, as new threats and countermeasures continue to evolve.

Indeed, if one lesson stands out from the past fifteen years, it's that terrorism is a dynamic threat, complex and multi-factorial, continuously adapting and morphing in response to our actions, and not a static phenomenon. Thus, current conditions may not last long. Indeed, the rise of ISIS coincided with a spike in self-radicalized attacks, and as Western governments act to prevent fighters travelling to join the group these attacks may spike further, with people who can't get to Syria deciding to act where they live. Clearly, there's only a limited role for military force here, and no one-size-fits-all answer. The threat, in democracies, must be handled primarily through political leadership, law enforcement and public engagement. There are also differences in dealing with communities from which remotely radicalized individuals may emerge.

The circumstances of French Muslims in the *banlieues* around Paris differ greatly from those of Asian communities in the British Midlands, Somali-Americans in Minnesota or Lebanese-Australians in Sydney (to use four not-quite-random examples). The types of violent radicalism that occur in each of these communities are different, and each society needs to decide for itself an appropriate response. Some Western governments have responded by Orientalizing Muslim immigrant populations, treating them as alien, exotic, potentially violent implants which have to be handled with kid gloves via self-appointed intermediaries (often old, male and socially and religiously conservative).[4] This is understandable, I suppose, but it treats young people, who may already feel marginalized and disenfranchised within the wider society, like second-class citizens in their own communities, and impedes integration of those communities into wider society. If anything, it may encourage radicalization, and partly explain why the average age of ISIS recruits is far younger than it was for AQ, and why a substantial number of ISIS recruits are young women.

The second threat, closely related to the first, is that of foreign fighters travelling to Iraq and Syria, and increasingly to Libya, Yemen and Somalia, to join terrorist organizations. We're not just talking about ISIS fighters here, though they are by far the largest group at present. This threat—and the potential for violence on their return—has received much attention, in part because a great deal of intelligence and domestic-security funding is tied to it. It's exacerbated by the fact that many ISIS recruits have Western passports, European faces and no known links to terrorist organizations (they're "clean-skins," in the jargon of counterterrorism bureaucrats) meaning that it would be relatively easy for them to reinfiltrate their parent societies after a stint with ISIS. In my view, this fear is a little overblown.

ISIS has gained recruits so quickly not only because its propaganda is slanted towards English-language media, making it highly accessible, but also because its standards are so low. If you want to join AQ, you need some knowledge of Salafi Islam, a certain level of physical fitness and some military potential. In contrast, ISIS pulls in large numbers of volunteers, many with no knowledge of

Islam, limited physical and mental aptitude, and no military skills to speak of. It selects and trains them in camps in Syria and Iraq, but uses most foreign fighters as cannon fodder (the term "useful idiots" comes to mind once again), masking the Ba'athist thugs, AQI veterans and alumni of the Chechen and Syrian wars who lie at the core of the group's combat capability.

My impression, from watching AQI develop in Iraq at first hand from late 2005 until 2007 (and from tracking its evolution into ISIS after 2011), is that it tends to "burn" Western volunteers for the most risky missions, to rid itself of newcomers who might challenge the existing power clique. This can be seen in some of the examples I gave in Chapter 13, where foreign suicide bombers led major attacks. Those who survived were often relegated to duties with little influence, and those who tried to leave were killed. Anyone thinking of joining ISIS needs to understand that the chance of being killed (by the organization, which takes an extremely dim view of waverers, or by its opponents) is extremely high, but the chance of contributing anything is extraordinarily low, as is the likelihood of making it back.

Rates of return for foreign fighters are fewer than 10 per cent for AQ fighters to date, and recent steps by governments to criminalize travel to join ISIS, and deny return to those who have done so, will lower these rates even further for ISIS supporters.[5] At the same time, many of those traveling to join ISIS in Syria and Iraq are better understood as "foreign volunteers" rather than foreign fighters—they are doctors, engineers, administrators or tradesmen, responding to Baghdadi's call to "come to Syria and help us build the state." For this reason, precisely because they see themselves as performing the *hijrah*, the migration of the faithful to a rightly governed Islamic State, many such ISIS volunteers may be even less likely to return than their predecessors in AQ. In any case, as with the first threat, dealing with foreign fighters involves mainly domestic measures: border security, visa and passport control, policing, immigration enforcement, intelligence liaison, community resilience and critical infrastructure protection.

As I've written elsewhere, and the British urban theorist Stephen Graham argued persuasively in a recent book on military urbanism, we're now seeing "boomerang effects" from the War on Terror.[6] Techniques from Iraq and Afghanistan—big data, biometrics, urban control and surveillance systems, drones and counter-IED technologies—have entered domestic policing (or, rather, re-entered it, since many of these techniques were originally adapted from law enforcement by the military after 9/11). Likewise, the militarization of police, with heavy weapons, armored vehicles, encrypted communications, military-style body armor, drones and training that inculcates the "warrior" mentality, has contributed to clashes in places like Ferguson, Missouri.[7] In the United States, much of this is surplus military gear, originally used in Iraq and Afghanistan, supplied to local police agencies by the federal government, while much of the rest is a product of the homeland-security–industrial complex that has emerged since 9/11.

On the other side, organized crime networks, street gangs and drug traffickers in the United States are beginning to import techniques and technologies—bomb-making methods, IED triggers, sniping and mortar systems, urban ambush techniques—from Iraq and Afghanistan, creating an increasing convergence between crime and war, something special operations analysts call a "grey zone".[8] To be sure, U.S. gangs and organized crime networks are not (or not yet) as militarized as those of Central America, Colombia or Brazil. But the trends are heading in that direction, and the proliferation of tactics, techniques and procedures (as well as easy-to-make lethal technologies) among different groups means that it would be foolhardy to rule out the possibility of such paramilitaries in the United States also. Thus, to critique gunned-up police forces without noticing how gunned-up the criminals are becoming is to do police officers, who operate today in a more dangerous environment, against a more sophisticated threat—a grave injustice. When the day comes that militarized gangs (or, for that matter, groups of citizens alienated by government intrusion and surveillance) using techniques imported from overseas activists, guerrillas and terrorists, and operating in this grey zone, begin to confront paramilitary police forces who employ counterinsurgency equipment and concepts from Iraq and Afghanistan in the cities of Western democracies, the War on Terror will truly have come home to roost. And that day—normality bias aside—may be much closer than many people think.

This issue of grey zone convergence matters hugely to any future strategy. President Bush often argued that the United States was "taking the fight to the terrorists abroad, so we don't have to face them here at home," or "fighting these terrorists with our military in Afghanistan and Iraq and beyond so we do not have to face them in the streets of our own cities."[9] This was somewhat unconvincing to most people, even at the time, and given what I've explained of AQ and ISIS strategy and ideology (in Chapters 5 and 6), it seems unrealistic to think that if the anti-ISIS coalition were to withdraw from Iraq and Syria, or NATO's Resolute Support Mission were to pull out from Afghanistan, that terrorists would immediately follow to attack us at home.

Given that AQ has its own internal struggles and is primarily focused on overthrowing "apostate regimes," with attacks on the United States and other Western countries mainly a means to that end, and given that ISIS (at the level of its central, state-building entity in Syria and Iraq) has its hands full with the Arab–Persian, Sunni–Shi'a war now in full swing within its region, it seems reasonable to think that "ending America's wars,"[10] as President Obama puts it, might actually bring about a short-term *drop* in terrorist incidents in Western countries. But the key word here is "short-term." The problem with a retrenchment strategy, or with the more isolationist option of U.S. disengagement (apart from the obvious point that pulling U.S. troops out of a conflict doesn't equate to ending it) is what happens next.

A policy of disengagement—or, perhaps closer to President Obama's vision, one of incremental retreat from onerous overseas commitments and leadership responsibilities, that would rely more on regional partners to manage conflicts while emphasizing home-land security in our own societies and light-footprint counterterrorism abroad—would actually multiply medium-term risks. In the broadest sense, these would come from the damage that U.S. disengagement would do to the international system.

Like it or not, the prosperity, security and stability of the United States and its allies (and even many of its adversaries) depend on a system designed by a group of nations led by Washington after 1945. President Putin is exactly correct, in this sense, in his assessment that the world system as we know it rests on a foundation, informal in some key respects, and hidden from most people most of the time, that's nonetheless very real. That foundation is Western diplomacy, backed by Western military and economic power, and shored up by Western (especially U.S.) financial and military credibility, global persistent presence and positive engagement.

Together, these things underpin a post-Cold War system of international political, economic and military norms, the spread of which has correlated with the greatest increase in human wellbeing in history. This global order wouldn't long survive if the United States decided to withdraw from it. And the United States would suffer as much as, if not more than, other countries in this scenario, because America is a major beneficiary of that Western-centric world system. To me, however, this macro-scale argument isn't the most compelling reason for dealing with today's threat overseas. Rather, the most persuasive reason for a forward strategy is the one I've already mentioned—namely that a truly effective domestic defensive strategy might turn our societies into police states.

A purely defensive stance, to succeed in completely thwarting terrorist threats from within and without, would have to include some or all of the following: perimeter defenses on major buildings, restrictions on public spaces, intrusive powers of search, arrest and seizure, larger and more heavily armed police forces, with more permissive rules for use of lethal force, enhanced surveillance, pre-emptive disarming of citizens, movement controls, enhanced national identity and biometrics databases, and a raft of limitations to freedom of expression and assembly. It would also, of course, impose limitations on international trade, require increased state interference in society and prompt greater spending on government programs—an even more burdensome version of what I described earlier as a "terrorism tax." Many of these things have been mooted, and quite a few (in relatively attenuated forms) are already in place. But accepting these impositions as permanent, and developing them to the level at which they could actually—in their own right, as the centerpiece of a counterterrorism strategy—protect against the atomized, self-radicalized terrorist threat of tomorrow, would amount to destroying society in order to save it.

Thus, I respectfully dissent from President Obama's approach of strategic divestment, not just because (as this book shows) it has been ineffective in its stated purpose, but more importantly because it could too easily become a recipe for domestic tyranny. And Americans are better off than most others in his regard, because the United States has robust constitutional safeguards (the Bill of

Rights) that make government abuses harder to enact and sustain. Other countries—the UK, for example, or Australia—lack many of these, and in these countries the risk of abuse is comparatively greater. To be clear, I'm noting a tendency rather than a present reality, pointing out the destination we might eventually reach if we continue down the road of strategic disengagement. Based on that, I think there's a strong case for a forward strategy of Active Containment—with the emphasis on Active—dealing with the threat overseas, to avoid the restrictions to liberty that a domestically focused strategy would entail.

The third threat is the effect of the rise of ISIS on other terrorist groups. As our discussion of Taliban resurgence and the growth of JN (in Chapter 13) demonstrated, Baghdadi's declaration of the caliphate has created a competitive dynamic that's having a massively invigorating effect on Salafi-jihadist groups globally. As we noted, Islamic State has provinces (*wilayat*) in eleven countries worldwide as of early 2016, and numerous other individuals and groups swore *bayat* to al-Baghdadi after his declaration. But the invigorating effect of ISIS isn't confined to its supporters. ISIS has already inspired rivals like AQAP, al-Shabaab and the Taliban to adopt its tactics, increasing the threat from all extremist groups. This suggests that fond hopes that the competing strains of global Salafi-jihadist terrorism might neutralize one another ("the enemy of my enemy is my friend") are unrealistic. Sometimes the enemy of my enemy is just another enemy.

This is one area where military efforts could make a huge difference, through carefully targeted assistance to countries under threat. The mechanisms for this are already in place—and have been since before 9/11—but they've been inadequately funded, haphazardly executed, and undermined by unilateral strikes that destroyed emerging partnerships. One lesson from the past fifteen years is that security assistance alone, without comparable efforts on government reform, human rights, rule of law and economic development, can backfire—as has happened in several African and Asian countries. Making bent cops more efficient, or helping the militaries of repressive regimes shoot straight, doesn't bring greater security. But with appropriate safeguards, a properly funded joint civil–military effort (ideally, involving several donor countries) can make a difference. Recent developments in Nigeria and Kenya suggest that governments are more open to cooperation in the face of the increased threat—that the rise of ISIS may invigorate friends as well as enemies.

You could argue that this is exactly what President Obama has been describing in speeches since 2013. It's not. The president's pitch was about winding down a conflict, using overseas assistance to substitute for military action in the face of a declining threat, but I'm talking about an expanded effort, in conjunction with *increased* conventional military operations abroad, against an escalating threat. One historical example of a successful effort, similar in kind (though vastly larger in scale) to what I'm suggesting, was the Lend-Lease Program during the Second World War, when U.S. military aid to Great Britain, the Commonwealth and the Soviet Union shored up allies against Nazi Germany, gave the U.S. government time to rally American public opinion, and preserved regional bases in Europe that proved essential for D-Day. Another (again, much larger in scale but similar in kind) was the Marshall Plan when U.S. assistance helped rebuild Western Europe as a bulwark against Soviet expansion during the Cold War, and formed part of an integrated strategy that included limited military interventions in developing countries, covert operations and intelligence activity (the original "rollback") along with military containment of the Warsaw Pact.

To succeed this time around, the approach would need to be funded at a higher level than in the past few years, it would require a long-term commitment linked to governance and human-rights norms (as was successfully done with Colombia against the FARC), and there would need to be more boots, both civil and military, on the ground.[11] It would also have to focus on substance and function, not the mimicry of Western forms of government or Eurocentric models of how to organize, govern and fight—what economists Lant Pritchett, Michael Woolcock and Matt Andrews have called "isomorphic mimicry," or "the adoption of the *forms* of other functional states and organizations which camouflages a persistent lack of *function*."[12] Put more bluntly, we have to stop training civil servants and soldiers to mimic our methods, and instead work with them to design and fund systems that work in their own environments. The biggest difference, though, would be the focus on protecting communities, stabilizing governments and rebuilding trust, rather than (as too often in the past) focusing on killing and capturing terrorists. This will not always be possible—for example, in places like Somalia, Pakistan or Libya—and in these places the choice may be to tolerate the existence of terrorist cells rather than run the risk of taking down fragile governments.

That would mean far stricter limits on raids and drone strikes, and always—*always*—preferring operations by, with and through local partners, conducted in their own way and in accord with their own priorities. As we saw in the case of Libya, one unilateral strike can destroy an entire government's legitimacy, undoing the work of years in less than an hour. The single terrorist captured in the October 2013 Tripoli raid, Abu Anas al-Libi, was wanted for an attack fifteen years earlier, was already seriously ill with liver cancer, and died in January 2015, ten days before his trial could begin. It's hard to see how that outcome justifies the government collapse, the fragmentation of Libya and the deaths of ordinary Libyans that resulted, in part, from the raid.

Thus, for an expanded assistance program to work, we need to help policy-makers get over their addiction to unilateral strikes, lest our obsession with killing terrorists in the short term undo our ability to defeat them over the long term. That's not a criticism of special operations or drones—on the contrary, both of these are outstanding, war-winning capabilities, which have contributed hugely to effective surveillance and targeting since the mid-1990s. Rather, it's a criticism of decision-makers (sometimes, not always, sitting in safety thousands of miles away, who've never heard a shot fired in anger) who succumb to the allure of Predator Porn, misusing these enormously powerful strategic assets, which should be applied as part of a broader plan, as stand-alone tactical tools, to substitute for lack of strategic thought, or (worse) who send others into harm's way in order to make themselves look tough.

This brings us to the final, most military element of the ISIS threat: the catastrophic war that the rise of the Islamic State, and the regional and global response to it, is inflicting on the Middle East and North Africa—primarily Iraq and Syria, but with destabilizing effects radiating to Europe and North Africa, as well as to Turkey, Lebanon, Israel, Jordan, Yemen, Egypt, Saudi Arabia and the Gulf.

This conflict threatens not only to destroy the lives of millions of people, but also to destabilize the world economy by massively disrupting global energy flows, shipping routes, air transportation and telecommunications systems. It has already created huge refugee flows into Europe that pose the risk—both through a rapid influx of individuals radicalized by war, and a backlash against those same immigrants—of radical violence and fundamental shifts in the political and cultural makeup of the countries concerned. More immediately, the conflict threatens to redraw the borders of half-a-dozen nation-states with huge loss of life in the process, to drag regional and world powers (Iran, Israel, Russia, Turkey, Egypt, Pakistan, Saudi Arabia) into an escalating—and potentially nuclear—regional confrontation, to encourage radical violence in scores of countries, and to enable the aggressive expansion of the Islamic State by means of military conquest into Jordan, Lebanon, Yemen the Palestinian Territories, Egypt (via the Sinai) and North Africa, all of which have been put forward by ISIS supporters as objectives for the next phase of the caliphate's expansion. Some of this is already happening, as Israeli strikes into Syria, Arab countries' armed intervention in Libya, the Saudi–Egyptian campaign in Yemen, confrontations in the Gulf of Aden among Iranian, U.S. and other naval forces—and of course the Turkish and Russian interventions in Syria—indicate.

This is the right strategic context in which to consider Russia's move into the Middle East conflict, and President Putin's broader "breakout" from the post-Cold War system. In strategic terms, Western policy-makers have three broad options in responding to Russia's incursion, and it's worth briefly charting them. The first—which we might call Compliance—would be to step back, wash our hands of this mess, and let Russia take a leadership role, with Iran, in attempting to defeat ISIS and negotiate a solution in Syria and Iraq. Given how long the United States and its allies have carried the burden, and the fact that Russian engagement may force Moscow to play a more constructive role, it's tempting to let Putin take a turn. But it also carries enormous risk.

Stepping back and allowing the Russian–Iranian alliance to take the lead against ISIS would provoke greater support for radical groups from Sunni states. It would also reinforce the ISIS narrative of a global sectarian conflict with Sunni Islam on one side, and Shi'a heretics and Christian states on the other. And there's the more prosaic risk that a Russian and Iranian-led effort would simply fail. Iranian-backed efforts against ISIS in Syria and Iraq in 2014–

15 failed everywhere they were tried, except when supported (as in Tikrit) with Western airpower. Likewise, Russian efforts in Syria—even given Russia's military modernization since 2011—will be extraordinarily hard to sustain for more than a few months. And the backlash from jihadists will be severe—as the downing of a Russian airliner over the Sinai in early October foreshadowed.

The second possible response—Competition—would be equally bad. Running our own anti-ISIS operation in parallel, competing with the Russian–Iranian–Syrian effort, would force the Iraqi government to choose between two rival sets of allies, creating the same dynamics Saddam Hussein was able to exploit during the Cold War, or pushing Iraq completely into the orbit of Russia and Iran. In Syria, where the two coalitions have starkly different war aims, it would also run a high risk of a proxy war or even of direct military clashes between the coalitions. President Obama's decision in November 2015 to deploy a small special operations team to Syria to assist the rebels—too little, and laughably late, as a response to the actual needs of the Syrian opposition—increases the risk of a clash even further. Overall, a competitive dynamic would also almost certainly create gaps in which ISIS (or its inevitable successor group) could thrive.

Given all this, Cooperation—the third possible response to Russian intervention—seems a more acceptable, though far from perfect, option. In this approach, we would take Russia at its word, join wholeheartedly in a coalition with Russia and Iran, seek to use cooperation on ISIS to create opportunities for broader rapprochement, and pool and coordinate all our efforts to crush ISIS, create a peaceful outcome in Syria, and stabilize Iraq.

There are huge disadvantages to this response—the morally reprehensible character of the Assad regime, for one thing, along with the implied acceptance of Russia's actions in Ukraine, and the fact that existing allies (from Israel to the Gulf to Saudi Arabia to Turkey to the Syrian rebels) would be massively alienated by such a move. It's possible, though, that allies might be persuaded to participate in joint action alongside both Russia and the United States, as long as that action was tied to very specific, limited objectives. Likewise—if my operational analysis is correct and the Russians lack the resources, and the Iranians the combat capability, to sustain operations for more than a few months without Western help—then our participation would give us increasing leverage over time.

As for the character of Assad's regime, Russia and Iran have shown no great personal commitment to Assad, and both are—to some degree—realist, rational actors with real-world objectives that could be compatible with our own under some circumstances. By intervening so forcefully in Syria, Moscow and Tehran have side-lined Assad as much as anyone else, so it's not beyond the bounds of possibility that a negotiated solution could emerge from the changed facts on the ground, whether Assad likes it or not. And several Syrian groups have indicated they might be willing to see the regime play a role in a peace settlement, provided Assad himself steps down.

With these caveats (and noting that this would still be enormously problematic, especially for Israel, Turkey and Saudi Arabia, and would require a degree of determination, strength of commitment and diplomatic finesse we've not shown so far) I do think Cooperation is worth considering—both as a way of focusing effort on the most important threat (the growth of a state-like ISIS entity in the heart of the Middle East) and as a way of forestalling, or at the very least influencing, the Russian attempt to break out of the post-Cold War order, helping to minimize its most negative consequences. That said, Cooperation is only the least bad of a series of terrible options, arising from the years of vacillation that created the vacuum that Russia and Iran are filling.

More immediately, how to deal with ISIS on the ground in Iraq and Syria? As I've explained, I see ISIS as primarily a state-like entity, or a state-building enterprise. That, and the way ISIS fights, make it a conventional adversary—not a counterinsurgency or counterterrorism problem *per se*—and one with which we need to deal quickly and decisively before it does even more damage. Indeed, holding our noses and cooperating with Russia and Iran—as distasteful as that is, makes sense only because the horror of Syria and the growing threat of ISIS are so vastly worse.

Yet the counterterrorism strategist Audrey Cronin has argued: "A full-on conventional war against the group, waged with the goal of completely destroying it … would be folly. After experiencing more than a decade of continuous war, the American public simply would not support the long-term occupation and intense fighting that would be required to obliterate ISIS. The pursuit of a full-fledged military campaign would exhaust U.S. resources and offer little hope of obtaining the objective. Wars pursued at odds with political reality cannot be won."[13] I take this objection, from such a respected source, very seriously indeed.

In an earlier version of this discussion—published in April 2015, before all the dramatic shifts of the summer—I suggested we were already in a full-on conventional war with ISIS, and that the longer we refused to recognize that fact, the worse things would become. As I saw it at that time, a conventional-style conflict against ISIS need not involve large Western combat units, or an open-ended commitment to occupation and reconstruction. On the contrary, I thought (and still think) that we should explicitly rule out any occupation and commit only a moderately larger number of ground troops—but under very different rules of engagement, and with a radically increased weight of air power to back them. I argued that we should limit the war's objectives to removing those characteristics that make ISIS a state-like entity: its control of territory, its ability to dominate a captive population, its government (including its military and administrative structures and strategic economic resources) and its ability to engage with other states. Adopting that approach, in the late spring or early summer of 2015, would have generated an intervention on about the same scale as Kosovo in 1999, Afghanistan in 2001 (but not the occupation and counterinsurgency) or Libya in 2011. The final part of my argument then (which was less prescient than it looks now, since people on the ground were already saying it was a possibility) was that if we didn't intervene on our own terms, then others would fill the vacuum, and we might not like the result.

This view, when I first put it forward, drew a lot of criticism as overly hawkish. Despite that, and even after everything that's happened since, I still think there's a solid, reasoned and humane case for a full-scale conventional campaign to destroy ISIS, because even (or especially) with the Russian-led intervention in Syria, the downing of the Russian airliner over the Sinai, the bombings in Beirut and the horrendous Paris massacre of November 2015, ISIS has clearly shown itself to be an escalating threat that's growing and worsening.

The longer it takes to deal with the Islamic State, the further its influence spreads, the more recruits it attracts, the harder it is to dislodge from the cities it has captured, the more deeply it's able to harm the communities it controls, the more civilians will ultimately be killed, and the greater the military response ultimately required to defeat it. This is immediately obvious if you look at what has happened in Iraq and Syria since the fall of Mosul. Indeed, this is one of those relatively rare occasions when the job will become much harder, require much more lethal force and do more harm as time goes on: as I argued in the spring of 2015, if we didn't go in hard then, we'd end up having to go in much harder, and potentially on a much larger scale, later. The risk, as I saw it, was that of a regional conflagration in the absence of an effective international (which, like it or not, meant Western-led) response. Things have changed hugely since then, of course. But U.S. policy-makers' responses to two of the transformative events of the summer bear mentioning, because they reinforce Cronin's point about political limits on military responses.

The first was the reaction to the fall of Ramadi, which was to deploy 450 more trainers, and loosen slightly the restrictions on U.S. advisers accompanying supported Iraqi units. The loss of Ramadi was an enormous strategic setback—it delayed the campaign to recapture Mosul by nine to twelve months, severely damaged Iraqi leaders' confidence in the coalition, empowered Iranian-backed sectarian militias and weakened the inclusive and reformist government of Prime Minister Abadi. To any impartial observer, it suggested that our entire light-footprint strategy—the strategy we'd been running since the fall of Mosul—was failing. The under-reaction by U.S. leaders was, at best, an utterly inadequate tweak; at worst, it was a signal that they had no intention of really addressing the problem, and many Iraqi leaders read it that way: hence their openness to Russian cooperation a few months later.

A second example was the U.S. reaction to the fall of Kunduz. Again, as we've seen, this was a huge setback: for the first time in the war the Taliban seized a major city and a provincial capital. The enemy commander at Kunduz, Mullah Abdul Salam, had just sworn allegiance to the new Taliban leader, Akhtar Mohammed Mansoor, so the Kunduz victory cemented Mansoor's leadership, which had been severely contested after Mullah Omar's death became known, and gave the Taliban a boost, while prompting a crisis in Kabul. While ANSF did eventually retake the city, the strain involved in sustaining the fight without NATO combat troops was clearly starting to tell. Likewise, once again, the light-footprint approach failed at Kunduz, as seen in the horrendous MSF hospital attack. In 2016–17, with even fewer NATO advisers, less situational awareness, an even smaller footprint, and less air support (due to increased commitments in Iraq and Syria)—these problems can only worsen. We now run the risk of a collapse and an ISIS blitzkrieg in Afghanistan in 2017 that could be at least as bad as what we saw in Iraq in 2014—and could literally take us back to square one, with a terrorist safe haven in Afghanistan as existed before 9/11.

Again, though, President Obama's response was a tiny tweak: drawing down to 5,500 troops in 2017, rather than 1,000 as originally planned. If 13,000 allied troops (including 9,800 Americans) couldn't stop the Taliban taking Kunduz in 2015, it's not clear why the president expects that fewer than half that number will be able to do the same job in 2017, when ANSF will have suffered another fighting season with even fewer resources, against an array of enemies that now includes both a resurgent Taliban and a new ISIS *wilayat*.

Based on this, I'm sorry to say that Cronin's critique looks even more compelling as time goes on. Especially now that Russia has entered the war, the likelihood of President Obama reversing the whole strategic tendency of his presidency, actually engaging in a wholehearted attempt to destroy ISIS as a state, taking meaningful action to curb the suffering of the Syrian population, or contemplating the commitment of ground troops to the kinds of post-conflict stabilization efforts that would be needed in the event of a peace deal, is next to nonexistent.

And while U.S. strategy remains non-committal, regional partners and allies will not (and should not) get too far out in front. Similarly, the chance that moderate Syrian rebels will fight ISIS (when their real goal, overthrowing Assad, looks increasingly remote) or that Iraqi politicians can create an inclusive political process and get enough Sunnis and Kurds behind them for a successful campaign against ISIS, is vanishingly slim.

Thus the real questions, as of late 2015, are about what can be done within a broader framework of active containment of ISIS, how bad things can get before a new administration takes office in

Washington, and what options might be open to the next president, of whichever party. If my experience over the last eleven years of the Disaggregation strategy tells me anything, it's that political will and timing are everything: an Active Containment strategy, though I do think it's the best of a bad lot of strategic choices now, will be over-taken by events if we wait too long, and end up being stillborn.

EPILOGUE

Insights From the Forever War

On the evening of Friday, 13 November 2015—ten months after the *Charlie Hebdo* attacks, two weeks before world leaders were to attend a climate conference in Paris, and hours after President Obama assured a CNN interviewer that ISIS was "contained"— Islamic State fighters struck Paris. They launched coordinated attacks on the Stade de France soccer stadium in the city's north, the Bataclan concert hall (near *Charlie Hebdo* in the 11th arrondissement) and a string of cafés and restaurants. The final death toll was 130 killed and 368 wounded, with eighty in critical condition. Commentators dubbed the attack "France's 9/11."

There was some truth to that—much as the 2001 AQ attacks led George W. Bush to declare a "Global War on Terror," Paris prompted President Francois Hollande to announce a "pitiless war against the Islamic State."[1] France launched airstrikes into Syria within days, and deployed its aircraft carrier, *Charles de Gaulle*, to the eastern Mediterranean for further strikes.[2] Just as NATO had invoked Article V of the North Atlantic Treaty after 9/11, enabling collective defense commitments toward the United States from its allies, President Hollande became the first European leader to invoke Article 47.2, the collective defense clause of the EU's Treaty of Lisbon. In response, twenty-eight European nations pledged "aid and assistance by all means within their power" to support France— triggering a continent-wide crackdown by military, police and security services. Hollande later called on Russia and the United States to join a global coalition against ISIS, and French and Russian planners met in late November, with added urgency since Russian investigators had now concluded that ISIS Wilayat Sinai had planted the bomb that brought down a Russian airliner, Metrojet Flight 9268, in the Sinai desert on 31 October, killing 224.

Hollande's chances of uniting Washington and Moscow in a Grand Alliance against ISIS—a variant of the "Cooperation" strategy I just described—seemed slim, however, given sharp disagreements over the future of Bashar al-Assad in Syria, and ongoing tensions among Russia, NATO and the United States over Russia's seizure of Crimea and invasion of Ukraine. These tensions spiked on 24 November, when Turkish F-16s shot down a Russian Sukhoi-24M bomber—one of four dozen warplanes now based in the expanding Russian airbase in Syria—after claiming it had strayed into Turkish airspace and ignored repeated warnings to leave. The pilot, Lieutenant Colonel Oleg Peshkov, was was killed by ground fire from Turkish-backed rebels as he and the navigator parachuted after ejecting over Syrian territory. The Su-24's navigator was rescued by Syrian special forces but a Russian marine died when a search-and-rescue helicopter sent to recover Peshkov's body crashed in northern Syria. This was the first downing of a Soviet or Russian aircraft by a NATO member since the 1950s, and a furious Vladimir Putin described it as "a stab in the back."[3]

Despite these tensions, the change in Europe—the sense of a new phase in the war against the Islamic State, of a new resolve from European politicians, and of a new tension around terrorism threats and the influx of Middle Eastern immigrants—was palpable. It was as if (after all that had happened, after *Charlie Hebdo*, Sousse, the refugee crisis, the Russian intervention) it had taken this large-scale attack in the heart of European civilization finally to bring the war home.

The Paris attacks were, in some ways, more concerning than 9/11, though casualties were much lower, because rather than a one-off attack from outside the country (the "expeditionary terrorism" model), they signaled the existence of a paramilitary underground—a better-organized, more capable version of the ISIS Internationale though not yet at the level of a full-blown *wilayat*—operating in cities within France, Belgium and Germany, and possibly also Denmark and the Netherlands. Early indications suggested that Paris might represent the start of a sustained urban guerrilla campaign—and perhaps not just in Europe.

EPILOGUE

The eight ISIS assaulters in Paris—seven of whom died in the attacks, while one, Saleh Abdeslam, fled from France into Belgium the morning afterward and remained on the run several weeks later—were organized into two groups of three operatives, and one of two. Each team operated independently, but they synchronized their efforts using text messages on cellphones, helping them launch eight separate attacks across the city in just thirty-three minutes (from 9:20pm, the moment of the first bombing at Stade de France, to 9:53pm when the last bomb exploded, by which time the Bataclan theater siege was well underway). This was what military analysts call a "complex attack," and its main targets were the soccer stadium (where a friendly match was under way between France and Germany, attended by President Hollande and German foreign minister Frank-Walter Steinmeier) and the Bataclan concert hall, with shootings and bombings at cafés and restaurants acting as a diversion, to draw off first responders and create confusion.

It could have been even worse. Thanks to a sharp-eyed security officer, the first bomber was turned away from the entrance to the soccer stadium, detonating his suicide belt a few seconds later—had he made it inside, the toll would have been far higher. And when police assaulted the Bataclan theater after a three-hour siege (and after the attackers had murdered eighty-nine people, firing and lobbing explosives into the crowd) the attackers detonated their suicide belts immediately: had they instead hunkered down for an urban siege or sought to preserve their standoff with authorities, the incident could have lasted days.

The attackers moved calmly and professionally throughout the assault, showed good weapons skills and tactical sense, and displayed a high degree of what soldiers call "battle discipline"—covering each other, maintaining all-round security while moving and halted, and seeking alternate targets when their first efforts were blocked. They wore a loose uniform and were well-equipped, with standardized gear: Kalashnikov-style assault rifles, hand grenades, at least one Browning 9mm automatic pistol, and seven suicide vests—the first time these had been used in France—all built to an identical, and relatively sophisticated design using TATP, a peroxide-based explosive whose use in suicide attacks had been pioneered by AQ-linked terrorists after 9/11.

One issue that worried investigators immediately after the attack was where the vests were made: had they been smuggled into Europe, or built near the target? Each possibility raised different concerns: the first suggested border security failures (two attackers were known, from fingerprints, to have entered Europe through Greece as asylum-seekers in October 2015) while the second implied that an underground cell had manufactured the devices inside Europe, under the noses of police, and close to the target: TATP is an easily-manufactured but delicate and volatile explosive that doesn't travel well. Then on 19 November, French police arrested Mohamed Khoualed, a 19-year-old from Roubaix in northern France, who turned himself in at a police station in Lille, and who they claimed was the bomb-maker, suggesting the latter explanation was correct—a disturbing admission given that French security services had been on high alert since *Charlie Hebdo* and ahead of the COP21 climate talks scheduled to begin in Paris on 30 November.

The tactics used in Paris were reminiscent of Lashkar-e Tayyiba's attack on Mumbai in November 2008—a series of small, coordinated teams, launching diversionary attacks to draw off first responders and shut the city down, then moving to their main targets.[4] Mumbai was a more sophisticated attack than Paris, given the complex seaborne approach and coastal infiltration involved, and the way the assault teams maintained an urban siege for sixty hours (as against only three in Paris). In part the longer duration of the 2008 attack was because the Mumbai waterfront is a much more complex and cluttered environment than central Paris, which was designed in the nineteenth century specifically to facilitate police response to security incidents.[5] In part it was because the state of high alert of French security services, though it didn't prevent the attack, allowed a faster and more coherent response once they began. In part, also, it was because the Mumbai attack was sponsored and supervised by former (and, allegedly, current) intelligence and special operations officers from Pakistan, whereas Paris was pulled together by a guerrilla group on the ground close to the target.

That said, the Paris attacks represented a dramatic escalation beyond the drive-by shootings and lone-wolf attacks previously seen from Islamic State supporters in Europe. Police now faced an enhanced threat including suicide bombers and "mobile active shooter" scenarios (where an attacker goes mobile—in this case, using stolen or rented cars—to commit a rapid string of shootings in multiple locations) along with large numbers of military-grade weapons: in addition to the rifles used in the assault, police discovered several caches of AK-47s, automatic pistols, explosives and ammunition in the days after the attack.

Beyond their professionalism, the attackers clearly had access to safe houses, stolen vehicles, weapons caches and false documents, suggesting a wider support network (the auxiliary and underground components that I described earlier). These components take longer to organize, and are harder to build than actual guerrilla fighting units—and therefore in many ways are more important for the long-term viability of a guerrilla movement. Police later estimated that at least twenty people played supporting roles in the attack, and in the weeks after the attack they carried out dozens of raids and arrested hundreds of suspects thought to be connected to the group.

This network wasn't limited to France—the attack planner, Abdelhamid Abaaoud, was a Belgian of Moroccan descent, who had founded an Islamic State cell in the Brussels suburb of Molenbeek in 2014, and had spent time with ISIS in Syria. The Molenbeek cell, raided by police after the *Charlie Hebdo* massacre, also sponsored several other attacks including an attempted shooting on a French train in mid-September. The weapons used in Paris were probably also acquired in Belgium, where several urban areas have a thriving black market for military-grade arms. Police suspected that weapons seized in Germany in early November were also linked to the same guerrilla group, and in the weeks after the Paris attacks German, Danish, Dutch and Belgian security forces all mounted counterterror sweeps or closed high-profile events and locations as a precautionary measure. In Belgium, in particular, a terrorism alert was put in place immediately after the attack and police and troops conducted security sweeps in the Brussels neighborhoods of Laeken, Uccle, Jette and Molenbeek, searching for members and associates of the group. This—plus the existence of paramilitary underground groups like the "Parc des Buttes-Chaumont" network, linked to the *Charlie Hebdo* massacre—suggested that the Paris attack was best thought of not as a single terrorist incident, but as one operation in a sustained campaign of urban guerrilla warfare.

That campaign—including attacks linked to ISIS in Lebanon, Turkey, Tunisia, France, Belgium, Kuwait and Denmark—had killed 1,000 civilians outside war zones by the end of 2015, contributing to a spike in global terrorism (including a disturbing rise in mass-casualty attacks). ISIS claimed responsibility for the Paris attack, though there was no evidence that Islamic State leaders selected targets, directed the attack, or put the team together. But as we've seen, that's not how Islamic State operates—as a disaggregated movement, applying methods such as leaderless resistance, guerrilla terrorism and remote radicalization, ISIS leaders don't have actively to direct every attack. Such methods also make detecting attacks ahead of time vastly more difficult—more akin to preventing school shootings than to classic counterterrorism.

On 18 November French police foiled a follow-on attack against the Paris business district, La Defense, fighting a seven-hour battle in the northern suburb of St. Denis against a cell (Paris prosecutor François Molins aptly called it a "commando") that was holed up in a rented apartment and included Abdelhamid Abaaoud, his cousin Hasna Aït Boulahcen, and an unidentified man. This pitched urban gunfight, in which police fired more than 5,000 rounds of ammunition and which ended when Abaaoud's unidentified companion detonated a suicide vest, appears to have foiled a further planned assault intended for 19 November. Other smaller attacks also took place in the days that followed. In Marseilles, Islamic State supporters stabbed a Jewish teacher, threats were made against public venues in Denmark, Germany and France, and a jihadist in Sarajevo killed two Bosnian soldiers. A major security crackdown was launched across Europe in response.

Jean-Charles Brisard, a French terrorism expert and co-author of the first full-length biography of AQI founder Abu Musab al-Zarqawi, called the Paris attacks "a change of paradigm."[6] In strategic terms, the attack seemed to be partly intended as retaliation for French attacks on ISIS territory, partly to deter further attacks, and partly to force adversaries to focus on defending their own populations and critical infrastructure, thereby reducing pressure on the central, state-like level of the "caliphate" in Iraq and Syria. In a tactical sense, however, the attack looked a lot like those we've discussed in Iraq and Syria, where ISIS used terrorism against urban targets to force police and military forces into a defensive, garrison mode, denuding other outlying areas of security presence and thereby creating space for themselves to organize. As of late 2015, it remains unclear whether ISIS leaders plan to conduct this kind of wider campaign, or might opportunistically exploit the post-Paris crackdown to the same end.

It's also unclear, as yet, whether the Paris attack was specifically designed to provoke a backlash against refugees and asylum seekers—800,000 of whom had flooded into the EU by the end of 2015, including a monthly record total of 216,000 in the month of October alone. But given Islamic State's proven talent for provoking sectarian conflict, it's reasonable to assume that this may have been part of the intent. As I explained earlier, in both Iraq and Syria, ISIS (and before it, AQI) specialized in provoking sectarian atrocities. The goal was to push Sunnis into a corner, where they would be forced to support the group, which posed as their defender against Shi'a and others. In Europe, the refugee influx (along with the alienation of Muslim immigrant communities as in Molenbeek or the Paris *banlieues*) had already generated significant anti-Muslim and anti-immigrant rhetoric from right-wing political parties, even before the Paris attacks. In the aftermath, tension spiked across many Western countries, spreading concerns about terrorist infiltration of the refugee flow into the political mainstream.

Perhaps aware of this danger, Islamic organizations in France quickly condemned the Paris attack—but public calls for solidarity with Muslims were muted by comparison to those after *Charlie Hebdo* in January, and a mainstream public backlash against separationist Muslim communities, and against asylum-seekers, quickly gathered steam. If Islamic State were indeed planning a sustained urban guerrilla campaign in Europe, the group would be perfectly positioned to exploit that backlash.

Looking at this from Australia or the United States, it was tempting to feel a certain complacency: Australia's offshore refugee processing system, thorough vetting of asylum seekers and tight border controls, for all the controversy they had generated over the years, sharply reduced the risk of terrorist infiltration into Australia via refugee flows. Likewise, neither North America nor Australia shares borders with Syria, unlike Europe (which does, indirectly, through

Turkey)—and distance may seem to mitigate the threat. In Australia's case, strict gun laws also limit the risk of a Paris-style urban guerrilla underground acquiring military-grade weapons.

But it was already clear by late 2015 that these laws hadn't protected Australian cities from attackers like fifteen-year-old Farhad Jabar, who used an automatic pistol to kill police employee Curtis Cheng in the western Sydney suburb of Parramatta in October 2015, or Man Haron Monis, who used a shotgun in the Lindt Café siege in Martin Place. And Australian gun laws, though extremely restrictive for urban-dwellers, allowed rural producers such as farmers to maintain weapons for use on their own properties, prompting outlaw motorcycle gangs (several with identified connections to Middle Eastern organized crime and some with links to religious extremists) to mount "gun runs" in rural areas, breaking-and-entering to steal weapons to be sold or re-used in the cities.

Likewise, Americans and Australians might look at the increasingly marginalized Muslims of many parts of urban Europe and congratulate themselves on their record of inclusiveness, but that would be hugely unwise. Young, alienated men and women in all Western countries have traveled to the Middle East to fight for Islamic State, and many more remain radicalized at home. What happened in Paris might not occur on the same scale in Australia, Canada, or the United States—but something like it could very well happen in the near future.

It wasn't all bad news: the solidarity of the French and German soccer teams during the Paris attacks—the Germans had to sleep on mattresses in Stade de France because it was considered unsafe to return to their hotel, so the French insisted on staying with them—was a case in point. The courage of Europeans at all levels, from German foreign minister Frank-Walter Steinmeier, who refused to be evacuated from the stadium, to Parisians who used the hashtag *#portesouvertes* ("open doors") to offer shelter to people stranded by the attacks, offered hope that communities could remain resilient in the face of this threat.

But, at some level, the attacks underlined the need for an honest conversation about the risks of massive immigration (especially illegal immigration) from war zones, and the dangers posed by marginalized, non-integrated communities within Western democracies. The fear, described by some commentators as "irrational," that terrorists would infiltrate Western countries along with the flow of refugees, was actually perfectly rational—as the infiltration of attackers for the Paris attacks showed. But almost all of these attackers were EU citizens, so a focus on screening immigrants (as distinct from tracking the movements of radicalized citizens) would not have helped in this case. In any case, the fear of radicalized illegal immigrants might be overblown, especially for countries like the United States and Australia that already had robust border protection and immigration vetting processes. In some ways, it was the EU's open borders that were most at risk here—and the greatest threat might be that an overreaction against domestic Muslim populations outside Europe could create opportunities ISIS can exploit, or generate marginalized and radicalized communities that could serve as the basis for a future guerrilla campaign in the West.

Clearly, whatever President Obama may have told CNN, the Islamic State was far from contained. And given the atomized, highly connected nature of the threat—and the possible emergence of low-grade urban guerrilla warfare in Europe—it may be worth asking whether containment, like Disaggregation before it, might already be overtaken by events.

* * *

We're now in the fifteenth year since 9/11 and, horrible though it is to contemplate, we may be nowhere close to the end of the War on Terror. The great war correspondent Dexter Filkins nailed the sense of boundless, endless conflict—wars like zombies, creeping, slow, unstoppable and unkillable—in his brilliant 2008 book *The Forever War*. Speaking to Taliban leaders in Kandahar, Filkins realized that "what lay at the foundation of the Taliban's rule was fear, but not fear of the Taliban themselves, at least not in the beginning. No: it was fear of the past. Fear that the past would return, that it would come back in all its disaggregated fury. That the past would become the future. The beards, the burqas, the whips, the stones; anything, anything you want. Anything but the past."[7]

But Filkins sat with those Talibs in September 1998, a lifetime ago, and the cycle of wars that started when we invaded their world (and thereby brought it into our own) is no closer to ending. For a while, it looked like things were improving: we were getting on top of the threat, and it seemed as if the wars we'd started so blithely after 9/11 might not turn out to be endless after all. But that was before ISIS began crucifying children, before the Taliban swept back out of the mountains to seize the cities, before the bodies of asylum-seekers began washing up on the beaches, before the first Russian cluster bomb fell on a Syrian village, before the first suicide vest exploded in a Paris concert hall.

As I've tried to explain in this book, all these things were avoidable, and it would be thoroughly wonderful if we could just walk away from this mess. But the fact is, we didn't avoid them, and we can't just walk away. We live in an age of persistent conflict, and adapting to that—working through it, dealing with the reality of the forever war, not trying to return to a fabled pre-9/11 age of peace that never really existed anyway—is the key challenge.

The story I've tried to tell in this book is a sad one, but it's relatively straightforward. The war in Iraq (commencing only fifteen months after 9/11) alienated a host of potential partners and ultimately created AQI. The disaggregation strategy, after 2005, atomized the terrorist threat, just as social media and electronic connectivity were exploding in such a way as to spread the pathogen throughout our societies, enabling remote radicalization and leaderless resistance to an unprecedented degree. The precipitate withdrawal from Iraq in 2011 revived AQI in the nick of time after it had been reduced by 90 per cent and almost annihilated during the Surge. The precipitate pullout from Iraq, the killing of Osama bin Laden, the AQ succession crisis that followed, and the failure of the Arab Spring—all in the same key year of 2011—helped turn AQI into ISIS and gave it a global leadership role it proceeded to exploit with utter and unprecedented ruthlessness. And complacency and hubris after bin Laden's death, along with vacillation in the face of the colossal tragedy of the Syrian War, created the basis for a conflict that's now consuming the Middle East and drawing regional and global powers into a hugely dangerous, and still escalating conflict. I don't propose to describe again the approaches I think we need to pursue as we deal with the next stage of this long conflict. But I do want to share some broader insights ("lessons" is too strong a word) that I've picked up along the way. In no particular order, then—and by way of conclusion—here are five insights.

EPILOGUE

Don't confuse bad management with destiny

In October 2007, at the height of the Surge, I had the honour of talking with the great American conversationalist Charlie Rose. He put it to me that the war in Iraq might be unwinnable. I said I thought it was absolutely winnable, but that didn't mean *we* could win it, or that we would. Since 9/11, many people have written off various efforts as unwinnable, challenges as impossible, or operating environments as unsuitable. Some describe the relative decline of the West as destiny, arguing that we should be managing that decline rather than pushing back against the inevitable. But I think it was Kin Hubbard (or maybe it was Will Rogers) who said: "Lots of folks confuse bad management with destiny." After fifteen years of this war, I don't believe there's anything pre-destined about failure. The fact that we're not getting something done doesn't mean it's undoable. It just means *we're* failing: decline is a choice that we make. Which means it's a choice we can unmake, if enough of us decide that we need better management.

Never think: "This is as bad as it gets"

The 9/11 Commission described the 2001 attacks as a "failure of imagination"—they were simply beyond what anyone could imagine would really happen. Then, after 9/11, we used to talk of AQ terrorists as if they were utterly without any self-imposed limits, a terrorist threat as bad as it could possibly get. Then Zarqawi turned up, and we realized that actually things could get a lot worse. And then ISIS emerged from AQI, and the ISIS fighters were so extreme that even the old AQI—today's Jabhat al-Nusrah—started to look moderate in comparison. The lesson I learned in Iraq, Afghanistan, Libya and Somalia, and that my contacts in Syria have reinforced ten times over, is never, ever to make the mistake of thinking that "this is as bad as it gets." Today, in the wake of the Paris attacks, people seem to think that ISIS is as bad as it gets, but that's far from the case: there are threats out there that make ISIS look tame. I'm not talking about a worse version of today's terrorism—I'm talking about things beyond terror altogether. Getting out in front of the imagination curve—breaking out of our normality bias, thinking ahead, rather than endlessly ratcheting up security measures in response to whatever happens to be the most recent atrocity the latest crop of bad guys can devise—is going to be even more critical in the future.

Strategy, without resources and sequencing, is fantasy

Strategy isn't just about deciding on goals, it's about resourcing and sequencing the actions needed to achieve them. After defeating the Taliban in 2001, the international community articulated a series of enormously ambitious nation-building objectives—and then utterly failed to commit the resources, people and time needed to achieve them. Before Iraq there was a huge debate in the Pentagon about the "light footprint" approach, and about how much was the bare minimum to get the job done. As I've explained, we ended up going in—thanks in part to Secretary Rumsfeld—with far too few resources to do the job, but then sticking around and trying to do it anyway. It was only when ends, ways and means briefly aligned during the Surge that we finally began to see success, and even that proved unsustainable because political leaders weren't prepared to commit the time needed to make it work. Then in 2009 President Obama announced a "fully resourced counterinsurgency strategy" for Afghanistan, which turned out to be anything but that: far fewer troops were deployed than were needed to achieve the policy goals that were set, and for far too little time, a fact that Afghans are living with today. Likewise, after Mosul, the president articulated a goal to "dismantle and defeat" ISIS. When the light footprint approach failed to achieve that goal, we needed to change the resourcing, change the goal, or both—but so far we've done neither. The lesson here—and it applies equally to the Bush and Obama administrations—is that a strategic vision, without the ability to resource and sequence a program of action to achieve it, is just empty rhetoric.

Battlefield success is not *victory*

Over the past fifteen years, we've repeatedly achieved battlefield success, only to fail to translate it into viable political outcomes. In 2001, U.S. and coalition forces (with enormous support from Afghans, as I've explained) routed the Taliban in less than seven weeks. But Western political leaders, Afghan warlords and international bureaucrats failed to use that victory to a launch a genuine peace process, undertake political reconciliation with the Taliban, or lay the foundation for stable and effective Afghan government—and so the Taliban came back. Six years later in Iraq, during the Surge, at a cost of hundreds of American and Allied lives, and from an absolutely horrendous start point, U.S. and coalition military forces cut both violence and insurgent activity to a tiny fraction of what it had been, creating the preconditions for reconciliation. But then U.S. political leaders walked away (against the advice of military commanders), Iraqi politicians pursued personal and sectarian goals at the expense of peace, and ISIS came roaring back out of the desert—this time with tanks. Call me cynical, but I think it's worth considering the possibility that our problem here is not fundamentally a military one.

Maybe the issue is that we don't know, or have forgotten, how to translate battlefield victory into enduring and stable peace. If that's true, it suggests that more attempts to "fix" the military—to better resource it, make it bigger, train it differently, give it different technology, and so forth—are misguided, that we need to focus instead on civilian agencies of government, educating policy-makers on both military strategy and conflict transformation, building greater capacity for peacemaking and war termination, and developing civilian officials who can operate effectively in the grey area between war and peace, the space of armed politics where translating battlefield victory into a better peace is the goal. It also suggests that we should educate our own public, helping them understand that (in a democracy, at any rate) war is not a spectator sport. To paraphrase Clemenceau, war is too important to be left to the generals, and peace is too important to be left to the politicians—the people must have their say on both, and continuously, not just at the outset.

You can't fight without fighting

I think it was the writer Fred Kaplan who pointed out that Rumsfeld's "transformation"—the high-tech weapons, the omniscient surveillance and communications devices, the whole stand-off precision system-of-systems thing—looked a lot, when all was said and done, like President Obama's light footprint. Both approaches failed drastically. This is not a dig at high-tech systems. On the contrary: technology offers hugely important advantages that we should exploit to the full. But whether it's fought with stones or drones, with swords or guided missiles, war is still War: an act of force to compel our enemies to do our will. Its surface character may change, but its underlying nature remains the same. War is nothing more or less than interpersonal violence, organized at a societal level, and it has been endemic in almost every known human civilization. That's not a value judgment; it's just a statement of fact. No technology, however advanced, changes that, and to the extent that we try to substitute technology for bodies, we're really admitting that we don't have the stomach for the fight. Policy-makers need to ask themselves, "Am I ready to put flesh against steel—to kill their people and lose ours—in order to win?" If the answer is No, then we shouldn't get into these conflicts at all.

Conversely, if (as it turns out—and as I've tried to argue in this book) we're already in a fight, whether we want one or not, then we need leaders with the moral force and clarity of will to see the thing as it truly is: to look at it without flinching, and to actually fight it. No amount of high-tech weaponry will help, because the problem isn't one of technology or intellect, but of character and will, and the harsh reality is that you can't fight without *fighting*. The Islamic State understands that; so do the Taliban and al-Qaeda. Do we?

NOTES

PREFACE

1. One symptom of our lack of clarity about Islamic State is that we've yet to settle on what to call it. The organization, whose name in Arabic is ad-Dawlah al-Islāmiyah fī 'l-'Irāq wa-sh-Shām, is variously known as Islamic State, IS, ISIS, ISIL, or (from Arabic abbreviation) as Da'ish or Da'esh. For reasons I get into in more detail later, I mostly call it ISIS, and sometimes Islamic State.
2. See President Obama's introduction to the 2012 Defense Strategic Guidance in *Sustaining U.S. Global Leadership: Priorities for 21ˢᵗ Century Defense*, United States Department of Defense, Washington D.C., 2012, p. 3 at http://archive.defense.gov/news/Defense_Strategic_Guidance.pdf

1. DEBACLE

1. Mohammed Kathieb, "Children freeze to death in Aleppo refugee camp," *Al-Monitor*, 20 January 2015, online at http://www.al-monitor.com/pulse/originals/2015/01/syria-refugees-children-death-bab-al-salameh-camp.html#
2. President Obama's "jayvee" remark has of course been subject to political spin from both directions, but its original intent is strikingly clear. See David Remnick, "Going the Distance," *The New Yorker*, 27 January 2014, and the non-partisan analysis of the remark in Glenn Kessler, "Spinning Obama's Reference to ISIS as a 'JV' Team," *The Washington Post*, 3 September 2014.
3. Barack Obama, Remarks by the President at the United States Military Academy Commencement Ceremony, 28 May 2014.
4. *Ibid.*
5. "Drone" as used here refers to remotely-piloted aircraft like the General Atomics MQ-1 Predator and MQ-9 Reaper, controlled by ground stations that may be on the other side of the planet, and carrying missiles

and surveillance equipment to target terrorists. These are not true "drones" in that they're not fully autonomous—I use the term simply because it's in widespread usage and is well understood by non-specialist readers.

2. DISAGGREGATION

1. David Kilcullen, "Countering Global Insurgency," 2004, www.cademia. edu/7026837/Countering_global insurgency.

2. "Either you are with us, or you are with the terrorists": President Bush made this statement, or a variation of it, many times during his first term. One of the earliest and most public was during his Address to the Nation on 20 September 2001, less than two weeks after 9/11. See "President Bush Addresses the Nation," *The Washington Post*, 20 September 2001.

3. For a description of the Maher Arar case see *Maher Arar: Rendition to Torture*, New York: Center for Constitutional Rights, n.d., online at https://ccrjustice.org/sites/default/files/assets/files/rendition%20 to%20torture%20report.pdf, and for the official report describing the case and exonerating Mr Arar see Government of Canada, *Report of the Events Relating to Maher Arar, Vol. 1, Factual Background*, Ottawa: Commission of Inquiry into the Actions of Canadian Officials Relating to Maher Arar, 2006, online at http://www.sirc-csars.gc.ca/pdfs/cm_arar_bgv1-eng.pdf

4. Kilcullen, 2004, *op. cit.*

5. For an unclassified description of the *National Implementation Plan* see http://nsp_intro.golearnportal.org/lesson6/natImplementation/. For the 2006 *National Security Strategy*, see http://nssarchive.us/national-security-strategy-2006/, and for a description of CONPLAN 7500 by its key architect, Navy SEAL Admiral Eric T. Olson, who commanded Special Operations Command when the plan was developed, see "Keynote Address: Admiral Eric T. Olson" in *Proceedings of the Unrestricted Warfare Symposium, 2008*, Baltimore: Johns Hopkins University, Applied Physics Research Laboratory, 2008, online at http://www.jhuapl.edu/urw_symposium/proceedings/2008/Authors/Olson.pdf

6. Olson, *ibid.*

7. For the original version of Contest see HM Government, *Countering International Terrorism: The United Kingdom's Strategy, July 2006*, online at https://www.gov.uk/government/uploads/system/uploads/attachment_data/file/272320/6888.pdf; for the 2011 version see HM Government, *CONTEST: The United Kingdom's Strategy for Countering Terrorism, July 2011* at https://www.gov.uk/government/uploads/system/uploads/

attachment_data/file/97995/strategy-contest.pdf. For the equivalent Australian document see Australian Government, *Counterterrorism White Paper: Securing Australia | Protecting Our Community*, Canberra: 2010, at https://www.asio.gov.au/img/files/counter-terrorism_white_paper.pdf and Council of Australian Governments, *Australia's Counter-Terrorism Strategy: Strengthening our Resiliency*, July 2015, at http://www.nationalse-curity.gov.au/Media-and-publications/Publications/Documents/Australias-Counter-Terrorism-Strategy-2015.pdf

8. Matthew Engel, "Scorned General's Tactics Proved Right: Profile of the army chief sidelined by Rumsfeld," *The Guardian*, 29 March 2003.

9. James Fallows, "Blind into Baghdad," *The Atlantic*, January–February 2004, online at http://www.theatlantic.com/magazine/archive/2004/01/blind-into-baghdad/302860/

10. David Margolick, "The Night of the Generals," *Vanity Fair*, April 2007, online at http://www.vanityfair.com/news/2007/04/iraqgenerals200704

11. Discussion with officer serving in Ramadi, Anbar province, May–October 2003.

12. Interview with former deputy chief of CIA Station Baghdad, Green Zone, April 2007.

13. Joel Roberts, "Top General: Insurgency not fading," CBS News online, CBS/AP, 23 June 2005.

3. ABYSS

1. For Iraqi civilian casualties, I rely in this essay on a combination of data produced by Iraq Body Count (IBC) and unclassified reports from the U.S. Department of Defense. This figure is from IBC—see www.iraq-bodycount.org/analysis/numbers/2006/; note: I have made no use of any data derived from WikiLeaks' "Iraq War Logs," as that material remains classified. If anything, including the WikiLeaks data would raise rather than lower this estimate.

2. The precise number, as of 28 November 2005, was 157,982 U.S. troops, and there were another 23,000 troops in Iraq, from a total of twenty-seven allied and coalition countries, supporting the effort. See Linwood B. Carter, *Iraq: Summary of U.S. Forces*, CRS Report for Congress, Washington DC, updated 28 November 2005, p. 1.

3. Michael Isikoff and David Corn, *Hubris: The Inside Story of Spin, Scandal, and the Selling of the Iraq War*, New York: Crown/Archetype, 2006, Kindle Edition, location 962.

4. *Ibid.*, locations 513–25.

5. Nate Fick, quoted in Evan Wright, *Generation Kill*, New York: Berkeley Publishing Group, 2004, p. 421.

6. Fallows, *op. cit.*

7. Isikoff and Corn, *op. cit.*, locations 327–29.

8. For a critical analysis of Secretary Rumsfeld's view of Transformation see Peter Dombrowski and Andrew L. Ross, "The Revolution in Military Affairs, Transformation and the Defense Industry," *Security Challenges*, Vol. 4, No. 4 (Summer 2008), pp. 13–38. See also Frank G. Hoffman, "Complex Irregular Warfare: The Next Revolution in Military Affairs," *Orbis*, Summer 2006, 395–411.

9. Fallows, *op. cit.*

10. See Lloyd C. Gardner, *The Long Road to Baghdad: A History of U.S. Foreign Policy from the 1970s to the Present*, New York: The New Press, 2008, pp. 207–210. See also David L. Phillips, *Losing Iraq: Inside the Postwar Reconstruction Fiasco*, New York: Basic Books, 2005, pp. 74–7.

11. For a detailed description of this construct, see David Kilcullen, *The Accidental Guerrilla: Fighting Small Wars in the Midst of a Big One*, New York/London: Oxford University Press/Hurst, 2009.

12. Central Intelligence Agency, *Iraq's Continuing Programs for Weapons of Mass Destruction*, National Intelligence Estimate 2002–16HC, October 2002, unredacted version approved for public release 9 December 2014, p. 68.

13. See Craig Whittock, "Zarqawi building his own terror network," *The Washington Post*, 3 October 2004.

14. Mustafa Hamid and Leah Farrell, *The Arabs at War in Afghanistan*, London: Hurst, 2015, p. 257.

15. Author's field notes, drawn from interviews with Iraqi colleagues at the Iraqi army counterinsurgency school, Taji, 21 and 26 June 2007.

16. CNN, "Al-Zawahiri: U.S. faltering in Afghanistan—CIA analysing al Qaeda videotape that appeared on Al-Jazeera," CNN online, 9 November 2004.

17. Audrey Kurth Cronin, "Correspondence: Response to Blood Year" in *Quarterly Essay* No. 59, August 2015.

18. Secretary of State Condoleezza Rice, *Remarks at the American University in Cairo*, 20 June 2005, online at http://2001–2009.state.gov/secretary/rm/2005/48328.htm

19. Robert M. Gates, *Duty: Memoirs of a Secretary at War*, New York: Alfred Knopf, 2014, p. 23.

20. Abbas Milani, "The Shah's Atomic Dreams," *Foreign Policy*, 29 December 2010. Milani refers to declassified U.S. documents showing Western support (mixed with concern about nuclear weapons proliferation) for Iranian nuclear energy programs under the Shah.

21. Charles Krauthammer, remarks at the American Enterprise Institute, Washington DC, panel, "U.S. Foreign Policy and the Future of Iraq," 22nd April 2003, C-SPAN video transcript at http://www.c-span.org/video/?176282–1/us-foreign-policy-future-iraq, quoted passage begins at 16:05.

22. Discussion with CIA operations officer RM, Baghdad, March 2007.

23. Civilian deaths in Iraq, the majority inflicted by sectarian killings, averaged 661 per week for the last quarter of 2006—more than 50 per cent of these happening inside Baghdad or the belts. See Iraq Body Count, www.iraqbodycount.org/analysis/numbers/2006/.

24. Andrew Buncombe and Patrick Cockburn, "Iraq's Death Squads: On the Brink of Civil War," *The Independent on Sunday*, 26 February 2006, at http://www.independent.co.uk/news/world/middle-east/iraqs-death-squads-on-the-brink-of-civil-war-6108236.html

25. Ibid.

26. Damien Cave, "Iraq's No. 2 Health Official Is Held and Accused of Financing Shiite Militants," *New York Times*, 7 February 2007, at http://query.nytimes.com/gst/fullpage.html?res=9E07E3D7113FF93AA357 51C0A9619C8B63&sec=&spon=&&scp=2&sq=zamili&st=cse

27. Author's personal observation, Baghdad, March 2006.

28. This example is drawn from two incidents, one described to me by a cavalry officer operating in Tal Afar in 2005–6, and one that I observed myself in northwest Baghdad in April 2007.

29. This description is drawn from an interview with my Iraqi interpreter in Baghdad in May 2007, based on his eyewitness account of what happened to his twelve-year-old younger brother and several boys from his neighbourhood in 2005–6.

30. For a profile of Abu Deraa and a link to the famous YouTube video, see Lydia Khalil, "The Shiite Zarqawi: A Profile of Abu Deraa," *Terrorism Monitor*, vol. 4, no. 22, 16 November 2006.

31. Author's personal observation and field notes, Baghdad, March 2007—based on accounts from patrol members from a U.S. airborne battalion operating in northern Baghdad, 2006.

32. Author's field notes from geothermal power plant, AO Commando, near Mahmudiyah, June 2007.

33. English translation of a letter from Ayman al-Zawahiri to Abu Musab al-Zarqawi, available online from the Combating Terrorism Center, 9 July 2005, p. 3.

34. Ibid, pp. 8–9.

35. For this insight, I'm indebted to Professor Mary Habeck of Johns Hopkins University. See Mary R. Habeck, *Knowing the Enemy: Jihadist Ideology and the War on Terror*, New Haven: Yale University Press, 2007.

4. WATERFALL

1. See http://council.smallwarsjournal.com/showthread.php?t=3177 for an unclassified extract from the *Multi-National Force Iraq Counterinsurgency Guidance*, issued in early June 2007.

2. For a detailed account of these events, see SGT Christopher Alexander, CPT Charles Kyle and MAJ William S. McCallister, *The Iraqi Insurgent Movement*, 14 November 2003, www.comw.org/warreport/fulltext/03alexander.pdf.

3. For a copy of this slide and related data, see "Overall Weekly Attack Trends," *OIF—Iraq Significant Activities (SIGACTs)*, GlobalSecurity.org, www.globalsecurity.org/military/ops/iraq_sigacts.htm.

5. CROCODILE

1. Martin Fletcher, "Al-Qaeda leaders admit: 'We are in crisis. There is panic and fear'," *The Times*, London, 11 February 2008.

2. Civilian casualty figures, as well as incident numbers, are drawn from the Iraq Body Count database.

3. Data come from the Iraq Coalition Casualty Count at http://icasualties.org/Iraq/ByMonth.aspx (for U.S. killed in Iraq, all causes) and from http://icasualties.org/Iraq/USCasualtiesByState.aspx (for U.S. wounded).

4. World Health Organization and Iraq Ministry of Health, *Iraq Family Health Survey 2006/2007*, Baghdad, Ministry of Health, 2008, p. 19.

5. For example, *Newsweek*'s cover story on 3 March 2010 was "Victory at Last: The Emergence of a Democratic Iraq" by Babak Dehghanpiseh, while the Institute for the Study of War, a Washington-based think-tank, issued a DVD entitled *The Surge: The Untold Story*, which described the Surge as "one of the most successful military operations in a generation of war fighting." See www.understandingwar.org/press-media/event/premier-event-surge-untold-story-never-seen-interviews.

6. Reported to the author by an American military officer who was in the meeting, June 2007, Baghdad.

7. Thomas E. Ricks, *The Gamble: General David Petraeus and the American Military Adventure in Iraq*, New York: Penguin, 2009.

8. Jack Serle, "Almost 2,500 Now Killed by Covert U.S. Drone Strikes Since Obama Inauguration Six Years Ago," *Common Dreams*, online, 2 February 2015.

9. For this insight, I'm indebted to Dr Janine Davidson of the Council on Foreign Relations.

10. Michael Gordon and Bernard Trainor, *The Endgame: The Inside Story of the Struggle for Iraq, from George W. Bush to Barack Obama*, New York: Vintage Books, 2013, pp. 360–1.

11. For a detailed account of growing authoritarian behavior under Maliki, including the "stacking" of command positions with political and sectarian loyalists, see Marisa Sullivan, *Maliki's Authoritarian Regime*, Institute for the Study of War, Middle East Security Report No. 10, April 2013.

12. Ted Carpenter, "A New Dictator? Nouri al-Maliki is exhibiting worrying authoritarian tendencies," *The National Interest*, 19 January 2010.
13. Sullivan, *op. cit.*, p. 9.

6. TSUNAMI

1. For the first detailed account of the raid, including the rough timeline, see Nicholas Schmidle, "Getting Bin Laden: What happened that night in Abbottabad," *The New Yorker*, 8 August 2011.
2. John Hudson, "Succession Battle Threatens to Split Al Qaeda," *The Atlantic*, 18 May 2011.
3. See, for example, "Veterans group to Obama: 'Heroes Don't Spike the Football'," *The Daily Caller*, 5 March 2012, http://dailycaller.com/2012/05/03/veterans-group-to-obama-heroes-don't-spike-the-football-video/.
4. Mark Mazzetti, "C.I.A. Closes Unit Focused on Capture of Bin Laden," *The New York Times*, 4 July 2006.
5. U.S. National Counterterrorism Center, "Al Qaeda in the Arabian Peninsula," www.nctc.gov/site/groups/aqap.html.
6. For the Fort Hood shooting, see Josh Rubin and Matt Smith, "'I am the shooter,' Nidal Hasan tells Fort Hood court-martial," CNN News, 6 August 2013.
7. Will McCants, "How Zawahiri Lost Al Qaeda," 19 November 2013, www.brookings.edu/research/opinions/2013/11/19-how-zawahri-lost-al-qaeda-mccantsw.
8. For a more detailed exposition of this history, see Abdel Bari Atwan, *The Secret History of Al Qa'eda*, updated edn, Berkeley: University of California Press, 2008.
9. Osama bin Laden, quoted in Mark Fineman and Stephen Braun, "Life Inside Al Qaeda: A Destructive Devotion," *Los Angeles Times*, 24 September 2001.
10. Niall Ferguson, *Civilization: The West and the Rest*, New York: Penguin, 2011, preface.
11. Peter Knoope and Anno Bunnik, "Why the People of Tunisia and Egypt Confirm the Bankruptcy of al Qaeda's Tactics," International Centre for Counter-Terrorism, the Hague, 31 January 2011, at http://icct.nl/publication/why-the-people-of-tunisia-and-egypt-confirm-the-bankruptcy-of-al-qaedas-tactics/
12. Barack Obama, "Obama says Egypt's transition 'must begin now,'" CNN News, 2 February 2011.
13. Barack Obama, quoted in Scott Wilson and Joby Warrick, "Asad must go, Obama says," *The Washington Post*, 18 August 2011.
14. Adolph "Spike" Dubs, killed in a kidnapping in Kabul in February 1979, was the last U.S. ambassador murdered in the line of duty.

Arnold Raphel (who died in a plane crash with Pakistani President Zia ul-Haq in August 1988) was arguably another—though the cause of the crash remains unclear, and it may have been simply an accident.

7. REBIRTH

1. *New Yorker* writer Laura Secor produced some of the most insightful reportage on the Green Revolution, as it unfolded in 2009. Her forthcoming *Children of Paradise: A Biography of Iran's Democracy Movement* (Penguin Canada, 2016) examines these issues in more detail.

2. Laura Secor, "Behind Iran's Silence," *The New Yorker*, 15 July 2009, online at http://www.newyorker.com/news/news-desk/laura-secor-behind-irans-silence

3. There is also a strong urban–rural and social class dynamic in the conflict. See David Kilcullen and Nathaniel Rosenblatt, "The Rise of Syria's Urban Poor: Why the War for Syria's Future Will Be Fought Over the Country's New Urban Villages," *Prism*, vol. 4, Syria Supplement, 2014, pp. 3–10.

4. For the full text of the UN Security Council resolution, see United Nations, *Security Council Approves 'No-Fly Zone' over Libya, Authorizing 'All Necessary Measures' to Protect Civilians, by Vote of 10 in Favour with 5 Abstentions*, 17 March 2011, www.un.org/press/en/2011/sc10200.doc.htm.

5. John Barry, "America's Secret Libya War," The Daily Beast, 30 August 2011, www.thedailybeast.com/articles/2011/08/30/americas-secret-libya-war-u-s-spent-1-billion-on-covert-ops-helping-nato.html.

6. For the discussion between Secretary Clinton and her staff about the Libya operation as a signature foreign policy achievement, see Michael S. Schmidt, "Benghazi Emails Put Focus on Hillary Clinton's Encouragement of Adviser," *New York Times*, 29 June 2015. For Secretary Clinton's comment on Gaddafi's death, see CBS News, "Clinton on Qaddafi: 'We came, we saw, he died'," 20 October 2011, at http://www.cbsnews.com/news/clinton-on-qaddafi-we-came-we-saw-he-died/

7. See Joby Warrick, "Hillary's war: How conviction replaced skepticism in Libya intervention," *The Washington Post*, October 30, 2011.

8. *Ibid.*

9. Wilson and Warrick, *op. cit.*

10. Author's discussion with a clandestine services officer with extensive Iraq experience, Rabat, Morocco, October 2013.

11. These "facts" (which need to be taken with some skepticism due to their source) come from a brief bio of al-Baghdadi published by ISIS in July 2013 under the title *Moments from the Life Journey of our Master the Emir of the Believers Abu Bakr al-Husseini al-Qurashi al-Baghdadi—May Allah*

Preserve Him—Emir of the Islamic State in Iraq and the Levant, translation available online at SITE Group, http://news.siteintelgroup.com/blog/index.php/entry/226-the-story-behind-abu-bakr-al-baghdadi.

12. This discussion of developments in Syria, and in Iraq after the U.S. pullout, draws on reporting from our field networks and analysts in Iraq and Syria, as well as reports by Bill Roggio's *Long War Journal*, ongoing analysis by the Institute for the Study of War and the Jamestown Foundation, and independent researchers. See www.caerusassociates.com and www.firstmilegeo.com for our reporting, as well as www.longwarjournal.org, www.jamestown.org, and www.understandingwar.org.

13. Ben Hubbard and Eric Schmitt, "Military Skill and Terrorist Technique Fuel Success of ISIS," *The New York Times*, 27 August 2014.

14. See "Al Qaeda in Iraq claims Hilla attack, vows revenge," *Dawn* (Pakistan), 9 May 2011, www.dawn.com/news/627307/al-qaeda-in-iraq-claims-hilla-attack-vows-revenge.

15. Associated Press in Baghdad, "Baghdad bomb attacks leave scores dead and hundreds injured," *The Guardian*, 23 December 2011.

16. For example, see Christoph Reuter, "The Terror Strategist: Secret Files Reveal the Structure of Islamic State," *Der Spiegel*, 18 April 2015, which explores a document cache allegedly removed from an SUV near the house in Syria where Haji Bakr was killed in January 2014 that demonstrates ISIS's roots in Saddam-era secular intelligence and covert operations structures.

17. References to Syrian respondents, unless otherwise noted, draw on interviews, survey responses and field team research conducted by Caerus Associates in Syria and Iraq between 2011 and 2015. For safety reasons, individual respondents are not identified.

18. Ian Black, "Why Bashar al-Assad stresses al-Qaida narrative: Syria has seen influx of foreign fighters, but regime has been spinning terror line since last March to help justify state violence," *The Guardian*, 19 May 2012.

19. Maamoun Youssef, "Al-Qaida: We're returning to old Iraq strongholds," Associated Press, 22 July 2012, https://news.yahoo.com/al-qaida-were-returning-old-iraq-strongholds-131645698.html.

20. Kristina Wong, "Royce: U.S. ignored calls to strike ISIS for months," *The Hill*, 23 July 2014, http://thehill.com/policy/defense/213091-royce-us-ignored-calls-to-strike-isis-for-months.

21. Jessica D. Lewis, *Al Qaeda in Iraq Resurgent: The Breaking the Walls Campaign, Part I*, Middle East Security Report No. 14, Institute for the Study of War, Washington DC, September 2013, p. 7.

22. *Ibid.*

23. Daniel Klaidman, "Obama: I Make the Drone Decisions," The Daily

Beast, 23 May 2013, www.thedailybeast.com/articles/2013/05/23/obama-i-make-the-drone-decisions.html.

24. Barack Obama, quoted in Glenn Kessler, "President Obama and the 'red line' on Syria's chemical weapons," *The Washington Post*, 6 September 2013.

25. *Ibid.*

26. *Ibid.*

27. Telephone discussions with activists in Aleppo, Idlib and Damascus, 20 and 24 August 2012.

28. It was aided in this, incidentally, by the *New York Times*, which quietly revised its report from "Syrian Rebels Accuse Government of Chemical Attack" to "Scores Killed in Syria, with Signs of Chemical War" and finally to "Images of Death in Syria, but No Proof of Chemical Attack." For the original version of this story, see: Ben Hubbard and Hwaida Saad, "Syrian Rebels Accuse Government of Chemical Attack," *The New York Times*, 21 August 2013, www.newsdiffs.org/diff/300484/300584/www.nytimes.com/2013/08/22/world/middleeast/syria.html, but the evening it was posted, the full text was replaced with new copy based on the same reporting but with a different editorial slant, entitled "Scores Killed in Syria, with Signs of Chemical War." The following day the headline was changed to "Images of Death in Syria, but No Proof of Chemical Attack", and copy added to support the White House attempt to raise doubts on the veracity of the Syrian eyewitnesses. This (twice revised) version remains on the *New York Times* website at www.nytimes.com/2013/08/22/world/middleeast/syria.html and the revision took place without any explanation from the *Times*.

29. *Ibid.*

30. Kevin Drum, "Kerry Gaffes, But Maybe It's the Good Kind of Gaffe," *Mother Jones*, 9 September 2013, www.motherjones.com/kevin-drum/2013/09/kerry-gaffe-syria-chemical-weapons-russia.

31. Chemical attacks, which international investigators concluded were carried out by the regime, continued to occur, including on 11 April 2014 and 17 March 2015. See Arms Control Association, "Timeline of Syrian Chemical Weapons Activity 2012–14," July 2014, www.armscontrol.org/factsheets/Timeline-of-Syrian-Chemical-Weapons-Activity for the April 2014 attack, and Hugh Naylor, "Chemical Weapons Attack Alleged in Syria," *The Washington Post*, 17 March 2015, for the 2015 incident.

32. Caerus Associates, *Mapping the Conflict in Aleppo*, Washington DC, February 2014, http://caerusassociates.com/wp-content/uploads/2014/02/Caerus_AleppoMappingProject_FinalReport_02–18–14.pdf.

8. COLLAPSE

1. Associated Press in Baghdad, "Iraq Vice-President sentenced to death amid deadly wave of insurgent attacks," *The Guardian*, 10 September 2012.
2. Michael R. Gordon, "Tensions Rise in Baghdad with Raid on Official," *The New York Times*, 20 December 2012; Associated Press, "Bomb hits convoy of Iraq's Sunni finance minister after demonstrations by his backers," Fox News online, 13 January 2013.
3. For more detail, see this piece on the fall of Mosul by two Caerus analysts—Yasir Abbas and Dan Trombly, "Inside the Collapse of the Iraqi Army's Second Division," *War on the Rocks*, 1 July 2014, http://waron-therocks.com/2014/07/inside-the-collapse-of-the-iraqi-armys-2nd-division/.
4. Anzela Armero (channel), "Nuri al-Maliki sectarian violence continues," YouTube, 28 May 2014, www.youtube.com/watch?v=rDrVt_TFU M4.

9. RETRIBUTION

1. This study was later published as Dickie Davis, David Kilcullen, Greg Mills and David Spencer, *A Great Perhaps? Conflict and Convergence in Colombia*, London: Hurst & Co., 2015.
2. Abbas and Trombly, *op. cit.*
3. *Ibid.*
4. Mustafa Habib, "The Iraqi Army Did Not Desert Mosul; They Were Ordered To Leave," Muftah, 16 June 2014, at http://muftah.org/the-iraqi-army-desert-mosul-ordered-leave/#.VhEhVdYrjdk
5. Abbas and Trombly, *op. cit.*
6. C.J. Chivers, "After Retreat, Iraqi Soldiers Fault Officers," *New York Times*, 1 July 2014, at http://www.nytimes.com/2014/07/02/world/middleeast/after-retreat-iraqi-soldiers-fault-officers.html?ref=todays paper&_r=1
7. *Ibid.*
8. *Ibid.*
9. *Ibid.*
10. The White House, Press Briefing by Principal Deputy Press Secretary Josh Earnest, 6/10/2014, at https://www.whitehouse.gov/the-press-office/2014/06/10/press-briefing-principal-deputy-press-secretary-josh-earnest-6102014
11. For an assessment of the situation one year after the rescue, see Vian Dakhil, "The Islamic State Is Raping 8-Year-Olds. And the World Is Doing Nothing," *Politico*, 7 October 2015.

12. White House, Remarks by President Obama and President Ilves of Estonia in Joint Press Conference, 3 September 2014, at https://www.whitehouse.gov/the-press-office/2014/09/03/remarks-president-obama-and-president-ilves-estonia-joint-press-confer-0

13. *Ibid.*

14. *Ibid.*

10. ROLLBACK?

1. Fraser Nelson, "Petraeus: America can't serve as an air force for a Shi'ite militia," *The Spectator*, 18 June 2014, at http://blogs.new.spectator.co.uk/2014/06/petraeus-america-cant-serve-as-an-air-force-for-a-shiite-militia/

2. This quote is drawn from, and portions of the preceding section are adapted from, David Kilcullen, "We can beat Isis. What happens after that is the hard bit," *The Sunday Times*, 17 August 2014.

11. INTERNATIONALE

1. For a paraphrased version of this conversation, published approximately one month later (and less than twenty-four hours before the Martin Place attack) see Kevin Chinnery, "David Kilcullen: how to beat the Islamic extremists," *Australian Financial Review*, 13 December 2014, at http://www.afr.com/lifestyle/arts-and-entertainment/art/david-kilcullenhow-to-beat-the-islamic-extremists-20141212-126c3y

2. The full motto, which appears on Islamic State documents, in media releases and on social media, is *ad-Dawlah al-Khalifya al-Islamiya, baqiya wa tatamaddad fi izin illah*—"the State of the Caliph of Islam, remaining and expanding by the grace of God."

3. Jamelle Wells, "Sydney siege inquest: Lawyer says Man Haron Monis was a pest and not very intelligent," ABC News (Australia), 29 May 2015, at http://www.abc.net.au/news/2015–05–29/lindt-cafe-siege-man-haron-monis-lawyers-give-evidence/6506312

4. Peter Kuitenbrouwer, "'Canada getting a taste of their own medicine': Jihadists sneer at Ottawa shooting on Twitter," *National Post* (Canada), 23 October 2014, at http://news.nationalpost.com/news/canada/canada-getting-a-taste-of-their-own-medicine-jihadists-sneer-at-ottawa-shooting-on-twitter

5. See "Le suspect de Montrouge, Amedy Coulibaly, était bien le tireur de Vincennes," *Le Monde*, 9 January 2015, at http://www.lemonde.fr/societe/article/2015/01/09/fusillade-de-montrouge-suspect-identifie-deux-nouvelles-interpellations_4552503_3224.html#1qPwV5wDUUjywSkj.99

6. David Gauthier-Villars, Asa Fitch and Raja Abdulrahim, "Islamic State Releases Video Calling Grocery Store Gunman Its 'Soldier,' Purports to Show One of the Paris Attackers," *Wall Street Journal*, 11 January 2015, at http://www.wsj.com/articles/video-appears-to-show-paris-kosher-grocery-attack-suspect-coulibaly-swearing-allegiance-to-islamic-state-1420977506

7. Andrew Higgins and Maia de la Baume, "Two Brothers Suspected in Killings Were Known to French Intelligence Services," *New York Times*, 8 January 2015, at http://www.nytimes.com/2015/01/08/world/two-brothers-suspected-in-killings-were-known-to-french-intelligence-services.html?_r=0

8. Angelique Chrisafis, "Charlie Hebdo attackers: born, raised and radicalised in Paris," *The Guardian*, 12 January 2015, at http://www.theguardian.com/world/2015/jan/12/-sp-charlie-hebdo-attackers-kids-france-radicalised-paris

9. For the British government account of the bombings see House of Commons, *Report of the Official Account of the Bombings in London on 7th July 2005*, London: The Stationary Office, 2006, also at https://www.gov.uk/government/uploads/system/uploads/attachment_data/file/228837/1087.pdf

10. For a discussion of the urban siege aspect of the Mumbai attacks see David Kilcullen, *Out of the Mountains: The Coming Age of the Urban Guerrilla*, London/New York: Hurst & Co./Oxford University Press, 2013, p. 52–66.

11. For a good introduction to this concept, with case studies, see Simson L. Garfinkel, "Leaderless Resistance Today," *First Monday*, Vol. 8, No. 3, 3 March 2003, at http://firstmonday.org/ojs/index.php/fm/article/view/1040/961

12. Parts of the preceding section on terrorist adaptation appeared as David Kilcullen, "Democracy in an Age of Evolving, Persistent Terrorism," *The Weekend Australian*, 17 January 2015.

12. WILAYAT

1. See Aaron Y. Zelin, *The Salafi Challenge to Tunisia's Nascent Democracy*, Washington Institute for Near East Policy, 8 December 2011, at http://www.washingtoninstitute.org/policy-analysis/view/the-salafi-challenge-to-tunisias-nascent-democracy

2. See Daveed Gartenstein-Ross, Bridget Moreng & Kathleen Soucy, *Raising the Stakes: Ansar al-Sharia in Tunisia's Shift to Jihad*, The Hague: International Centre for Counter-Terrorism, February 2014.

3. Lin Noueihed, "Radical Islamists urge bigger role for Islam in Tunisia," Reuters, 21 May 2012, at http://in.reuters.com/article/2012/05/21/tunisia-salafis-idINDEE84K03420120521

4. For official reports of the Benghazi attacks see United States House of Representatives, Permanent Select Committee on Intelligence, *Investigative Report on the Attacks on U.S. Facilities in Benghazi, Libya, September 11–12, 2012*, Washington DC: U.S. House of Representatives, 113th Congress, 21 November 2014, at https://intelligence.house.gov/sites/intelligence.house.gov/files/documents/Benghazi%20Report.pdf and United States Department of State, *Report of an Accountability Review Board (ARB) to examine the facts and circumstances surrounding the September 11–12, 2012, killings of four U.S. government personnel, including the U.S. Ambassador to Libya, John Christopher Stevens, in Benghazi, Libya*, at http://www.state.gov/documents/organization/202446.pdf

5. House of Representatives, Permanent Select Committee on Intelligence, *op. cit.*

6. See Hillary Clinton, "In my Office," email to "Diane Reynolds" (Chelsea Clinton) at 11:12pm, 12 September 2012, at http://benghazi.house.gov/sites/republicans.benghazi.house.gov/files/documents/Tab%2050.pdf

7. Abdallah Suleiman Ali, "Global jihadists recognize Islamic State," *al-Monitor*, 3 July 2014, at http://www.al-monitor.com/pulse/security/2014/07/syria-iraq-isis-islamic-Caliphate-global-recognition.html#

8. Jamel Arfaoui, "Tunisia: Ansar Al-Sharia Tunisia Spokesman Backs Isis," *AllAfrica*, 8 July 2014, at http://allafrica.com/stories/201407090299.html

9. Associated Press, "ISIS Claims Responsibility For Tunisia Museum Attack In Audio Message," 19 March 2015, at http://www.huffingtonpost.com/2015/03/19/isis-tunisia-museum-attack_n_6902244.html

10. Chris Stephen, Kareem Shaheen and Mark Tran, "Tunis museum attack: 20 people killed after hostage drama at tourist site," *The Guardian*, 18 March 2015, at http://www.theguardian.com/world/2015/mar/18/eight-people-killed-in-attack-on-tunisia-bardo-museum

11. Lizzie Dearden, "Tunisia attack: Isis-affiliated group sent tweet threatening Western tourists with massacre," *The Independent*, 30 June 2015, at http://www.independent.co.uk/news/world/africa/tunisia-attack-isis-affiliated-group-posted-tweet-threatening-western-tourists-with-massacre-10356183.html

12. Aaron Y. Zelin and Sami David, "ICSR Insight: Between The Islamic State and al-Qaeda in Tunisia," International Centre for the Study of Radicalisation, 11 May 2015, at http://icsr.info/2015/05/icsr-insight-islamic-state-al-qaeda-tunisia/

13. Richard Spencer, "Senior Tunisian jihadist and Osama bin Laden associate 'killed by US strike in Libya'," *The Telegraph*, 3 July 2015, at http://www.telegraph.co.uk/news/worldnews/africaandindianocean/tunisia/11715933/Senior-Tunisian-jihadist-and-Osama-bin-Laden-associate-killed-by-US-strike-in-Libya.html

14. Reuters, "Most Tunisia hotel attack victims were British: Tunisia premier," 27 June 2015, at http://www.reuters.com/article/2015/06/28/us-tunisia-security-idUSKBN0P61F020150628

15. See Berny Sèbe, "Sousse shows the deadly potential of the Isis franchise," *The Guardian*, 28 June 2015, at http://www.theguardian.com/commentisfree/2015/jun/28/sousse-isis-islamist-tunisia

16. Ben Hubbard, "Terrorist Attacks in France, Tunisia and Kuwait Kill Dozens," *The New York Times*, 26 June 2015, at http://www.nytimes.com/2015/06/27/world/middleeast/terror-attacks-france-tunisia-kuwait.html?hp&action=click&pgtype=Homepage&module=a-lede-package-region&region=top-news&WT.nav=top-news

17. Karen Yourish, Derek Watkins and Tom Giratikanon, "Where ISIS Has Directed and Inspired Attacks Around the World," *New York Times*, 20 August 2015, at http://www.nytimes.com/interactive/2015/06/17/world/middleeast/map-isis-attacks-around-the-world.html?_r=0. Note that these data only include ten ISIS *wilayat*, but were published before the creation of the *wilayat* in Russia (Wilayat al-Kavkaz) in September 2015.

13. KHILAFAH

1. Among many examples, see Nick Butler, "New Lines in the Sand: who will win as the borders of the Middle East are redrawn?", *Financial Times*, 2 March 2015, at http://blogs.ft.com/nick-butler/2015/03/02/new-lines-in-the-sand-who-will-win-as-the-borders-of-the-middle-east-are-redrawn/

2. See World Bank, Urban Population (% of total) at http://data.worldbank.org/indicator/SP.URB.TOTL.IN.ZS

3. Kilcullen, 2013, *op. cit.*

4. Bill Roggio, "Analysis: ISIS, allies reviving 'Baghdad belts' battle plan," *Long War Journal*, 14 June 2014, online at http://www.longwarjournal.org/archives/2014/06/analysis_isis_allies.php

5. *Ibid.*

6. David Kilcullen and Nathaniel Rosenblatt, *Mapping the Conflict in Aleppo, Syria*, Washington DC: American Security Project, 2014.

7. Hillary Clinton, *Hard Choices*, New York: Simon and Schuster, 2014, p. 138.

8. Kalyan Kumar, "US Pumping Weapons Into Iraq Ahead Of Mosul Offensive: Retaking Mosul Expected To Cripple ISIS Strength," *International Business Times*, 26 February 2015, at http://www.ibtimes.com.au/us-pumping-weapons-iraq-ahead-mosul-offensive-retaking-mosul-expected-cripple-isis-strength-1425134

9. *Ibid.*

10. See (among many eyewitness accounts) Tim Arango, "Escaping Death in Northern Iraq Video Feature: Surviving an ISIS Massacre," *New York Times*, 3 September 2014.

11. BBC News, "Iraqi forces seek to encircle IS forces in Tikrit," 4 March 2015, at http://www.bbc.com/news/world-middle-east-31727470

12. Ahmed Rasheed and Dominic Evans, "Iraqi forces try to seal off Islamic State around Tikrit," Reuters, 4 March 2015, at http://uk. reuters.com/article/2015/03/04/uk-mideast-crisis-iraq-idUKKBN0 LZ0Z020150304

13. Matt Bradley, "Iraq's battle to take back Tikrit slows," *Wall Street Journal*, 19 March 2015, at http://www.wsj.com/articles/iraqs-battle-to-take-back-tikrit-slows-1426795245

14. BBC News, "Islamic State Conflict: US launches Tikrit Air Strikes," 25 March 2015, at http://www.bbc.com/news/world-middle-east-32035340

15. Al jazeera, "Shia militias pull back as US joins battle for Tikrit," 27 March 2015, at http://www.aljazeera.com/news/middleeast/ 2015/03/shia-militias-step-joins-battle-tikrit-150327010352355.html

16. Arwa Damon, Hamdi Alkhshali and Ralph Ellis, "Mass graves in Tikrit might contain 1,700 bodies," CNN, 8 April 2015, at http:// edition.cnn.com/2015/04/06/middleeast/iraq-mass-graves/index. html

17. Simon Tomlinson and Tom Wyke, "Now it's ISIS's turn to be the victims of atrocities. Iraqi forces 'take revenge' with beheadings, mutilations and brutal executions by throwing people from buildings," *Daily Mail* (UK) at http://www.dailymail.co.uk/news/article-2993300/ Mutilated-beheaded-thrown-deaths-tall-buildings-time-pictures-claim-ISIS-fighters-subjected-wartime-atrocities-allegedly-carried-Iraqi-forces.html#ixzz3oPVxnMQt

18. BBC News, "Iraq Conflict: Saddam's tomb destroyed in Tikrit fighting," 16 March 2015, at http://www.bbc.com/news/world-middle-east-31901568

19. For an excellent analysis of ISIS tactics, written just after the Tikrit attack, see Alexandre Mello and Michael Knights, "The Cult of the Offensive: the Islamic State on Defense," CTC Sentinel, 30 April 2015, at https://www.ctc.usma.edu/posts/the-cult-of-the-offensive-the-islamic-state-on-defense

20. *Ibid.*

21. Terri Moon Cronk, "Strategy to Defeat ISIL is Working, Military Official Says," U.S. Department of Defense News, 15 May 2015, at http://www.defense.gov/News-Article-View/Article/604654

22. Ken Dilanian, "Iraqi Forces Routinely Leave U.S.-Supplied Weapons On Battlefield For Islamic State," *Chicago Tribune*, 25 May, 2015,

http://www.chicagotribune.com/news/nationworld/ct-iraqi-army-islamic-state-20150525-story.html

23. Margaret Coker, "How Islamic State's Win in Ramadi Reveals New Weapons, Tactical Sophistication and Prowess," in *Wall Street Journal*, 25 May 2015, at http://www.wsj.com/articles/islamic-states-gains-reveal-new-prowess-on-battlefield-1432592298

24. *Ibid.*

25. Iraqi military source, via email, 26 May 2015.

26. For more detail see Patrick Martin, Genevieve Casagrande and Jessica Lewis McFate, *ISIS Captures Ramadi*, Institute for the Study of War, 18 May 2015, at http://www.understandingwar.org/sites/default/files/ISIS%20Captures%20Ramadi%20—%20May%202015.pdf

27. Barbara Starr, "Carter: Iraqis showed 'no will to fight' in Ramadi," CNN, 24 May 2015, at http://www.cnn.com/2015/05/24/politics/ashton-carter-isis-ramadi/

28. This sequence of obstacle breaching is common to both NATO and former Soviet doctrine, and dates back to eighteenth-century siege warfare. ISIS's adoption of these tactics may reflect the presence of Syrian- or Iraqi-trained former officers (who would have been schooled in Soviet-style breach tactics) or Western-trained defectors from the post-2003 Iraqi Army, or both. It may also reflect the presence of numerous Chechen fighters within ISIS, some of whom had fought in heavy urban engagements in Grozny against the Russians, and many of whom had previous military service as conscripts in the Russian Federation.

29. The following account of the fall of Palmyra, unless otherwise footnoted, is drawn from reporting (via phone, email or in person) from the author's Syrian contacts in the town and surrounding areas. Where feasible verbatim quotes are used, but names are withheld since the region is ISIS-controlled at the time of writing.

14. TRANSFORMATION

1. CBS News International, "Following the trail of Syria's looted history," 9 September 2015, at http://www.cbsnews.com/news/isis-looted-syrian-ancient-artifacts-black-market-us-and-europe/

2. Ben Hubbard, "Shielding Syrian Antiquities, to a Grisly Death at ISIS' Hands," *New York Times*, 19 August 2015, at http://www.nytimes.com/2015/08/20/world/middleeast/isis-palmyra-syria-antiquities-scholar-beheaded.html?_r=0

3. Kareem Shaheen and Ian Black, "Beheaded Syrian scholar refused to lead Isis to hidden Palmyra antiquities," *The Guardian*, 19 August 2015, at http://www.theguardian.com/world/2015/aug/18/isis-beheads-archaeologist-syria

4. For an example of a purported effort to reconcile, see Syrian Observatory for Human Rights, "Abo Baker al-Baghdadi allows for the people of al-Shaitaat tribe to come back home" (sic), 6 November 2014, at http://www.syriahr.com/en/2014/11/abo-baker-al-baghdadi-allowes-for-the-people-of-al-shaitaat-tribe-to-come-back-home/

5. Reporting from field sources in Palmyra. See also Wissam Abdallah, "Tribal disputes heat up in Syrian desert," *al-Monitor*, 8 July 2015, at http://www.al-monitor.com/pulse/politics/2015/07/syria-desert-tribes-division-oil-geography.html, and Richard Spencer, "Islamic State begins beheading regime fighters in Palmyra," *The Telegraph*, 21 May 2015, at http://www.telegraph.co.uk/news/worldnews/middleeast/syria/11621055/Islamic-State-begins-beheading-regime-fighters-in-Palmyra.html

6. Muhannad Haimour, former U.S. contractor and now Special Advisor to the Governor of Anbar, speaking to *Daily Mail* reporters, 18 May 2015.

7. Reporting by phone from a source in Ramadi, 20 and 21 May 2015.

8. Author's personal observation, Sadr al-Yusufiya and Doura, May–July 2007.

9. Erin Cunningham, "In Ramadi, the Islamic State settles in, fixing roads and restoring electricity," *The Washington Post*, 2 July 2015, at https://www.washingtonpost.com/world/middle_east/in-ramadi-the-islamic-state-settles-in-fixing-roads-and-restoring-electricity/2015/07/01/db32ccec-19e2-11e5-bed8-1093ee58dad0_story.html

10. See Kilcullen, 2013, *op. cit.*, pp. 116–68.

11. Cunningham, *op. cit.*

12. Agence-France Press, "Isis closes Ramadi dam gates, cutting off water to pro-government towns," 2 June 2015, at http://www.theguardian.com/world/2015/jun/03/isis-closes-ramadi-dam-gates-cutting-off-water-to-pro-government-towns

13. International Crisis Group, *Defeating the Iraqi State, One Victory at a Time*, 26 March 2015, at http://www.crisisgroup.org/en/publication-type/media-releases/2015/middle-east-north-africa/statement-defeating-the-iraqi-state-one-victory-at-a-time.aspx

14. Personal observation, and perusal of the list (which remained in the contact's possession), Washington DC, May 2015.

15. Guy Taylor, "Kurdish leader says his people will one day declare independence," *Washington Times*, 6 May 2015, at http://www.washingtontimes.com/news/2015/may/6/massud-barzani-independence-kurds-is-coming/?page=all

16. Conversation with pro-regime peace negotiator, Washington DC, October 2013.

17. Michael Pizzi, "Syria Al-Qaeda leader: Our mission is to defeat

regime, not attack West," Al Jazeera, 28 May 2015, at http://america.aljazeera.com/articles/2015/5/28/syria-al-qaeda-leader-our-mission-is-to-defeat-regime.html

18. President Obama, "Remarks by the President on the Iran Nuclear Deal," 5 August 2015, at https://www.whitehouse.gov/the-press-office/2015/08/05/remarks-president-iran-nuclear-deal

19. Michael Crowley, "Rift in Obama administration over Putin," *Politico*, 13 October 2015, at http://www.politico.com/story/2015/10/syria-obama-putin-russia-discord-214677

20. Hillary Clinton, videotaped remarks, "Hillary Clinton addresses the Iran nuclear deal," Brookings Institution, 9 September 2015, at http://www.brookings.edu/events/2015/09/09-clinton-iran-nuclear-deal

21. Conversations with White House and State Department staffers in Washington D.C., August and September 2015.

22. Michael Doran, "Obama's Secret Iran Strategy," *Mosaic*, 2 February 2015, at http://mosaicmagazine.com/essay/2015/02/obamas-secret-iran-strategy/

23. Jay Solomon and Carol E. Lee, "Obama Wrote Secret Letter to Iran's Khamenei About Fighting Islamic State," *Wall Street Journal*, 6 November 2014, at http://www.wsj.com/articles/obama-wrote-secret-letter-to-irans-khamenei-about-fighting-islamic-state-1415295291; see also Spencer Ackerman and Dan Roberts, "Obama pens secret letter to Iran's Ayatollah Khamenei as nuclear deadline looms," *The Guardian*, 6 November 2014, at http://www.theguardian.com/us-news/2014/nov/06/obama-letter-ayatollah-khamenei-iran-nuclear-talks

24, Jared M. Feldschreiber, "Officials: Iranian General Soleimani Visited Russia in Defiance of Travel Ban," United Press International, 10 August 2015, at http://www.upi.com/Top_News/World-News/2015/08/10/Officials-Iranian-General-Soleimani-visited-Russia-in-defiance-of-travel-ban/5321439232413/

25. Reuters, "Russian, Iranian foreign ministers to discuss nuclear plan, Syria," 15 August 2015, at http://www.reuters.com/article/us-mideast-crisis-russia-iran-idUSKCN0QK0AH20150815#fSwUH69WZ6Q94p3f.97

26. Isabel Kershner, "Iran Deal Denounced by Netanyahu as 'Historic Mistakee'," *The New York Times*, 14 July 2015, at http://www.nytimes.com/2015/07/15/world/middleeast/iran-nuclear-deal-israel.html?_r=0

27. Elizabeth Whitman, "Iran Deal 2015: Israel and Saudi Arabia offer contrasting responses," *International Business Times*, 16 July 2015, at http://www.ibtimes.com/iran-deal-2015-israel-saudi-arabia-offer-contrasting-responses-2012393

28. Adam Taylor, "Saudi Prince Bandar: The U.S. nuclear pact with North Korea failed. The Iran deal is worse," *Washington Post*, 16 July 2015 at https://www.washingtonpost.com/news/worldviews/wp/2015/07/16/saudi-prince-bandar-says-iran-nuke-deal-worse-than-failed-north-korea-deal/; for the original Arabic article, see, Bandar bin Sultan, "Déjà vu Again," *Elaph* at http://elaphjournal.com/Web/News/2015/7/1024259.html

29. Ismael el-Kholy, "Cairo, Riyadh pledge cooperation as each weighs nuclear deal," *al-Monitor*, 5 August 2015, at http://www.al-monitor.com/pulse/originals/2015/08/egypt-saudi-arabia-iran-deal-stance-foreign-relations.html#ixzz3oqGOq7ag

30. Simeon Kerr, "Gulf states publicly praise, privately fear Iran nuclear deal," *Financial Times*, 15 July 2015, at http://www.ft.com/intl/cms/s/0/c740cae0–2644–11e5-bd83–71cb60e8f08c.html#axzz3oq2Kq8HF

15. SPILLOVER

1. European Commission, *Asylum in the European Union*, September 2015, at http://ec.europa.eu/dgs/home-affairs/e-library/docs/infographics/asylum/infographic_asylum_en.pdf

2. BBC News, "Migrant 'chaos' on Greek islands—UN refugee agency," 7 August 2015, at http://www.bbc.com/news/world-europe-33818193

3. BBC News, "Europe Migrant Crisis: Germany will cope with surge," 19 August 2015, at http://www.bbc.com/news/world-europe-33992563

4. NATO, International Security Assistance Force—Facts and Figures, 1 December 2014, at http://www.nato.int/nato_static_fl2014/assets/pdf/pdf_2014_12/20141201_141201-ISAF-Placemat-final.pdf

5. *Ibid.* The main contingents (in order of decreasing size) were drawn from the United States, Italy, Germany, Georgia, Jordan, UK, Turkey, Bulgaria, Poland, Romania, Spain, Australia, the Czech Republic, Denmark, the Former Yugoslavian Republic of Macedonia, and smaller detachments from another twenty-seven countries.

6. See Anthony H. Cordesman, *Afghan Forces on the Edge of Transition–IV: Progress in Afghan Force Development*, Washington DC: Center for Strategic and International Studies, 17 November 2014, pp. 61, 131, at http://csis.org/files/publication/141118_IV_Security_Transition_in_Afghanistan_17_NOV_2014_0.pdf

7. Bill Roggio and Caleb Weiss, "Taliban controls or contests scores of districts in Afghanistan," *Long War Journal*, 5 October 2015, at http://www.longwarjournal.org/archives/2015/10/taliban-controls-or-contests-scores-of-districts-in-afghanistan.php

8. Mujib Mashal, Joseph Goldstein and Jawad Sukhanyar, "Afghans Form

Militias and Call on Warlords to Battle Taliban," *New York Times*, 24 May 2015, at http://www.nytimes.com/2015/05/25/world/asia/as-taliban-advance-afghanistan-reluctantly-recruits-militias.html

9. This account of the battle draws on media reports, as well as research by the Afghanistan Analysts network, and the author's discussions (by phone or email) with contacts in Pakistan and Afghanistan in October 2015. Unless otherwise noted, identity of field sources is withheld for safety reasons.

10. Personal observation and discussions with French officers during the author's deployments with French forces in Kapisa, December 2009, September 2010 and June 2011.

11. Jane's Terrorism and Insurgency Monitor, *JTIC Brief: Assessing the Taliban's capture of Kunduz and its ongoing implications*, IHS Global, October 2015, pp. 2–3.

12. *Ibid.*, p. 4.

13. *Ibid.*

14. Civilian source familiar with conditions in Kunduz, 21 October 2015 (via email).

15. Bethany Matta, "The failed pilot test: Kunduz' local government crisis," Afghanistan Analysts' Network, 5 June 2015, at https://www.afghanistan-analysts.org/the-failed-pilot-test-kunduz-local-governance-crisis/

16. Jane's, op. cit., p. 5

17. Joseph Goldstein and Mujib Mashal, "Taliban Fighters Capture Kunduz City as Afghan Forces Retreat," *New York Times*, 28 September 2015, at http://www.nytimes.com/2015/09/29/world/asia/taliban-fighters-enter-city-of-kunduz-in-northern-afghanistan.html; see also Sune Engel Rasmussen, "Taliban capture key Afghan provincial capital Kunduz," *The Guardian*, 28 September 2015, at http://www.theguardian.com/world/2015/sep/28/taliban-attempt-to-invade-key-afghan-city-kunduz

18. Outlook Afghanistan, "Kunduz Governor Omar Safi Flees to UK," 30 September 2015, at http://outlookafghanistan.net/national_detail.php?post_id=13188#sthash.iaaL0zPi.dpuf

19. BBC News, "Taliban Kunduz attack: Afghan forces claim control of city," 1 October 2015, at http://www.bbc.com/news/world-asia-34409292

20. Jane's, *op. cit.*, p. 4.

21. MSF, "Afghanistan: MSF Opens Surgical Hospital in Kunduz," 17 October 2011, at http://www.doctorswithoutborders.org/news-stories/press-release/afghanistan-msf-opens-surgical-hospital-kunduz

22. Deutsche Welle, "US-Angriff auf Klinik in Kundus ein Kriegsverbrechen?", 3 October 2015, at http://www.dw.com/de/us-angriff-auf-klinik-in-kundus-ein-kriegsverbrechen/a-18759857

23. Kate Clark, "MSF Investigation: US Hospital Strike Looking More Like a War Crime," Afghanistan Analysts' Network, 10 November 2015, at https://www.afghanistan-analysts.org/msf-investigation-us-hospital-strike-looking-more-like-a-war-crime/

24. Thomas Gibbons-Neff, "U.S. military struggles to explain how it wound up bombing Doctors Without Borders hospital," *Washington Post*, 5 October 2015, at https://www.washingtonpost.com/news/checkpoint/wp/2015/10/05/afghan-forces-requested-airstrike-that-hit-hospital-in-kunduz/

25. Mirwais Harooni and Andrew Macaskill, "Medical charity MSF demands independent probe into strike on Afghan hospital," Reuters, 5 October 2015, at http://www.reuters.com/article/2015/10/05/us-afghanistan-attack-idUSKCN0RW0HC20151005

26. Roberta Rampton and Stephanie Nebehay, "Obama apologizes for Kunduz attack, MSF demands independent probe," Reuters, 7 October 2015 at http://www.reuters.com/article/2015/10/07/us-afghanistan-attack-msf-idUSKCN0S10SX20151007

27. Abū Jarīr ash-Shamālī, "Al-Qa'idah Of Waziristan: A Testimony From Within," *Dabiq*, Issue 6, Rabi al 'Awwal 1436 (December 2014) pp. 40–55, at http://media.clarionproject.org/files/islamic-state/isis-isil-islamic-state-magazine-issue-6-al-qaeda-of-waziristan.pdf

28. Bill Roggio, "US drone strike kills mufti of Islamic State Khorasan Province," *Long War Journal*, 15 October 2015, at http://www.longwar-journal.org/archives/2015/10/us-drone-strike-kills-mufti-of-islamic-state-khorasan-province.php

16. MASKIROVKA

1. For President Putin's speech as prepared and translated by the United Nations, see http://www.scribd.com/doc/283010015/Vladimir-Putins-2015-Address-to-the-United-Nations. For a video of the speech as delivered, with English simultaneous translation, see https://www.youtube.com/watch?v=q13yzl6k6w0

2. *Ibid.*

3. Oryx blog, "From the Ukraine to Syria, Russian Orlan-10 and Eleron-3SV drones in Syria's skies," 21 July 2015, at http://spioenkop.blogspot.com/2015/07/from-ukraine-to-syria-russian-orlan-10.html

4. Oryx blog, "From Russia with Love: Syria's BTR-82As," 24 August 2015, at http://spioenkop.blogspot.com/2015/08/from-russia-with-love-syrias-btr-82as.html

5. Mike Eckel, "Evidence Suggests Key Russian Brigade In Crimea Seizure Deploying To Syria," Radio Free Europe/Radio Liberty, 11 September 2015, at http://www.rferl.org/content/russian-troops-syria-brigade-crimea-putin-assad-islamic-state/27240966.html

6. Oryx blog, 24 August 2015, *op cit.*

7. Lucas Tomlinson and Jennifer Griffin, "Russia, Syria and Iran Set Up Military Coordination Cell in Baghdad," 25 September 2015, at http://www.military.com/daily-news/2015/09/25/russia-syria-and-iran-set-up-military-coordination-cell-baghdad.html

8. RT News, "Russia, Iran, Iraq & Syria setting up 'joint information center' to coordinate anti-ISIS operations," 26 September 2015, at https://www.rt.com/news/316592-russia-syria-islamic-state/

9. For a detailed analysis of the Russian deployment see Hugo Spaulding et al., *Russian Deployment to Syria: Putin's Middle East Game Changer*, Warning Intelligence Note, Washington DC: Institute for the Study of War, 17 September 2015, at http://understandingwar.org/sites/default/files/Russian%20Deployment%20to%20Syria%2017%20September%202015%20%281%29.pdf

10. Andrew Buncombe, "Syria bombing: Russian three star general warned US officials 'we request your people leave'," *The Independent*, 30 September 2015, at http://www.independent.co.uk/news/world/middle-east/syria-bombing-russian-three-star-general-warned-us-officials-we-request-your-people-leave-a6674166.html

11. BBC News, "Syria crisis: Russian air strikes against Assad enemies," 30 September 2015, at http://www.bbc.com/news/world-middle-east-34399164

12. Sputnik News, "Russian Aircraft in Syria Carry Out 88 Sorties in 24 Hours," 13 October 2015, at http://sputniknews.com/middleeast/20151013/1028456707/russia-airstrikes-syria.html#ixzz3p4b519G8

13. Phillip Smyth, "Iran-backed Iraqi militias are pouring into Syria," 2 October 2015, at http://uk.businessinsider.com/iran-backed-iraqi-militias-are-pouring-into-syria-2015-10?r=US&IR=T

14. Leith Fadel, "Russian Marines and Iranian Revolutionary Guardsmen Build a Protectorate in Western Syria," *Al Masdar*, 26 September 2015, at http://www.almasdarnews.com/article/russian-marines-and-iranian-revolutionary-guardsmen-build-a-protectorate-in-western-syria/

15. Luis Martinez, "Russian troops fire artillery and rockets in Syria," ABC News (US), 7 October 2015, at http://abcnews.go.com/Politics/russian-troops-fire-artillery-rockets-syria/story?id=34322668

16. Eliot Higgins, "Mounting Evidence of Russian Cluster Bomb Use in Syria," 6 October 2015, at https://www.bellingcat.com/news/mena/2015/10/06/mounting-evidence-of-russian-cluster-bomb-use-in-syria/

17. Loveday Morris, "Iraqi prime minister says he would 'welcome' Russian airstrikes in Iraq," *The Washington Post*, 1 October 2015, at https://www.washingtonpost.com/world/iraqi-prime-minister-says-he-would-welcome-russian-airstrikes/2015/10/01/4177cf3c-684b-11e5-8325-a42b5a459b1e_story.html

18. For an early analysis of the offensive see Chris Kozak, "Joint Syrian-Iranian-Russian Offensive Achieves Only Limited Gains," Institute for the Study of War, 14 October 2015, at http://www.understandingwar.org/backgrounder/joint-syrian-iranian-russian-offensive-achieves-only-limited-initial-gains

19. Alistair Bell and Tom Perry, "Obama warns Russia's Putin of 'quagmire' in Syria," Reuters, 3 October 2015, at http://www.reuters.com/article/2015/10/03/us-mideast-crisis-syria-airstrikes-idUSKCN0RW0W220151003

20. Club Orlov, "Putin to Western elites: Play-time is Over," 29 October 2014, at http://cluborlov.blogspot.com/2014/10/putin-to-western-elites-play-time-is.html

21. See CBS News, "All eyes on Putin," *60 Minutes*, 27 September 2015, at http://www.cbsnews.com/news/vladimir-putin-russian-president-60-minutes-charlie-rose/ for a recent example.

22. Russian Federation, "Meeting of the Valdai International Discussion Club—Remarks of President Vladimir V. Putin," Sochi, Russia, 24 October 2014, at http://en.kremlin.ru/events/president/news/46860

23. *Ibid.*

24. Dmitri Trenin, *Russia's Breakout From the Post-Cold War System: The Drivers Of Putin's Course*, Moscow: Carnegie Russia Center, 2014, pp. 7–8, at http://carnegieendowment.org/files/CP_Trenin_Putin2014_web_Eng.pdf

25. *Ibid.*, p. 2.

17. AGE OF CONFLICT

1. James Traub, "America Has Abdicated Its Guiding Role in the Middle East to a Sectarian Arab Military Force. What Could Go Wrong?," *Foreign Policy*, 10 April 2015.

2. Sara Murray and Maeve Reston, "Jeb Bush again changes Iraq answer," CNN News, 15 May 2015, at http://www.cnn.com/2015/05/13/politics/jeb-bush-iraq-2016/

3. Quoted in Matthew Cella and Paul D. Shinkman, "The Great Iraq Mistake," *U.S. News and World Report*, 26 May 2015, at http://www.usnews.com/news/the-report/articles/2015/05/26/gop-agrees-bush-was-wrong-to-invade-iraq-now-what

4. See Maajid Nawaz, *Radical: My Journey Out of Islamic Extremism*, London: W.H. Allen, 2013 and Akbar Ahmed, *Journey Into Islam: The Crisis of Globalization*, Washington DC: Brookings Institution Press, 2008. See also Akbar Ahmed, *The Thistle and The Drone: How America's War on Terror*

Became a Global War on Tribal Islam, Washington DC: Brookings Institution Press, 2013.

5. For a comprehensive (pre-ISIS) discussion of this issue, see Thomas Hegghammer, "The Rise of Muslim Foreign Fighters: Islam and the Globalization of Jihad" in *International Security*, Vol. 35, No. 3 (Winter 2010–11), pp. 53–94.

6. Stephen Graham, "Foucault's Boomerang—The New Military Urbanism," *Development Dialogue*, no. 58, April 2012, pp. 37–8.

7. For an excellent study of this phenomenon in its U.S. context, see Radley Balko, *Rise of the Warrior Cop: The Militarization of America's Police Forces*, New York: Public Affairs, 2013.

8. See Michael Miklaucic and Jacqueline Brewer (eds), *Convergence: Illicit Networks and National Security in the Age of Globalization*, Washington DC: National Defense University Press, 2013, for a range of perspectives on this phenomenon.

9. For the sources of quotes from President Bush, see "Taking the Fight to the Terrorists," *Sourcewatch*, www.sourcewatch.org/index.php?title= Taking_the_fight_to_the_terrorists

10. For commentary on this from a progressive (i.e. left-wing) perspective, see Will Marshall, "Obama Goes Back to War," Progressive Policy Institute, online, 10 September 2014, www.progressivepolicy.org/ issues/military/obama-goes-back-war/

11. For a recent assessment of the situation in Colombia, see Dickie Davis, David Kilcullen, Greg Mills and David Spencer, *op. cit.*

12. See Lant Pritchett, Michael Woolcock and Matt Andrews, *Capability Traps? The Mechanisms of Persistent Implementation Failure*, Harvard: Kennedy School of Government, May 2010, conference paper, at http:// www.ksg.harvard.edu/fs/lpritch/Governance/capability_traps(june 2010).pdf

13. Audrey Cronin, "ISIS Is Not a Terrorist Group," Foreign Affairs, March/April 2015.

EPILOGUE

1. Some portions of this section appeared as David Kilcullen, "Paris Attacks: Terrorism in for long campaign of urban warfare," *The Australian*, 21 November 2015, at http://www.theaustralian.com.au/news/ inquirer/paris-attacks-terrorism-in-for-long-campaign-of-urban-warfare/story-e6frg6z6-1227617543969

2. The French carrier had been scheduled to replace a U.S. aircraft carrier in the Eastern Mediterranean since earlier in 2015, but the Paris attacks prompted a more rapid turnover and a higher rate of strike sorties when *Charles de Gaulle* reached the flight line in mid-November.

3. Joshua Keating, "Turkey downing that Russian Fighter Jet is Terrible News for the War on ISIS," Slate, 24 November 2015, at http://www.slate.com/blogs/the_slatest/2015/11/24/fighter_jet_is_terrible_news_for_the_war_on.html

4. For a detailed discussion of the Mumbai attacks see Kilcullen, 2013, *op. cit.*, pp. 58–73.

5. *Ibid.*

6. Patrick J. McDonnell and Alexandra Zavis, "Slain Paris plotter's Europe ties facilitated travel from Syria," *Los Angeles Times*, 19 November 2015, at http://www.latimes.com/world/europe/la-fg-paris-attacks-master-mind-20151119-story.html

7. Dexter Filkins, *The Forever War*, New York: Knopf Doubleday Publishing Group, Kindle Edition, pp. 33–4.

INDEX

Abaaoud, Abdelhamid, 223, 224
al-Abadi, Haider, 107–8, 136–8,
    140–1, 156, 191, 216
Abbas, Yasir, 87–8, 90, 108
Abbott, Anthony John 'Tony', 111
Abbottabad, Pakistan, 53, 56
Abdeslam, Saleh, 221
Abdilal, Sadiq Rasheed, 92
Abdullah Abdullah, 171, 172, 177
Abdulmutallab, Umar Farouk, 55,
    116, 118, 122
Abizaid, John, 14
Abu Abed, 137
Abu Alaa al-Afri, 142
Abu Anas al-Libi, 64, 211
Abu Ayyub al-Masri, 73
Abu Bakr al-Baghdadi, 2, 3, 72–8,
    85, 99, 108, 109, 110, 112, 115,
    116, 136, 142, 143, 151, 152,
    159, 182, 200, 205, 209
Abu Deraa, 33
Abu Dhabi, United Arab Emir-
    ates, 1, 111
Abu Ghraib prison, Baghdad, 78,
    137
Abu Jarir ash-Shamali, 182
Abu Muhammad al-Adnani, 131,
    182
Abu Muhammad al-Jolani, 76–7,
    81, 95, 99, 158–9

Abu Musab al-Zarqawi, 21–2, 25,
    29, 31–2, 40, 73, 103, 134–5,
    224
Abu Omar al-Baghdadi, 73
Abu Suleiman, 135
Abu Walid, 152
Abyan, Yemen, 55, 127
accidental guerrillas, 21
Active Containment, 209, 218
al-Adel, Saif, 58
Aden, Yemen, 55, 127, 212
Adhamiyah, Baghdad, 31
al-Adnani, Abu Muhammad, 131,
    182
Afghan National Air Force, 173
Afghan National Security Forces
    (ANSF), 170–9, 217
Afghan Services Bureau, 60
Afghanistan, ix, x, 3, 4, 12, 14,
    16, 18–21, 23, 24, 26, 27, 42,
    48, 49, 55, 57, 60, 70, 77, 95,
    96, 101, 102–4, 109, 112, 115,
    118, 125, 127, 132, 151, 167,
    169, 170–83, 193, 197, 199,
    200, 203, 205, 206–7, 215, 217,
    227–8, 229, 230
    1979–89 Soviet-Afghan War, 21,
        60, 179
    1988 mujahideen capture Kun-
        duz, 179

INDEX

1999 *at-Tawhid wa'l-Jihad* establish training camp in Herat, 21

2001–14 US-led War, ix, x, 3, 4, 14, 16, 18–19, 20–1, 23, 26, 27, 42, 48, 49, 55, 57, 95, 96, 101, 102–4, 112, 115, 125, 167, 193, 199, 200, 203, 206–7, 215, 230–1

2001 Abu Musab al-Zarqawi flees to Iran, 21, 22, 103; Bonn Conference, 17; Battle of Tora Bora, 16

2003 Quetta Shura launch insurgency, 23

2004 renewed Taliban insurgency, 23

2008 French troops take control of Kapisa, 175

2010 ISAF Surge begins; Lisbon NATO Summit, 173

2011 date set for withdrawal of NATO troops, 55, 95; Médecins Sans Frontières (MSF) establish hospital in Kunduz, 180

2013 Taliban launch offensives across country, 171; death of Mullah Omar, 182

2014 arrival of ISIS representatives, 181–2; Ashraf Ghani wins Presidential election, 171; USS *George H.W. Bush* and Carrier Strike Group Two redeployed to Iraq, 96, 173; withdrawal of NATO combat mission, 55, 95, 170, 175, 197

2015 Operation Resolute Support begins, 170, 172, 207; establishment of IS *wilayat*, 127, 181–3, 217; death of Mullah Omar announced, 182–3, 216; Taliban launch

offensives across country; capture Kunduz, 174–81, 197, 200, 216, 217; IS attacks in Nangarhar, 151, 181; US bombing of MSF hospital in Kunduz, 180–1, 217

al-Afri, Abu Alaa, 142

aggregation, 8–11, 39, 54, 58, 118, 127

Ahmadinejad, Mahmoud, 68

Ahrar al-Sham, 77, 147

air campaigns, 101–3, 133, 138, 155

Air Force Intelligence Directorate (Syria), 69, 81, 148

air-to-surface missiles, 54

airport security, 118–19, 124

AK-47s, 131, 221, 223

AKSU-74 carbines, 53

Alawites, 75, 158, 159

Albu Fahd, 156

Albu Faraj, 143

Albu Mahal, 41

Albu Risha, 137

alcohol, 152

Alec Station, 54

Aleppo, Syria, 81, 136, 143, 159, 160, 164, 190–1

Algeria, 58, 59, 61, 63, 115, 116, 127

Aliabad, Afghanistan, 177

Allawi, Ayad, 108

ambushes, 31, 92, 122, 135, 141, 179, 206

al-Ameri, Hadi, 30, 71, 137, 140

American University, Cairo, 24

Ameriya, Baghdad, 73, 137

Amerli, Iraq, 96, 104, 108

Amman, Jordan, 21

amputations, 98, 153

Anbar Awakening, 40–1, 46–7, 50, 67, 74, 76, 94, 104, 137, 152, 153

INDEX

Anbar Operations Command
(AOC), 142–3, 153
Anbar province, Iraq, 13, 30, 72,
78, 83, 84, 137, 142, 145, 156
Andrews, Matt, 210
Ansar al-Islam, 29
Ansar al-Sharia (AS), 62, 65,
128–30, 131, 200
anti-aircraft systems, 147, 161
anti-armor missiles, 147, 177
anti-tank teams, 141
antiquities, 152
Antonov An-124 cargo aircraft,
187
apostasy, 34, 59–60, 207
Arab Spring (2010–11), ix, 2, 51,
58, 61–5, 67, 68, 69, 75, 83,
128, 186, 228
al-'Arak gas field, Syria, 146
Arar, Maher, 9
Arctic, 195, 196
armored vehicles, 85, 94, 105,
141, 143, 206
armoured personnel carriers
(APCs), 187
Army of Conquest, 159
Army War College (US), 19
artillery, 85, 94, 137, 139, 142,
145, 187
al-Asaad, Khaled, 152
al-Asad airbase, Iraq, 145
al-Askari shrine, Samarra, 29
al-Assad, Asma, 76
al-Assad, Bashar, xiii, 2, 3, 10, 62,
63, 67, 68, 69, 70, 71, 75, 76,
77, 79, 80, 81, 108–9, 146, 147,
148, 149, 152, 158, 159, 161,
162, 163, 164, 168, 189, 191,
196, 213, 214, 217, 220
al-Assad, Hafez, 60
al-Assad, Rifaat, 146
assassinations, 29, 32, 60, 74, 78,
83, 88, 91, 130, 175, 195

assault rifles, 114, 115, 131, 221,
223
asylum-seekers, 3, 167–9, 198,
222, 225, 228
atomized threat, 111, 113, 124,
130, 227
Australia, 2, 7, 10, 11, 12, 22, 23,
36, 42, 75, 96, 97, 105, 111–13,
117, 121, 145, 169, 174, 200,
201, 204, 225–6
    1999 intervention in East Timor,
    36
    2002 death of citizens in Bali
    bombings, 7, 8, 202
    2003 resignation of Andrew
    Wilkie, 10
    2004 publication of *Transnational
    Terrorism: The Threat to Australia*,
    7; David Kilcullen joins US
    Quadrennial Defense Review
    team, 11
    2007 David Kilcullen appointed
    Counterinsurgency Advisor to
    US Army, 36; David Kilcullen
    posted to Afghanistan, 42
    2008 withdrawal of troops from
    Iraq, 75
    2014 intervention against ISIS
    in Iraq, 96; advisers begin
    training Iraqi Army, 134;
    humanitarian aid supplied
    to Yazidis in Sinjar, 97, 98;
    Sydney hostage crisis, 111–13,
    121, 226
    2015 intention to accept 20,000
    refugees announced, 169; Par-
    ramatta shooting, 226
Australian Financial Review, 111
Australian Security Intelligence
Organisation, 112
Austria, 160, 168
authoritarianism, 21, 23, 24, 26,
42, 49, 50, 60, 62, 109

INDEX

al-Awadi, Hussein, 93
Awakening, 40–1, 46–7, 50, 67, 74, 76, 94, 104, 137, 152, 153
al-Awja, Iraq, 141
al-Awlaki, Anwar, 56, 116, 122
Axis of Evil, 9, 10, 26
Azzan mountains, Syria, 190

B-52 Stratofortresses, 102
Ba'ath Party of Iraq, 13, 22, 27, 28, 47, 50, 73, 74, 83, 94, 98, 139, 205
al-Bab, Syria, 164
Badakhshan, Afghanistan, 174
Badr Organisation, 25, 30, 32, 71, 108, 137
Baghdad International Airport, 16, 37, 96
Baghdad, Iraq, 3, 14, 15–16, 18, 22, 25, 27, 29, 30, 31, 33, 37–9, 73, 74, 84, 85, 88, 89, 95, 105 134–5, 137, 144, 154, 187, 201
al-Baghdadi, Abu Bakr, 2, 3, 72–8, 85, 99, 108, 109, 110, 112, 115, 116, 136, 142, 143, 151, 152, 159, 182, 200, 205, 209
al-Baghdadi, Abu Omar, 73
Baghlan, Afghanistan, 174, 179
Bagram, Afghanistan, 102, 172
Bahrain, 64, 98
Bali bombings (2002), 7, 8, 202
ballistic missiles, 146
Baltic States, 81, 195, 196
Baluch people, 27
banlieues, 205, 225
baqiya wa tatamaddad (remaining and expanding), 112
Baqubah, Iraq, 35, 137
Bardo Museum attack (2015), 130
Barqah, Libya, 127
barrel bombs, 79, 170, 189
Baryal, Qari, 175, 176, 178
Barzani, Masoud, 157

Basel al-Assad airport, Jableh, 187
Basra, Iraq, 45–6, 91, 92, 137
Bataclan concert hall, Paris, 219, 221, 228
al-Battar Military Camp, 58
battle discipline, 221
bayat (allegiance), 22, 130, 159, 182, 209
Bayji, Iraq, 91, 94, 96, 139, 142, 155
Beazley, Kim, 36
beheadings, 98, 152, 153, 168
Beirut, Lebanon, 26, 117, 215
Belgium, 117, 220, 221, 223, 224, 225
Belkacem, Smain Aït Ali, 116
Belmokhtar, Mokhtar, 131
belts, 15, 29, 39, 74, 78
belts strategy, 134–6, 143
Ben Ali, Zine el Abidine, 68, 128
Ben Hassine, Seifallah, 128–9, 131
Benghazi, Libya, ix, 63, 72, 129–30
Beyond Good and Evil (Nietzsche), v
BFM-TV, 115
Biden, Joseph, 42, 71
big data, 51, 205
Bill of Rights, 208–9
bin Laden, Osama, ix, 4, 8, 16–17, 22, 33, 51, 53–5, 56, 57, 60–2, 74, 118, 123, 129, 228
bin Sultan, Bandar, 162
biological weapons, 79
biometrics, 205, 208
Bissonnette, Matt, 53
Black Friday, 131, 151
Black Sea, 187
Black September, 117
Blackhawk helicopters, 39
Blood Year, 198
BM-30 multiple-launch rocket systems, 190
BMW, 1, 32, 93

INDEX

Bodrum, Turkey, 169
body armor, 206
bomb-making, 122, 206, 222
Bonn Conference (2001), 17
boomerang effects, 205
border fences, 169
Bosnia, 224
Bosporus Strait, 187
Boston Marathon bombing (2013), 122
Boulahcen, Hasna Aït, 224
Boumeddiene, Hayat, 115, 116
Brazil, 206
Breaking the Walls campaign, 78
Bremer, Lewis Paul 'Jerry', 13, 15, 43, 47
BRICS, 193
bridgeheads-in-depth, 128
Brisard, Jean-Charles, 224
Browning 9mm automatic pistols, 221
Brussels, Belgium, 223, 225
BTR-82A armored personnel carriers, 187
bulldozers, 143
Buncombe, Andrew, 30
Bush, George Herbert Walker, 17
Bush, George Walker, ix, x, 5, 9, 10, 16, 18, 24, 26, 35–6, 39–40, 42, 43, 46, 47, 49, 53, 80, 101, 161, 186, 193, 195, 199–200, 206–7, 219, 230
Bush, John Ellis 'Jeb', 199
Buttes Chaumont network, 116, 123, 223

C-130 Hercules, 37, 180
Cairo, Egypt, 24, 70
Caliphate, 2, 3, 33, 35, 59, 85, 98, 99, 108, 112, 115, 116, 124, 127–8, 130, 132, 134, 136, 144, 151, 181, 200–1, 209, 224
Camp Bucca, Iraq, 73–4, 76

Camp Speicher, Iraq, 140, 141
Camp Victory, Iraq, 16
Campaign Support Plan, 12
Canada, 7, 9, 12, 96, 105, 113–14, 117, 121, 134, 169, 226
Canal Hotel, Baghdad, 22
Canberra, Australia, 36
capitalism, 59, 193
car bombs, 31, 88, 118, 143, 144
Carnegie Moscow Center, 193
Carrier Strike Group Two, 96, 173
Carter, Ashton, 140, 141, 144, 156
Casey, George, 16
Caspian Sea, 188
Caucasus, 3, 8, 72, 127, 187, 188, 191, 205
CBS (Columbia Broadcasting System), 72
Center for Strategic and International Studies (CSIS), 19, 84
Central America, 206
Central Command (US), 11, 14, 16
Chalabi, Ahmad, 17, 20, 27, 83
change management, 37
Chardara, Afghanistan, 177
Charles de Gaulle, 219
Charlie Hebdo, 114–17, 121, 122, 123, 219, 220, 222, 223, 225
Chasseurs Alpins, 175
Chechnya, 8, 72, 187, 188, 205
checkpoints, 153
chemical weapons, 10, 79–81, 158, 191–2
Cheney, Richard Bruce 'Dick', 17, 19, 21, 35, 40
Cheng, Curtis, 226
China, 57, 160, 193
Chinnery, Kevin, 111
Chivers, Christopher John, 91, 92
Churchill, Winston, 16, 192
CIA (Central Intelligence Agency),

xiii, 8, 11, 15, 17, 19, 21, 54, 63, 103, 105, 124, 129
cigarettes, 152
Circassians, 191
Cirillo, Nathan, 113
civil disobedience, 61
clean-skins, 204
Clemenceau, Georges, 231
Clinton, Hillary Rodham, 42, 61, 71–2, 95, 96, 129, 136, 160, 186, 194
Clinton, William Jefferson 'Bill', 17, 162
CNN (Cable News Network), 219, 227
Coca-Cola, 33
Cockburn, Patrick, 30
Cohen, Eliot, 14
Coker, Margaret, 143
Cold War, 2, 102, 185, 192, 194, 197, 208, 210, 212, 213, 214
Colombia, 87, 206, 210
colonialism, 59, 109
columns, 84–5, 89, 92, 94, 95, 102, 138, 139, 147, 177, 178
Combat Search And Rescue, 105
combined arms assaults, 94
Combined Arms, 102, 144
Commonwealth, 210
communism, 59
Competition, 213
Compliance, 212
conflict entrepreneurs, 28, 33, 69
Congo, 167
Congress (US), 41, 42, 79, 103, 157, 200
CONPLAN 7500, 12
Contest strategy, 12
control by interdiction, 136
converts, 201
Cooperation, 213–14, 220
COP21 climate talks, 222
Copenhagen, Denmark, 12, 117, 121, 130, 224

Cordesman, Anthony, 83
corruption, 46, 50, 57, 90, 108, 137, 200
Coulibaly, Amedy, 115–17, 121
Counter-ISIL Coalition, 98, 105, 130, 189
counterinsurgency (COIN), x, 12, 14, 19, 35, 37, 41, 42, 47–8, 51, 145, 206, 214, 215, 230
counterterrorism, x, 4, 7, 11, 12, 14, 15, 22–4, 49, 55, 95, 119–20, 172, 198, 201–9, 214
Couture-Rouleau, Martin 114
crime, 21, 26, 28, 112–14, 116, 117, 134, 154, 168, 202, 206
Crimea, 2, 81, 186, 187, 195, 196, 220
Croatia, 168
Crocker, Ryan, 40
Cronin, Audrey Kurth, 23, 214, 216, 217
crucifixions, 3, 98, 153, 228
Crumpton, Hank, 14, 24
crypto radios, 157
cyber-security/warfare, 119, 195
Cyprus, 157
Cyrenaica, Libya, 63, 64

D'awa Party, 49, 107
da'wah (issuing an invitation), 128
Dabiq, 122, 182
Daghestan, 72, 191
Damascus, Syria, 2, 71, 80, 146, 148, 158, 159, 160, 187
dams, 94, 96
Daneshi, Hamdullah, 177
Darfur, 167
Dasht-e Archi, Kunduz, 177
ad-Dawlah al-'Iraq al-Islamiyah, 32
death squads, 30, 31, 32, 38, 67, 138
deep web, 124
Defense Intelligence Agency, 17

INDEX

La Defense, Paris, 224

Deir ez-Zor, Syria, 82, 146, 147, 152, 159, 160

Deliberate Obstacle Breach, 145

democracy, 24, 42, 61, 62, 64, 65, 69, 104, 128, 171, 185, 193, 194, 199, 201, 203, 206, 226, 231

Democratic Party (US), 5, 194

Dempsey, Martin, 103

Denmark, 12, 117, 121, 220, 223, 224

Department of Homeland Security (US), 11, 206

Deraa, Syria, 147, 159, 191

Desert One raid (1980), 26

destabilization, 2, 9, 27–9, 94, 108, 191, 203, 211

Disaggregation, 9–12, 15, 23, 46, 51, 54, 56, 93, 113, 127, 130, 201, 202, 218, 227, 228

disengagement, 5, 201, 207, 209, 210

displaced persons, 3, 164, 168, 170, 198

district-hardening, 38

diversionary assaults, 130

Diyala, Iraq, 74, 78

Diyarbakır, Turkey, 165

Doran, Michael, 161

Dostum, Rashid, 102–3

doublethink, 10

al-Douri, Izzat Ibrahim, 28, 73, 75, 84, 94, 142

drones, ix, 5, 23, 49, 54, 56, 79, 98, 124, 172, 173, 186, 187, 199, 206, 211

Dulaim tribal confederation, 84

Earnest, Josh, 95, 109

East African Embassy bombings (1998), 58, 64

East Timor, 36

Eastern Europe, 157

economic development, 51

economy of force, 173

education, 60, 167

EFPs (explosively-formed projectiles), 29

Egypt, 3, 9, 24, 56, 58, 59, 60–3, 64, 68, 70, 127, 128, 129, 162, 198, 199, 211, 212, 213, 215

1967 Six Day War, 59

1973 Yom Kippur War, 59

1978 Camp David Accords, 59, 63

1981 assassination of Anwar Sadat, 60

2011 Revolution, 58, 61, 62, 199

2012 Mohammed Morsi elected President, 62

2013 Morsi overthrown in coup d'état, 62, 63

2014 IS establish *wilayat* in Sinai, 127, 212

2015 restoration of US military aid, 63; intervention in Yemeni Civil War, 64, 162, 198, 212; clashes with IS in Sinai, 62; bombing of Metrojet Flight 9268 over Sinai, 213, 215, 220

Egyptian Islamic Jihad (EIJ), 59, 60

Eid ul-Adha, 176, 177

El Al, 118–19

electricity, 21, 30, 94, 136, 146, 149, 153, 154

electronic communications, 56, 134, 138

Email, 55

Empty Quarter, Arabian Peninsula, 1

encrypted communications, 177, 206

engineers, 139

INDEX

Eritrea, 167
Estonia, 195
ethnic cleansing, 30
Euphrates river, 134, 137, 145, 146, 153, 164
Eurasian Economic Union, 193
European refugee crisis, 3, 151, 167–70, 183, 198, 212, 220, 225, 227, 228
European Union (EU), 160, 167–70, 200, 211, 219, 225, 226, 227
Eurozone financial crisis, 167
expeditionary terrorism, 117–19, 220
extraordinary rendition, 9

F-16 Fighting Falcons, 37, 220
Facebook, 55, 113, 115
al-Fahd, 41
Faith Campaign, 28, 73
Fallows, James, 19
Fallujah, Iraq, 73, 84, 95, 99, 106, 136, 137, 142, 145, 152, 154, 155
FARC (Fuerzas Armadas Revolucionarias de Colombia), 87, 210
Farrell, Leah, 22
Feith, Douglas, 20
Ferguson, Missouri, 206
Ferguson, Niall, 61
Fezzan, Libya, 127
Fiasco (Ricks), 48
Fick, Nate, 17
Filkins, Dexter, 227
Fiumicino airport, Rome, 118–19
flame weapons, 134
floggings, 98, 153
Florida, United States, 39
Foley, James, 97
food distribution, 20, 94, 133, 149, 153
Ford pickup trucks, 177

foreign fighters, 24, 63, 67, 75–6, 142, 143, 197, 204–5
Foreign Legion, 175
Forever War, The (Filkins), 227
Fort Dix, New Jersey, 122
Fort Hood shooting (2009), 56, 122, 202
France, 10, 12, 26, 65, 80, 96, 98, 105, 114–17, 121, 122, 130, 131, 168, 175, 204, 209, 215, 219–27
    2001 transatlantic shoe bomb plot, 118
    2008 troops take control of Kapisa, Afghanistan, 175
    2010 Lisbon NATO Summit, 173
    2013 intervention in Mali, 65, 116
    2014 intervention against ISIS in Iraq, 96, 98, 105
    2015 Île-de-France attacks, 114–17, 121, 122, 123, 125, 130; IS attack on factory in Lyon, 131; signing of Iranian nuclear deal framework, 151, 160; Paris massacre, 215, 219–27, 228, 229; Jewish teacher stabbed by IS supporter in Marseilles, 224; airstrikes against IS in Syria, 219; COP21 climate talks, 222
Frederick, Jim, 201
free speech, 117, 202, 208
Free Syrian Army (FSA), 77, 80, 104, 109, 147, 159, 188, 191
Freedom and Justice Party (FJP), 62

Gaddafi, Muammar, 58, 61, 63, 64, 68, 69, 71, 72, 114, 127
Garner, Jay, 18
gas, 94, 146, 147, 195

INDEX

Gates, Robert, 25
Gaziantep, Turkey, 152, 164
Geneva, Switzerland, 165
genocide, 96
George H.W. Bush, USS, 96, 173
Georgia, 195
Germany, 10, 14, 16, 17, 25, 26, 62, 117–18, 160, 168, 169, 210, 220, 221, 223, 224, 226
al-Ghaab plain, Syria, 160, 188, 190
al-Ghanam, Naser, 90
Ghani, Ashraf, 171, 172, 177
ghost soldiers, 108
Ghouta, Damascus, 80, 104, 158
Golan Heights, 109
Golden Division, 142, 155
Google Earth, 122, 125
GoPro cameras, 115
Gor Tepa, Kunduz, 177
Graham, Stephen, 205
Grand Mosque, Mecca, 60
Grand Synagogue, Copenhagen, 117
Great Recession (2007–9), 49, 167
Greece, 167, 168–9, 222
Green Movement (Iran), 68
Green Zone, Baghdad, 14, 37, 39
grenades, 134
grey zone, 206
Guardianship Council (Iran), 69
guerrilla terrorism, 120, 123, 125, 131, 132, 206, 219–27
guerrilla warfare, x, 7, 19, 20, 21, 22, 28, 34, 62, 64, 68, 74, 76, 84, 85, 87, 93, 94, 120, 133, 139, 176
Gulf War (1990–1), 17, 28
gun laws, 226

Habbaniyah, Iraq, 154
Haditha, Iraq, 96, 145, 154
Haines, David, 98

Haji Bakr, 74, 75, 77
Hama, Syria, 188, 190
Hamadan, Iran, 187
Hamid, Mustafa, 22
Hamrin Mountains, 142
hand grenades, 221
Haqqani Network, 171, 173
Harakat Hazm, 104
Hasakah, Syria, 72, 159, 160
Hasan, Nidal, 56, 122, 202
Hashd al-Shaabi, 108
al-Hashimi, Tariq, 33, 83
Hawija, Iraq, 84
al-Hayl, gas field, Syria, 146
health services, 30, 59, 94, 133, 149, 153
heavy weapons, 64, 85, 89, 104, 140, 147, 177, 179, 206
Herat, Afghanistan, 21, 22, 103, 172
Hezbollah, 49, 70, 109, 146, 158, 159, 190
High Court (Australia), 112
hijrah, 205
hisbah (holding accountable), 128
Hit, Iraq, 154
Hitler, Adolf, 14, 16, 25, 62
Hizballah Brigades, 25
Hollande, Francois, 219–20, 221
homegrown terrorism, 121, 201
Homeland Security (US), 11, 206
homemade explosives, 122
Homs, Syria, 145, 148, 159, 160, 188, 190
House of Commons
    Canada, 114
    United Kingdom, 10
Houthis, 162
Howard, John, 10, 36
Hubbard, Kin, 229
human rights, 9–10, 30, 57, 123, 196, 208–9
humanitarian aid, 3, 70, 71, 76, 97, 164, 169

Humvees, 143, 177
Hungary, 167, 168, 169
El-Hussein, Omar Abdel Hamid
117
Hussein, Saddam, 13, 15, 17,
20–1, 26–8, 32, 38, 48, 49, 73,
75, 84, 94, 105, 141, 213

Idlib, Syria, 81, 143, 146–7, 159,
189, 190
Il-76 transport aircraft, 146
Imam Sahib, Kunduz, 177
Imperial Marhaba Hotel, Sousse,
131
improvised explosive devices
(IEDs), 78, 94, 140, 141–2, 144,
145, 153, 155, 179, 206
ncirlik, Turkey, 164, 165
Independent High Electoral Commission (Iraq), 50
Independent Naval Infantry Brigade (Russia), 187
India, 10, 120, 121, 123, 129, 176,
197, 222
Indonesia, 3, 7, 8
infantry, 15, 33, 36, 46, 94, 105,
139
infiltration, 58, 117–18, 120, 131,
140, 141, 143, 169, 177, 204,
222, 225, 226–7
infrastructure, 20–1, 94, 96, 143,
153, 154
inghemasiyoun (infiltrators), 143
Innocence of Muslims, The, 129
Inspire, 55, 122
Instagram, 122
Institute for the Study of War, 78
Intelligence Community, 53, 122
intelligence surveillance and
reconnaissance (ISR), 19
International Crisis Group, 156–7
International Security Assistance
Force (ISAF), 51, 172, 173

Internationale, 111–25, 132, 203,
220
Internet, 55, 85, 113, 114, 115,
117, 121–3, 124, 125, 129,
130–1, 143, 202, 228
Iran, x, 3, 8, 10, 21, 22, 25–8, 29,
32, 34–5, 45, 48, 49, 51, 59, 60,
64, 68–9, 70, 78, 83, 84, 92, 99,
107, 112, 138, 140, 141, 146,
154–5, 156, 158, 159, 160–5,
170, 186, 187, 188, 189–91,
195–6, 198, 199, 212–14, 216
1953 CIA sponsor coup against
Mohammad Mossadegh, 26
1959 nuclear reactor supplied by
US, 26
1979 Islamic Revolution; US
Embassy hostage crisis, 26,
60; Nouri al-Maliki arrives in
exile, 49, 71, 107, 108
1980–8 Iran-Iraq War, 26, 164
1980 US launch Desert One
raid, 26
1983 involvement in US Embassy bombing in Beirut, 26
1987–8 Iran-Iraq 'tanker war';
airliner shot down by US, 26
2001 Abu Musab al-Zarqawi
arrives seeking medical treatment, 21, 22, 103
2002 named part of 'Axis of
Evil' by George W. Bush, 9,
10, 26
2003 support for Shi'a militias in
Iraq War begins, 25, 27, 29
2007 Muqtada al-Sadr arrives in
exile, 45
2005 Mohammad Khatami
succeeded by Mahmoud
Ahmadinejad, 69
2009 Green Movement protests,
68, 199
2012 Iraq opens borders for

supply of aid to Assad regime, 71; Quds Force enters Syria, 70, 213–13

2013 Hassan Rouhani elected President, 160

2014 Barack Obama makes offer of cooperation in fight against IS, 161

2015 Quds Force joins offensive on Tikrit, Iraq, 139, 140, 155, 213; support for Houthis in Yemeni Civil War begins, 64, 162; signing of nuclear deal framework, 151, 160–2, 164, 165, 186, 198; delegations visit Russia, 161–2, 186; launch of ground offensive in Syria, 189–91, 212–13

Iranian Revolutionary Guards Corps (IRGC), 25, 69, 146, 159, 161, 189–90

Quds Force, 25, 27, 49, 69, 70, 108, 138, 139, 140, 164, 189

Iraq, ix, xiii, 1–4, 8, 9, 12–14, 15–36, 37–43, 45–51, 55, 59, 67–8, 70–6, 78, 81–2, 87–99, 101–10, 112, 115, 116, 125, 128, 131, 132, 133–45, 151, 153–8, 160, 161, 164, 167, 169, 170, 172, 173, 174, 179, 182, 183, 185, 186, 187–8, 189, 190, 191, 193–4, 195, 196, 197, 198, 199, 200, 203, 204, 205, 206–7, 211–14, 216–17, 224–5, 228, 229, 230, 231

1979 Nouri al-Maliki exiled to Iran, 49, 71

1980–8 Iran-Iraq War, 26, 164

1990–1 Gulf War, 17, 28

1993 launch of Faith Campaign, 28, 73

1995 CIA sponsored coup d'état attempt, 17

1998 Operation Desert Fox airstrikes, 17

2002 CIA reports al-Zarqawi operating in country, 21

2003–11 US-led War, ix, x, 1, 3, 4, 9, 10, 12–14, 15–36, 37–43, 45–51, 73, 101, 105, 107, 115, 125, 136, 167, 170, 185, 193–4, 199, 200, 203, 206–7, 228

2003 de-Ba'athification; disbanding of Iraqi Army, 13, 27, 47, 50, 185; bombing of Canal Hotel, Baghdad, 22; Saddam Hussein captured by US forces, 26

2004 Abu Bakr al-Baghdadi arrested in Fallujah, 73; al-Zarqawi pledges alligiance to bin Laden; foundation of al-Qaeda in Iraq (AQI), 22

2005 parliamentary elections; Sunni boycott, 30; AQI tricks disabled teenager into bombing polling station, 144; al-Zawahiri writes to al-Zarqawi criticizing AQI treatment of Shi'a Muslims, 33–5

2006 bombing of al-Askari shrine, 29; Abu Deraa vows to kill Tariq al-Hashimi in YouTube video, 33; al-Zarqawi killed by US airstrike, 35, 73, 134; formation of Anbar Awakening, 40–1; AQI joins Mujahidin Shura Council (MSC), 73, 74; establishment of Islamic State of Iraq (ISI), 32, 48, 73, 74; execution of Saddam Hussein, 27

2007 US Surge, 14, 35–6, 38, 40–3, 46–8, 67, 74, 75, 135, 173, 200, 229, 231; bombing in Adhamiyah, Baghdad, 31; Anbar Awakening campaign against AQI, 40–1, 67, 137, 153; Iraq Body Count releases assessment of civilian casualties, 45; Mahdi Army ceasefire; al-Sadr exiled to Iran, 45

2008 Iraqi Army campaign against Shi'a militias in Basra, 45–6; withdrawal of Australian troops, 75; US–Iraq Status of Forces Agreement, 47

2010 al-Maliki bars candidates from parliamentary election, 50; Abu Ayyub al-Masri and Abu Omar al-Baghdadi killed by US forces; Abu Bakr al-Baghdadi takes control of ISI, 73, 74; partial withdrawal of US troops, 49; al-Maliki takes control of Defence and Interior ministries, 50

2011 ISI launch terror campaign, 74–5; band of ISI fighters enter Syria, 72, 75, 76; withdrawal of UK troops, 75, 172; full withdrawal of US troops, 47, 55, 75, 78, 83, 172, 173, 194, 197, 200, 228; al-Maliki issues warrant for arrest of Tariq al-Hashimi, 83; ISI bombing campaign in Baghdad, 75

2012 al-Maliki opens borders for supply of aid to Assad regime, 71; ISI launch 'Breaking the Walls' campaign, 78, 85; Sunni demonstrations begin in Anbar, 83; Haji Bakr and senior ISI fighters enter Syria, 72, 75, 77; Tariq al-Hashimi sentenced to death in absentia, 83

2013 assassination attempt on Rafi al-Issawi, 83; Hawija massacre, 84; ISI splits with al-Qaeda; name changed to Islamic State in Iraq and al-Sham (ISIS), 77; ISIS breaches Abu Ghraib prison in Baghdad, 78; al-Maliki calls for US airstrikes against ISIS, 78–9

2014 ISIS launch offensive; capture Mosul, Fallujah and Tikrit, 2, 3, 4, 43, 78, 84–5, 87–95, 106, 107, 108, 136, 137, 139–40, 141, 142, 198, 216, 230; Camp Speicher massacre, 140, 141; formation of Popular Mobilization Forces (PMF), 108; US airstrikes against ISIS begin, 78, 95–6, 102; US deploys *George H.W. Bush* and Carrier Strike Group Two, 96, 173; IS declare Caliphate, 2, 3, 85, 112, 116, 124, 130, 136, 181, 200–1, 209; Fuad Masum becomes President, 106–7; IS advance on Kirkuk, Amerli and Sinjar; evacuation of Yazidis, 96–7, 98, 107, 108; al-Maliki replaced as Prime Minister by Haider al-Abadi, 106–7, 156; US-led 'Counter-ISIL Coalition' launched, 98, 105, 130, 189; al-Maliki seeks to create Sunni National Guard, 104; Baghdad-Kurdistan oil revenue-sharing agreement, 107

2015 Iraqi forces push IS back from Kirkuk and Irbil, 138; US releases plans for assault on Mosul, 138–9; Iraqi forces push IS back from Tikrit, 139–43, 155, 156–7, 213; IS capture Ramadi, 78, 142–5, 151–6, 181, 216; IS massacre civilians in Ramadi, 153; Masoud Barzani visits Washington D.C., 157; IS seize Ramadi dam, 154; arrival of additional US advisers, 155; anti-corruption protests, 156; Masoud Barzani extends term as Kurdistan President, 157; arrival of Russian intelligence team, 187–8; Iraqi forces push IS back from Jurf as-Sakhr, 155

Iraq Body Count, 45
Iraq Liberation Act (1998), 17
Iraqi Air Force, 140
Iraqi Army, 13, 31, 45–6, 47, 50, 51, 74, 83, 85, 87, 88–91, 102, 104, 108, 134, 136, 138–45, 154–5
Iraqi Border Police, 91–2
Iraqi National Congress, 17
Iraqi Police, 8, 30, 31, 38, 46, 50, 74, 78, 83, 84, 85, 87, 88, 90, 91, 108
Iraqi Security Forces, 87
Irbil, Iraq, 3, 96, 105, 138, 142, 154
Iron Curtain, 192
Islamic Movement of Uzbekistan, 176
Islamic State in Iraq and al-Sham (ISIS), xiii, ix–x, 2–5, 21–2, 25, 31–6, 40–1, 45, 48, 50, 51, 62, 65, 67, 72–82, 84–5, 87–99, 101–10, 111–17, 120, 121, 122, 124–5, 127–32, 133–49, 151–65, 168, 173, 176, 179, 181–3, 186, 188–9, 191, 194, 195, 197, 199–205, 207, 209, 211–17, 219–32

1999 inception as *at-Tawhid wa'l-Jihad* in Jordan and Afghanistan, 21
2002 CIA reports al-Zarqawi operating in Iraq, 21
2003 bombing of Canal Hotel, Baghdad, 22
2004 al-Zarqawi pledges alligiance to bin Laden; name changed to al-Qaeda in Iraq (AQI), 22
2005 disabled teenager tricked into bombing polling station, 144; al-Zawahiri writes to al-Zarqawi criticizing AQI treatment of Shi'a Muslims, 33–5
2006 bombing of al-Askari shrine, Samarra, 29; al-Zarqawi killed by US airstrike, 35, 73, 134; absorption into Mujahidin Shura Council (MSC), 73, 74; establishment of Islamic State of Iraq (ISI), 32, 48, 73, 74
2007 bombing in Adhamiyah, Baghdad, 31; conflict with Anbar Awakening, 40–1, 67, 137, 153
2010 Abu Ayyub al-Masri and Abu Omar al-Baghdadi killed by US forces; Abu Bakr al-Baghdadi becomes leader, 73, 74
2011 terror campaign launched in Iraq, 74–5; band of fighters enter Syria with al-Jolani, 72, 75, 76; bombing campaign in Baghdad, 75
2012 al-Jolani founds Jabhat an-Nusra (JN), 77; launch of 'Breaking the Walls' campaign in Iraq, 78, 85; Haji Bakr en-

ters Syria with senior fighters, 72, 75, 77

2013 split with JN and al-Qaeda; name changed to Islamic State in Iraq and al-Sham (ISIS), 77, 95; attack on Abu Ghraib prison in Baghdad, 78; offensive in Aleppo, capture of Raqqa, 81–2

2014 offensive in Iraq; capture of Mosul, Fallujah and Tikrit, 2, 3, 4, 43, 78, 84–5, 87–95, 106, 107, 108, 136, 137, 139–40, 141, 142, 198, 216, 230; Camp Speicher massacre, 140, 141; representatives sent to Afghanistan and Pakistan, 181–2; targeted by US airstrikes in Iraq, 78, 95–6, 102; declaration of Caliphate, 2, 3, 85, 112, 116, 124, 130, 136, 181, 200–1, 209; advance on Kirkuk and Amerli; Sinjar massacre, 96–7, 98, 107, 108; execution of James Foley, 97; execution of Steven Sotloff, 97; US-led 'Counter-ISIL Coalition' launched, 98, 105, 130, 189; execution of David Haines, 98; lone wolf attacks in Quebec and Ottawa, 113–14, 121; Battle for Kobani begins, 163; establishment of *wilayat* in North Africa and Middle East, 127; massacre of Sheitats in Deir ez-Zor, 152; Sydney hostage crisis, 111–13, 121, 226

2015 Île-de-France attacks, 114–17, 121, 122, 123, 125, 130, 219, 220, 222, 223, 225; Twitter account calls for attacks in Western nations, 117;

pushed back from Kirkuk and Irbil, 138; pushed back from Kobani, 138, 163; establishment of *wilayat* in Afghanistan and Pakistan, 127, 181–3; lone wolf attack in Copenhagen, 117, 121, 130, 224; establishment of *wilayat* in Nigeria and Caucusus, 127; claiming of Bardo Museum attack in Tunis, 130, 224; establishment of *wilayat* in Tunisia, 130; pushed back from Tikrit, 139–43, 155, 156–7, 213; capture of Ramadi and Palmyra, 78, 142–9, 151–6, 168, 181, 216; massacres in Ramadi and Palmyra, 153; demolition of Palmyra ruins; execution of Khaled al-Asaad, 152; Sousse attacks, 128, 131, 151, 224; attacks in Lyon, France, 131, 151; bombing of Shi'a mosque in Kuwait, 131, 151, 224; seizure of Ramadi dam, 154; clashes with Egyptian Army in Sinai, 62; clashes with Turkey on Syrian border, 151; capture of al-Qaryatayn; attacks on Deir ez-Zor and Hasakah, 160; attacks in Nangarhar, Afghanistan, 151, 181; targeted by Russian airstrikes in Syria, 188–9; pushed back from Jurf as-Sakhr, 155; bombing of Metrojet Flight 9268 over Sinai, 213, 215, 220; Beirut bombings, 215; Paris massacre, 215, 219–27, 228, 229; stabbing of Jewish teacher in Marseilles, 224; targeted by French airstrikes in Syria, 219

INDEX

Islamic State of Iraq (ISI), 32, 48, 67, 72–7
Islamism 3, 58–63, 69, 99, 199
isomorphic mimicry, 210
Israel, 2, 26, 29, 34, 59, 63, 79, 97, 99, 118–19, 162, 165, 211, 212, 213, 214
al-Issawi, Rafi, 83
Istanbul, Turkey, 187
Italy, 118–19, 167, 168, 170

Jabar, Farhad, 226
Jabhat al-Janubiya, 147, 159
Jabhat al-Nusra (JN), 77, 81, 99, 146–7, 152, 158–9, 163, 188, 209, 229
Jableh, Syria, 187
Jabr, Bayan, 30
jahiliyya, 59
Jaish al-Fatah, 188
Jalalabad, Afghanistan, 172
al-Janabi, Abdullah, 84
Japan, 144
Jaysh al-Fatah (JF), 159–60
al-Jazeera, 158
Jemaah Islamiyah, 7
Jette, Brussels, 223
jihad, 9, 28, 29, 30, 60, 61, 63, 64, 74, 76, 114, 162, 172, 201, 209
Jisr al-Shugour, Syria, 159
Joint Chiefs of Staff (JCS), 12, 17, 18, 19, 103
Joint Comprehensive Plan Of Action (JCPOA), 151, 160–2, 164, 165, 183
Joint Terminal Attack Controllers (JTACs), 103
al-Jolani, Abu Muhammad, 76–7, 81, 95, 99, 158–9
Jordan, 20, 21, 24, 58, 61, 98, 105, 117, 159, 168, 211, 212
Judaism, 115, 117, 121, 201, 224
Jurf as-Sakhr, Iraq, 155, 156

Kabul, Afghanistan, 103, 172, 175, 181, 217
Kafr an-Naboudeh, Syria, 190
Kagan, Frederick, 14
Kairouan, Tunisia, 128, 131
Kalashnikov assault rifles, 131, 221, 223
kamikaze pilots, 144
Kandahar, Afghanistan, 103, 172
kandaks, 179
el-Kantaoui beach resort, Sousse, 131
Kapisa, Afghanistan, 175
Kaplan, Fred, 231
Karbala, 93
Karzai, Hamid, 18, 20, 171, 172
Keane, Jack, 14, 200
Kelly, David 10
Kenya, 56, 120, 121, 123, 203, 209
Kerry, John, 42, 80, 160, 161
keyhole shots, 141
KGB (Komitet gosudarstvennoy bezopasnosti), 194
Khalid Sheikh Mohammed, 8
Khalidiyah, Iraq, 154
Khamenei, Ali, 161
Khan, Hafez Saeed, 182
Khan, Ismail, 103
Khan, Mohammed Sidique, 120
Khanabad, Afghanistan, 177
Khatami, Seyyed Mohammad, 68
Khorasan, 127
Khyber Pakhtunkhwa (KPK), Pakistan, 181, 182
Khyber Pass, 182
kidnappings, 29, 30, 32, 33, 67
Kirkuk, Iraq, 29, 84, 91, 94, 95, 96, 104, 138, 139
Kissinger, Henry, 164
knee-jerk responses, 118, 199
Kobani, Syria, 138, 163–4
Kos, Greece, 169

Kosovo, 102, 106, 215
Kouachi, Saïd and Chérif, 115–17, 118, 121, 122
Krauthammer, Charles, 27
Kunar, Afghanistan, 42
Kunduz, Afghanistan, 174–81, 200, 216, 217
Kurdi, Alan, 169–70
Kurdish Democratic Party (KDP), 28, 157
Kurdistan Regional Government (KRG), 84, 107, 157
Kurdistan Workers' Party (PKK), 29, 72, 157, 165
Kurds, Kurdistan, 3, 17, 18, 27, 28–9, 40, 45, 47, 49, 69, 70, 72, 83, 84, 85, 89, 94, 96, 97, 98, 104, 105, 107–8, 134, 136, 138, 142, 147, 154, 155, 156, 157–8, 163–5, 217
Kuwait, 18, 25, 131, 224

Laeken, Brussels, 223
Landing Zone Washington, Baghdad, 14
Lashkar-e Tayyiba, 120, 121, 176, 222
Latakia, Syria, 159, 160, 186, 187, 189, 190
Lavrov, Sergey, 80, 162
leaderless resistance, 120, 123–4, 125, 129, 132, 224, 228
Lebanon, 26, 59, 70, 109, 117, 146, 159, 168, 204, 211, 212, 215, 224
Leeds, England, 121
Lend-Lease Program, 210
Lewis, Jessica, 78
al-Libi, Abu Anas, 64, 211
Libya, ix, 2, 3, 4, 9, 56, 58, 59, 61, 63–4, 68, 69, 70, 71–2, 81, 96, 101, 106, 114, 117, 127–30, 131, 167, 185, 186, 194, 198, 199, 200, 203, 204, 211, 212, 215, 229
2011 Revolution, 2, 58, 61, 69, 114, 199; multi-national military intervention, 61, 63, 71–2, 96, 101, 106, 185, 186, 194, 212, 215; death of Gaddafi, 63, 68
2012 attack on US diplomatic compounds in Benghazi, ix, 63–4, 129–30
2013 US Special Forces raid in Tripoli; Zeidan flees country, 64
2014 Civil War breaks out, 167
2015 establishment of IS *wilayat*, 127; Seifallah Ben Hassine killed by US airstrike, 131
Libyan Shield, 64
light-footprint operations, 18–19, 49, 55, 63, 145, 155, 173, 181, 207, 217, 230, 231
Lindt Café, Martin Place, 111, 226
Lisbon Summit (2010), 173
London, England, 12, 120–1, 122, 123, 178, 202
lone wolf attacks, 54, 111–14, 117, 222
Long War, 200
Long War Journal, 174
looting, 20, 148
Lord of the Flies (Golding), x
Luck, Les, 7
Lyon, France, 131

M20 motorway, Syria, 146, 147
Macedonia, 168
Madrid train bombings (2004), 202
Mahdi Army, 25, 27, 45
Makarov pistols, 53
Malaysia, 3, 112, 118

INDEX

Malaysia Airlines Flight 17 shoot-down (2014), 195
Mali, 64–5, 115–16, 128, 203
al-Maliki, Ali Waham, 92, 93
al-Maliki, Nouri, 40, 45, 46–7, 49–51, 70–1, 76, 78–9, 82, 83, 84, 85, 88, 104, 106–7, 108, 137, 138, 156, 172–3
Manchester, England, 107
Mansoor, Mullah Akhtar Moham-med, 176, 216
Mansoor, Pete, 38
Mansour, Mullah Akhtar, 182–3
Mansoura, Syria, 190
Marine Corps (US), 18, 19, 96
Marine Corps University, 19
Marseilles, France, 224
Marshall Plan, 210
Martin Place, Sydney, 111–13, 226
Marxism, 34
maskirovka (deception), 194–5
al-Masri, Abu Ayyub, 73
mass surveillance, ix, 5, 19, 49, 124, 206, 208, 211
Massachusetts Institute of Tech-nology, 26
Mauritania, 128
Mazar-e Sharif, Afghanistan, 103, 172, 177
McChrystal, Stanley, 51
McMaster, Herbert Raymond, 14
Mecca, Saudi Arabia, 60
Médecins Sans Frontières (MSF), 180, 217
Medina, Saudi Arabia, 60
Mediterranean Sea, 71, 131, 146, 191, 197, 219
Medvedev, Dmitri, 71–2, 194
Merabet, Ahmed, 114
Metrojet Flight 9268 bombing (2015), 213, 215, 220
Mil Mi-17 helicopters, 87
militarization of police, 206

Military Operations Center (US), 159
Ministry of Health, Iraq, 32
Ministry of the Interior, Iraq, 30, 32, 88, 138
Minnesota, United States, 204
Missouri, United States, 206
al-Moallem, Walid, 80
mobile shooters, 117, 125, 130, 223
moderate rebels, 80–1, 158, 162–3, 164, 186, 188
Mohammed, Prophet of Islam, 73
Molenbeek, Brussels, 223, 225
Molins, François, 224
Monis, Man Haron, 112–13, 117, 121, 123, 226
Montería, Colombia, 87
Morocco, 58, 61, 128, 223
Morsi, Mohammed, 62, 63
mortars, 39, 94, 134, 206
Mosaic restaurant, Martin Place, 111
Mossadegh, Mohammad, 26
Mosul, Iraq, 3, 4, 43, 76, 85, 87–91, 94–6, 99, 102, 105–8, 136–9, 141–2, 152, 154–5, 157, 173, 191, 198, 216, 230
Mosul first plan, 136
Mousavi, Mir Hossein, 68
Moussa Hill, Syria, 146
MP-5 submachine guns, 157
Mubarak, Hosni, 58, 62, 63, 68, 69
mujahideen, 175, 179
Mujahidin Shura Council (MSC), 73, 74, 77
Multi-National Force Iraq Commander's Counterinsurgency Guidance, 38
Mumbai attacks (2008), 120, 121, 123, 176, 222
Munich massacre (1972), 117
Muslim Brotherhood, 58, 59, 62

Nairobi, Kenya, 120, 121, 123
Nangarhar, Afghanistan, 151, 181–3
Naqshbandi Order, 84, 94
Nasrati, Abdul Sabur, 177
National Counterterrorism Center (NCTC), 11, 12
National Defense Force (NDF), 147
National Defense University, Washington D.C., 79
National Directorate of Security (NDS), 175, 178
National Guard (Iraq), 104
National Implementation Plan for the War on Terror, 12
National Military Strategic Plan for the War on Terrorism, 12
National Security Council, 200
National Security Strategy of the United States of America, 12
nationalism, 27–8, 29, 50, 59, 69, 77, 80, 84, 94, 104, 147, 172, 208
NATO (North Atlantic Treaty Orgaization), x, 3, 10, 71, 72, 118, 170, 171–5, 193, 200, 207, 217, 219, 220
Navy SEALs, 53
Nawaz, Maajid, 199
Nazi Germany, 14, 16, 17, 25, 62, 106, 210
nerve gas, 80, 104, 158
Netanyahu, Benjamin, 162
Netherlands, 220, 223
New American Way of War, 19, 103
New York, United States, 55, 117, 162, 174, 185, 192
New York Times, 80, 91
New Yorker, 68
New Zealand, 7, 145
NGOs (non-governmental organizations), 45, 70

Niagara Falls, 41
Nietzsche, Friedrich, v
Niger, 167
Nigeria, 3, 8, 56, 116, 127, 203, 209
night vision goggles, 157
Nikolay Filchenkov, RFS, 187
Nineveh Operations Command (NOC), 88, 90, 142
Nineveh province, Iraq, 76, 85, 88–9, 108, 159
no-fly zones, 17, 71
Nobel Peace Prize, 181
Nørgaard, Finn, 117
North Korea, 26, 162
North-West Frontier Province, Pakistan, 181
Northern Alliance, 26, 27, 103, 104
Northwest Airlines bomb plot (2009), 55, 116, 118, 122
nuclear power/weapons, x, 3, 10, 25–7, 79, 151, 160–2, 164, 165, 183, 186
al-Nujaifi, Atheel, 89–90, 108
al-Nujaifi, Osama, 89
Nuristan, Afghanistan, 42

O'Neill, Robert, 53
Obama, Barack, ix, x, 3–5, 12, 42–3, 45, 48, 49, 51, 53, 54, 55, 57, 61–2, 70, 72, 79, 80, 87, 96, 97, 101, 103, 136, 158, 160, 161, 181, 186, 188, 191–2, 194, 195, 199–200, 207, 208, 210, 213, 217, 219, 227, 230, 231
al-Obeidi, Khaled, 108, 136, 137, 139
Occupy movement, 83
Odierno, Raymond Thomas, 38, 40
Office of National Assessments (Australia), 10

INDEX

Office of Special Plans (US), 20
Office of the Commander in Chief (OCINC), 50
oil, 47, 94, 96, 107, 139, 146, 152, 154, 195
Olson, Eric, 12
Olympic Games, 117, 192
Omar, Mullah Mohammed, 182, 216
one-member terror cells, 124
Operation Inherent Resolve, 142
Operation Resolute Support, 170, 172, 174, 207
operations rooms, 159
Orakzai, Afghanistan, 182
organized crime, 26, 28, 112–14, 117, 134, 154, 206
OTR (off the record) chat, 56
Ottawa, Ontario, 12, 113–14, 121
Ottoman Empire, 59, 127
Overseas Contingency Operations, 48

Pace, John, 30, 38
Pakistan, x, 3, 4, 8, 10, 16, 17, 23, 24, 25, 33, 34, 42, 49, 51, 53–4, 70, 77, 127, 171, 173, 175–6, 177, 181, 197, 203, 211, 212, 222
Pakistani Taliban, 23, 55, 176, 181, 182, 183
Palais Coburg Hotel, Vienna, 160
Palestine, 2, 117, 212
Palmyra, Syria, 78, 145–9, 151, 152–3, 159, 168, 191
Panjshir, Afghanistan, 177
Paris, France, 12, 80, 114–17, 121, 122, 123, 125, 130, 204, 215, 219–27, 228
Parramatta, Sydney, 226
Partiya Karkerên Kurdistanê (PKK), 29, 72, 157, 165
Partiya Yekîtiya Demokrat (PYD), 164

Pashtuns, 174, 177, 182
Pentagon, Virginia, 11, 13, 18, 19, 20, 54, 61, 95, 118, 161, 230
People's Protection Units (YPG), 147, 157
People's Union of Kurdistan (PUK), 28–9, 107, 157
Peshawar Shura, 175
Peshkov, Oleg, 220
Peshmerga, 72, 84, 97, 104, 138, 155, 157
Petraeus, David, 14, 35–6, 37, 40, 41, 109
PGP (Pretty Good Privacy), 56
Philippines, 8
police, ix, 1, 8, 21, 24, 30, 31, 38, 46, 50, 63, 64, 74, 78, 83, 84, 85, 87, 88, 90, 91, 108, 121, 169, 170, 171, 174, 175, 177–9, 181, 183, 194, 202, 206, 208, 209, 219, 221–6
police states, 206, 208
Popular Front strategy, 34, 77, 159
Popular Mobilization Forces (PMF), 108, 138, 139, 140, 141–2, 147, 154, 155, 156
Porte de Vincennes siege (2015), 115, 121, 122, 123
Portugal, 173, 219
post-traumatic stress disorder, 20
postwar planning, 18
Powell, Colin, 10, 17, 21
PowerPoint, 41
precision weapons, 19
Predator Porn, 211
Presidential Palace, Baghdad, 15, 37–8
pressure-cooker bombs, 122
Pritchett, Lant, 210
propaganda, 8, 22, 122, 124, 128, 133, 153, 182, 204
Provincial Reconstruction Teams (PRTs), 171

proxy wars, 29, 64, 164, 186, 198, 213

public safety, 51

public services, 94, 133, 148–9, 153

Putin, Vladimir, 71–2, 185–6, 188, 191–7, 207, 212, 220

al-Qaeda, 3, 4–5, 7–12, 16–17, 21, 22, 23, 26, 29, 31–6, 38, 40–1, 45, 46, 48, 50, 53–65, 67, 72–7, 81, 84, 85, 89, 95, 98, 99, 115–24, 127, 131, 135, 137, 153, 154, 158–9, 172, 173, 175, 181, 182, 193, 197, 199, 200, 201–7, 209, 219, 221, 224, 225, 228, 229, 232

1988 foundation of, 59–61

1998 bombings of US Embassies in Kenya and Tanzania, 58, 64

2001 September 11 attacks, 3, 4, 8, 10, 26, 61, 101, 113, 117–21, 124, 198–9, 202, 206, 219, 220, 221, 228, 229

2004 Madrid train bombings, 202; al-Zarqawi pledges alligiance to bin Laden; establishment of al-Qaeda in Iraq (AQI), 22

2005 AQI tricks disabled Iraqi teenager into bombing polling station, 144; London 7/7 bombings, 120–1, 122, 123, 202; al-Zawahiri writes to al-Zarqawi criticizing AQI treatment of Shi'a Muslims, 33–5

2006 AQI bombing of al-Askari shrine, Samarra, 29; Ontario terror plot, 122; al-Zarqawi killed by US airstrike, 35, 73, 134; AQI joins Mujahidin

Shura Council (MSC), 73, 74; AQI becomes Islamic State of Iraq (ISI), 32, 48, 73, 74

2007 foundation of al-Qaeda in the Islamic Maghreb (AQIM), 55, ISI bombing in Adhamiyah, Baghdad, 31; Fort Dix attack plot, 122; ISI conflict with Anbar Awakening, 40–1, 67, 137, 153

2009 foundation of al-Qaeda in the Arabian Peninsula (AQAP), 55; AQAP linked shooting in Fort Hood, Texas, 56, 122, 202; AQAP Northwest Airlines bomb plot, 55, 116, 118, 122

2010 Abu Ayyub al-Masri and Abu Omar al-Baghdadi killed by US forces; Abu Bakr al-Baghdadi becomes ISI leader, 73, 74

2011 Osama bin Laden killed by US Navy SEALS, ix, 51, 53–8, 74, 123, 129, 228; ISI launch terror campaign in Iraq, 74–5; ISI fighters enter Syria with al-Jolani, 72, 75, 76; ISI bombing campaign in Baghdad, 75

2012 al-Jolani founds Jabhat an-Nusra (JN), 77; al-Shabaab declares allegiance, 55; ISI launch 'Breaking the Walls' campaign in Iraq, 78; AQIM attack on US diplomatic compounds in Benghazi, ix, 63–4, 129–30; Haji Bakr enters Syria with senior ISI fighters, 72, 75, 77

2013 JN declares allegiance; split with ISI, 77, 95; al-Shabaab attack on Westgate Mall,

Nairobi, 120, 121, 123; Abu Anas al-Libi captured by US Special Forces in Tripoli, 64, 211

2014 IS condemns policies in Aghanistan-Pakistan region, 182

2015 AQAP linked attack on *Charlie Hebdo*, 114–17, 121, 122, 123, 125, 130, 219, 220, 222, 223, 225; JN assault on Idlib, 146–7

al-Qaeda in Iraq (AQI), 22, 31–6, 38, 40–1, 45, 46, 48, 50, 67, 73, 75, 77, 84, 85, 93, 116, 135, 137, 144, 154, 158–9, 173, 199, 205, 224, 225, 228, 229

al-Qaeda in the Arabian Peninsula (AQAP), 55, 115–17, 122, 209

al-Qaeda in the Islamic Maghreb (AQIM), 55, 129–30, 131

al-Qaim, Iraq, 91–2, 94, 98, 109

Qalamoun Mountains, 146, 159

al-Qaryatayn, Syria, 160, 191

Qatar, 98

Quadrennial Defense Review (QDR), 11

Quarterly Essay, xiii

Quds Force, 25, 27, 49, 69, 70, 108, 138, 139, 140, 164, 189

Quebec, Canada, 114

Quetta Shura, 23, 176, 182

Quick Reaction Force, 105

Quilliam Foundation, 199

Quneitra, Syria, 159, 191

radicalization, 54, 55–6, 60, 111–14, 117, 120, 121–3, 125, 130, 132, 197, 202, 203–4, 208, 226, 227, 228

Rafidah (rejecters), 162

Rafsanjani, Akbar Hashemi, 160

Rais, Seifeddine, 130

Ramadan, 131

Ramadi, Iraq, 78, 84, 136, 137, 142–5, 147, 148, 152–6, 181, 216

RAND Corporation, 11, 19

Raqqa, Syria, 76, 81, 97, 98, 136, 142, 147, 149

reconnaissance, 18, 19, 85, 106, 121, 186

red line, 79–80, 158

refugees, 3, 151, 152, 164, 167–70, 183, 198, 212, 220, 225, 227, 228

remaining and expanding (*baqiya wa tatamaddad*), 112

remote radicalization, 56, 120, 121–3, 125, 132, 202, 204, 228

remote-observation data, 51

renewable energy, 51

Republican Guard (Iraq), 17

Republican Party (US), 5, 194

responsibility to protect, 71, 96

Reuters, 139

Revolution in Military Affairs, 19

Revolutionary Command Council (Iraq), 28

Revolutionary Guards Corps (IRGC), 25

Rezgui Yacoubi, Seifeddine 131

Rhino Runners, 37

Rice, Condoleezza, 24, 36, 42, 57

Rice, Susan, 71

Ricks, Thomas Edwin, 48

ar-Rishawi, 41

roadside bombs, 39, 85, 134

Robertson, George, 193

rocket-propelled grenades (RPGs), 115

rockets, 37–8, 39, 42, 80, 85, 102, 134, 190

Rogers, Will, 229

Rojava, 164

Rome, Italy, 118–19

Rose, Charlie, 229
Rouhani, Hassan, 160
Route Irish, Baghdad, 37
rule of law, 57, 76, 123, 209
Rumsfeld, Donald, 12–14, 17,
    18–19, 20, 35, 40, 43, 47, 181,
    230, 231
Russia, x, 2, 14, 16, 17, 25, 26, 57,
    68, 71–2, 80, 81, 87, 99, 109,
    146, 160, 161–2, 165, 185–96,
    197, 198, 199, 207, 212–17,
    219–20, 228
  1941 German invasion, 14, 16,
    17; invasion of Iran, 188
  1942–3 Battle of Stalingrad, 106
  1979–89 Afghanistan War, 21,
    60, 179
  2000 Vladimir Putin begins first
    term as President, 193
  2001 support for US in Afghani-
    stan War, 193
  2008 invasion of Georgia, 195
  2011 vote on UN resolution
    on Libya abstained, 71, 186,
    194; veto of UN resolution on
    Syria, 71–2
  2013 Sergey Lavrov brokers
    negotiations on elimination of
    Syrian chemical weapons, 80,
    191–2
  2014 annexation of Crimea, 2,
    81, 186, 187, 195, 196, 220;
    Ukraine crisis begins, 81, 186,
    195, 196, 213, 220; shoot-
    down of Malaysia Airlines
    Flight 17, 195; kidnapping of
    Eston Kohver, 195; Vladimir
    Putin's Valdai speech, 192–3
  2015 signing of Iranian nuclear
    deal framework, 151, 160–2,
    164, 165, 186; visits from
    Iranian delegations, 161–2,
    186; intervention in Syria be-
    gins, 71, 186–8, 198, 212–13,
    220, 228; intelligence team
    deployed to Iraq, 187–8; claim
    on Arctic submitted to UN,
    195; Vladimir Putin addresses
    UN General Assembly, 185–6,
    188, 192, 194–5; *demarche* is-
    sued to US on Syria; airstrikes
    in Homs-Hama corridor,
    188–9; launch of ground
    offensive in Syria, 190–1,
    212–13; IS bombs Metrojet
    Flight 9268 over Sinai, 213,
    215, 220; Turkey shoots down
    Sukhoi-24M bomber, 220
Russian Black Sea Fleet, 187
Russian Naval Infantry, 190

S-300 anti-aircraft systems, 161
Sadat, Anwar, 59, 60
Saddam University, Baghdad, 73
al-Sadr, Muqtada, 25, 27, 45
Sadr City, Baghdad, 33
safe settlements, 164
Safi, Umar, 177, 178
Sahel region, 55, 64
Saladin province, Iraq, 91
Salafi Islam, 28, 74, 112, 201, 204,
    209
Salam, Mullah Abdul, 176, 177,
    178, 179, 216
Saleh, Ali Abdullah, 64, 68
Samarra, Iraq, 29, 73, 94, 139
Sanaa, Yemen, 127
sanitation, 21, 30
Sarajevo, Bosnia, 224
Sattar, Sheikh 137
Saudi Arabia, 1, 24, 29, 60, 64,
    98, 99, 118, 127, 147, 162, 198,
    211, 212, 213, 214
Scud Missiles, 38
Secor, Laura, 68
sectarianism, 29–36, 38, 41, 45–6,

INDEX

49–50, 70, 74, 75, 77, 78, 82–4, 89, 104, 107, 109, 137, 138, 140, 141, 144, 156, 158, 198, 206, 216, 225
secularism, 27, 33, 58, 59, 62, 65, 67, 69, 77, 80, 81, 104
security dilemma, 51
Seh Darak Hospital, kunduz, 178
self-radicalization, 54, 55–6, 111–14, 117, 121, 130, 203, 208
Senate Armed Services Committee, 17
September 11 attacks (2001), 3, 4, 8, 10, 26, 61, 101, 113, 117–21, 124, 198–9, 202, 206, 219, 220, 221, 228, 229
Serbia, 168
Sevastopol, Crimea, 187
sexual slavery, 3, 97
al-Shabaab, 23, 55, 120, 121, 200, 209
shabiha, 67, 70, 147, 148, 170
shahada, 178
ash-Shamali, Abu Jarir, 182
Shanghai Cooperation Organisation, 193
sharia law, 3, 59, 98, 128, 133, 153
Sheitat clan, 152–3
Shi'a Islam, 25, 27–8, 29–36, 40, 45, 46
Shi'a Islam, 25, 27–8, 29–36, 40, 45, 46, 48, 49–51, 70–1, 74, 75, 78, 83, 85, 89, 91, 92, 104, 105, 107, 108, 109, 112, 128, 131, 137, 138, 140, 141, 142, 156, 157, 159, 164, 182, 189–90, 198, 207, 212, 225
militias, 25, 27, 29–30, 41, 45–6, 48–9, 64, 71, 84, 92, 104, 108–9, 137–8, 140–2, 147, 154, 155, 156, 157, 159, 189–90, 216
Shinseki, Eric, 12

Shock and Awe, 19, 26, 103
shoe bomb plot (2001), 118
Shoygu, Sergey, 161
Sijariyah, Ramadi, 143
Sinai, Egypt, 62, 127, 212, 213, 215, 220
singleton terrorists, 124
Sinjar, Iraq, 96–7, 98, 104, 108
Sirte, Libya, 127
al-Sistani, Ali, 91
Six Day War (1967), 59
Sky, Emma, 38
slavery, 3, 97
Slovenia, 168
smuggling, 134
Snapchat, 122
snipers, 39, 85, 94, 134, 141–2, 143, 153, 157, 206
Snowden, Edward, xiii
snuff videos, 33
Sochi, Russia, 192
social media, 56, 85, 113, 114, 115, 117, 121–3, 124, 125, 129, 130–1, 143, 202, 228
socialism, 59, 60
Le Soir, 117
Soleimani, Qasem, 25–6, 69, 138, 140, 141, 154, 161, 164, 186, 190
Somalia, 8, 12, 23, 55, 58, 70, 167, 197, 200, 203, 204, 211, 229
Sons of Iraq, 46–7, 50, 104
Sotloff, Steven, 97
Sousse attacks (2015), 128, 131, 220
Southern Front, 147, 159
Soviet Union, 14, 16, 17, 71, 106, 179, 185, 188, 191, 192, 210
Soviet-Afghan War (1979–89), 21, 60, 179
Spain, 202
SPBE-D air-delivered cluster bombs, 191

Special Air Service (SAS), 96
Special Forces (US), 41, 63, 64, 97
Special Operations Command
    (US), 11, 12, 53
Special Operations Forces
    (Afghanistan), 171, 172
Special Operations Forces (Iraq),
    46
St. Denis, Paris, 224
stabilization, 13, 16–19, 24, 27,
    28, 93, 102, 105, 171, 173, 199,
    210, 213, 217
Stade de France, Paris, 219, 221,
    226
Stalin, Joseph, 17
Stalingrad, Battle of (1942–3), 106
State Department (US), 11, 14
Status of Forces Agreement
    (SOFA), 47, 51
Steinmeier, Frank-Walter, 221, 226
Stevens, Chris, 63, 64
Strait of Hormuz, 96
strategy, 230
student movements, 59
Su-25 strike aircraft, 187
Sudan, 167
Sufi Islam, 84, 94, 128
suicide bombings, 39, 85, 88,
    141–2, 143–5, 147, 154, 205,
    221–2, 223
as-Sukhnah, Syria, 146
Sukhnah, Syria, 147
Sukhoi-24 strike aircraft, 187, 220
al-Suleiman, Ali Hatem, 84
Sullivan, Marisa, 50
Sunni Islam, 13, 28, 30–6, 40, 45,
    46, 49–51, 70, 74, 78, 83–5, 89,
    91, 94, 97, 104, 105, 107, 108,
    109, 112, 137, 138, 140, 144,
    155, 156, 157, 162, 164, 198,
    207, 212, 217, 225
Supreme Command for Jihad and
    Liberation, 84

surgical strikes, 49
surveillance, ix, 5, 19, 49, 124,
    181, 206, 208, 211
SWAT teams, 157
Sweden, 168
Switzerland, 165
Sydney, New South Wales, 2, 12,
    111–13, 121, 204, 226
symbolic figures, 124
Syria, xiii, 2, 3, 4, 9, 12, 21, 24,
    26, 27, 29, 49, 56, 58, 59, 60,
    63, 67–72, 75–82, 87, 91, 97,
    98, 102, 104–5, 107, 108–10,
    112, 114, 115, 125, 128, 132,
    133–4, 136, 138, 143, 145–9,
    151–3, 158–65, 167, 169, 170,
    173, 182, 183, 186–91, 195–6,
    197, 198, 201, 202, 204, 205,
    207, 211, 212, 213–16, 217,
    219–20, 223, 224–5, 228
1980 Tadmur prison massacre,
    146
1982 Hama massacre, 60
2011 Revolution, 58, 63, 67–8,
    70, 104, 147; Assad regime re-
    leases jihadi prisoners, 67, 76;
    Russia begins sending advisers
    and aid to Assad regime, 71;
    ISI fighters enter country with
    al-Jolani, 72, 75; Russia vetoes
    UN resolution on interven-
    tion, 71–2
2012 foundation of Jabhat
    an-Nusra (JN), 77; Iraq opens
    borders for supply of aid to
    regime, 71; arrival of Hezbol-
    lah advisers, 70; Quds Force
    enters country, 70, 212–13;
    Geneva I Conference, 165;
    Haji Bakr enters country with
    senior ISI fighters, 72, 75, 77
2013 JN pledge allegiance to
    al-Qaeda; ISIS splits with al-

Qaeda, 77; Hezbollah combat units enter country, 70; regime chemical weapons attack in Ghouta, 80, 104, 158, 191–2; Framework for elimination of chemical weapons launched, 80, 191–2; ISIS launches offensive in Aleppo, captures Raqqa, 81–2; Genva II Conference postponed, 165

2014 IS declare Caliphate, 2, 3, 85, 112, 116, 124, 130, 136, 181, 200–1, 209; IS execute James Foley, 97; IS execute Steven Sotloff, 97; IS execute David Haines, 98; Battle for Kobani begins, 163; IS massacre Sheitats in Deir ez-Zor, 152

2015 IS pushed back from Kobani, 138, 163; JN and rebel groups capture Idlib, 146–7; Southern Front offensive on Deraa, 147; Jaysh al-Fatah (JF) capture Idlib, 159; Southern Front offensive in Quneitra, 159; US begins training rebels, 163; regime capture Moussa Hill, 146; IS capture Palmyra, 78, 145–9, 151, 168; IS massacre Sheitats in Palmyra, 153; IS demolishes Palmyra ruins; executes Khaled al-Asaad, 152; Turkish intervention against IS begins, 151, 183, 212; failed regime offensive on Palmyra, 159; JF/FSA offensive on Latakia and Aleppo, 159–60; IS captures al-Qaryatayn; attacks on Deir ez-Zor and Hasakah, 160; Russian intervention begins, 71, 186–8, 198, 212, 213,

220, 228; Russian airstrikes in Homs-Hama corridor, 188–9; Israeli airstrikes in Quneitra, 212; end of US rebel training program, 163; Turkey seeks to create safe zone in north, 164–5; Iran and Russia launch ground offensive, 189–91, 212–13; US special operations team arrives to assist rebels, 213; French airstrikes against IS, 219

Syrian Air Force Intelligence Directorate, 69, 81
Syrian National Coalition, 104
Syrian Opposition Council, 67
system of systems, 19

T-90 tanks, 187
Tadmur, Syria, 146, 147
Taji, Iraq, 135, 145
Tajikistan, 177, 178
takfir, 77
Takhar, Afghanistan, 174
Talabani, Jalal, 107
Taliban, xiii, 10, 14, 18, 20, 21, 23, 26, 77, 102–3, 171–83, 193, 197, 200, 209, 216–17, 227–8, 230–2
Tampa, Florida, 39
Tanker War (1984–8), 26
tanks, 85, 94, 104, 137, 139, 141
Tanzim Qaidat al-Jihad fi'l Bilad al-Rafidayn, 22
Tartus, Syria, 71, 159, 187, 190, 191
task saturation, 151
TATP (triacetone triperoxide, peroxyacetone), 221, 222
at-Tawhid wa'l-Jihad, 21
taxation, 94, 133
technicals, 64, 85, 89, 92, 94, 141, 177, 183

INDEX

Tehrik-e Taliban Pakistan (TTP), 23, 55, 176, 181, 182, 183
terrorism, ix, 2–4, 7, 9–12, 14–15, 21–6, 35–6, 41, 46, 48, 49, 50, 54–7, 60–1, 63–4, 78–9, 83, 85, 93–4, 110–25, 129–32, 136, 141, 154, 158, 168, 169, 171, 172, 175, 176, 181, 186, 189, 196, 197–209, 219–32
  homegrown terrorism, 121, 201
  and knee-jerk responses, 118, 199
  leaderless resistance, 120, 123–4, 125, 129, 132, 224, 228
  lone wolf attacks, 54, 111–14, 117, 222
  mobile shooters, 117, 125, 130, 223
  one-member terror cells, 124
  radicalization, 54, 55–6, 60, 111–14, 117, 120, 121–3, 125, 130, 132, 197, 202, 203–4, 208, 226, 227, 228
  terrorism tax, 118–19, 208
  urban sieges, 115, 120, 121, 125, 130, 219–27
Texas, United States, 56
theory of victory, 12
Tigris river, 134, 139
Tikrit, Iraq, 73, 84, 91, 94, 95, 99, 105, 106, 136, 137, 139–43, 147, 154, 155, 156, 213
Time, 201
Times Square, New York, 55
Timor-Leste, 36
Tokubetsu Kōgekitai, 144
Tor, 56
Tora Bora, Battle of (2001), 16
Toronto, Ontario, 122
torture, 9, 30, 32, 67, 146, 152
TOW anti-tank missiles, 104
Townsville, Queensland, 36
Toyota, 93

trade unions, 59
Train, Advise and Assist Commands (TAACs), 172
Transformation', 19, 181, 231
Transnational Terrorism: The Threat to Australia, 7
transport, 107, 134
Traub, James, 198
Treaty of Lisbon, 219
Trenin, Dmitri, 193, 194, 197
Tripoli, Libya, 64, 72, 127, 211
Trombly, Dan, 87–8, 90, 108
truck bombs, 141–2
Tsarnaev, Dzhokhar and Tamerlan, 122
Tuareg people, 64
Tunis, Tunisia, 129, 130
Tunisia, 58, 59, 61, 63, 65, 68, 127, 128–31, 224
Turkey, 3, 29, 59, 70, 72, 83, 138, 151, 152, 158, 163–5, 168, 169, 178, 183, 187, 198, 211, 212, 213, 214, 220, 224, 226
Twitter, 55, 85, 114, 115, 117, 122, 130–1

UAVs (unmanned aerial vehicles), 186
Uccle, Brussels, 223
Ukraine, 2–3, 81, 186, 187, 195, 196, 213, 220
Unconventional Warfare, 120, 163
underwear bomber, 55, 116, 118, 122
United Arab Emirates (UAE), 1, 98, 111, 130
United Kingdom (UK), 2, 7, 9, 10, 12, 23, 26, 75, 96, 98, 105, 107, 118, 120–1, 122, 131, 134, 143, 160, 168, 174, 177, 178, 200, 202, 204, 209, 210
  1941 invasion of Iran, 188
  1946 Winston Churchill's 'Iron Curtain' speech, 192

INDEX

1953 MI6 sponsor coup against Mohammad Mossadegh in Iran, 26

1977 Haider al-Abadi arrives in London, 107

2001 Richard Reid attempts to bomb transatlantic airliner, 118

2003 invasion of Iraq, 10, 23; suicide of David Kelly, 10

2005 London 7/7 bombings, 120–1, 122, 123, 202

2010 Lisbon NATO Summit, 173

2011 withdrawal of troops from Iraq, 75, 172

2014 Ansar al-Sharia declared a terrorist organization, 130; intervention against IS in Iraq, 96, 105, 131; advisers begin training Iraqi Army, 134; IS execute David Haines, 98

2015 suicide bombing by Abu Khalid al-Britani in Ramadi, 143; signing of Iranian nuclear deal framework, 151, 160 Umar Safi arrives in London, 177, 178

United Nations (UN), 10, 17, 22, 30, 63, 71–2, 107, 130, 161, 165, 177, 178, 185–6, 188

Educational, Scientific and Cultural Organization (UNESCO), 146

General Assembly, 162, 165, 167, 174, 185–6, 188, 192

High Commissioner for Refugees (UNHCR), 169

Security Council, 71–2, 185

United States (US), ix–x, 1–5, 7–14, 15–36, 37–43, 45–51, 53–8, 59, 61–4, 68, 71–2, 73–4, 75, 79–80, 87, 95–9, 101–10, 117–20, 122–4, 129–30, 131, 134, 136, 138–41, 142, 155, 158, 159, 160–5, 169, 170, 172–4, 179–81, 185–6, 188, 191–201, 204, 206–18, 219, 220, 225–30

1953 CIA sponsor coup against Mohammad Mossadegh in Iran, 26

1959 nuclear reactor supplied to Iran, 26

1978 Camp David Accords, 59, 63

1979–81 Iran hostage crisis, 26

1980 Desert One raid in Iran, 26

1983 bombing of Embassy in Beirut, 26

1987–8 intervention in Iran-Iraq 'tanker war'; shoot-down of Iranian airliner, 26

1990–1 Gulf War, 17

1994 failed North Korean nuclear deal, 162

1995 CIA sponsor coup attempt against Saddam in Iraq, 17

1996 CIA create of Alec Station to track bin Laden, 54

1998 East African Embassy bombings, 58, 64; Iraq Liberation Act; Operation Desert Fox, 17

1999 intervention in Kosovo War, 102, 106, 215

2001 September 11 attacks, 3, 4, 8, 10, 26, 61, 101, 113, 117–21, 124, 198–9, 202, 206, 219, 220, 221, 228, 229; Afghanistan War begins, 8, 16, 18, 19, 20, 22, 26, 101, 102–4, 115, 193, 199, 203, 206, 215, 230–1; Bonn Conference, 17; Battle of Tora Bora, 16; transatlantic shoe bomb plot, 118

2002 George W. Bush's 'Axis of Evil' speech, 9, 10, 26; CIA reports al-Zarqawi operating in Iraq, 21; detention and deportation of Maher Arar, 9; Congress passes Iraq Resolution, 42

2003–11 Iraq War, ix, x, 1, 3, 4, 9, 10, 12–14, 15–36, 37–43, 45–51, 73, 101, 105, 107, 115, 136, 167, 170, 185, 193–4, 199, 200, 203, 206–7, 228

2003 Paul Bremer launches de-Ba'athification in Iraq, 13, 27, 47, 50, 185; capture of Saddam Hussein, 27

2004 arrest of Abu Bakr al-Baghdadi in Fallujah, 73; Pakistan named major non-NATO ally, 10; renewed Taliban insurgency in Afghanistan, 23

2005 Condoleezza Rice's speech at American University, Cairo, 24, 57; closure of Alec Station, 54

2006 killing of al-Zarqawi in airstrike, 35, 73, 134; Robert Gates replaces Donald Rumsfeld as Secretary of Defense, 14, 25, 35

2007 Surge in Iraq, 14, 35–6, 38, 40–3, 46–8, 67, 74, 75, 135, 173, 200, 229, 231; David Kilcullen appointed Counterinsurgency Advisor to David Petraeus, 36; Tampa Conference, 39; Fort Dix attack plot, 122; Iraq Body Count releases assessment of civilian casualties, 45; Petraeus briefs Congress on Surge, 41;

David Kilcullen posted to Afghanistan, 42

2008 US–Iraq Status of Forces Agreement, 47

2009 inauguration of Barack Obama as President, 43, 45, 48, 57, 194; Fort Hood shooting, 56, 122, 202; Northwest Airlines Christmas Day bomb plot, 55, 116, 118, 122

2010 Pakistani Taliban Times Square bomb plot, 55; partial withdrawal of troops from Iraq, 49; killing of Abu Ayyub al-Masri and Abu Omar al-Baghdadi, 73; Lisbon NATO Summit, 173

2011 military intervention in Libya, 61, 63, 71–2, 96, 101, 106, 185, 186, 194, 215; killing of Osama bin Laden, ix, 51, 53–8, 74, 123, 129, 228; date set for withdrawal from Afghanistan, 55, 95; Obama calls for Bashar al-Assad to 'step aside', 62, 70, 72; full withdrawal of troops from Iraq, 47, 55, 75, 78, 83, 172, 173, 194, 200, 228

2012 Obama lays down 'red line' on Syrian WMDs, 79, 158; attack on diplomatic compounds in Benghazi, ix, 63–4, 129–30; storming of Embassy in Tunis, 129; Obama wins Presidential election, 43, 54

2013 White House declares Syrian use of WMDs would be 'game changer', 79; Boston Marathon bombing, 122; al-Maliki's calls for airstrikes in Iraq rebuffed, 78–9; negotiations on elimination of Syrian chemical weapons, 80, 191–2; Special Forces raid in Tripoli; capture of Abu Anas al-Libi, 64, 211

2014 Ansar al-Sharia declared a terrorist organization, 130; Obama's speech at West Point, 3–4, 12, 87; intervention against IS in Iraq, 78, 95–6, 102; USS *George H.W. Bush* and Carrier Strike Group Two deployed to Iraq, 96, 173; evacuation of Yazidis from Sinjar, 96–7, 98; Ferguson protests begin, 206; IS execute James Foley, 97; advisers begin training Iraqi Army, 134; IS execute Steven Sotloff, 97; 'Counter-ISIL Coalition' intervention in Iraq and Syria, 98, 105, 189; Obama makes offer of cooperation with Iran in fighting IS, 161; withdrawal of combat troops from Afghanistan, 55, 95, 170, 175, 197

2015 Operation Resolute Support begins in Afghanistan, 170; 172, 207; New York City raises terror threat levels, 117; plans for assault on Mosul released, 138–9; airstrikes against IS in Tikrit, 140–1, 213; restoration of military aid to Egypt, 63; suicide bombing by Abu Dawud al-Amriki in Tikrit, 142; Masoud Barzani visits Washington D.C., 157; training of rebels in Syria begins, 163; killing of Seifallah Ben Hassine in airstrike, 131; additional advisers sent to Iraq, 155; signing of Iranian nuclear deal framework, 151, 160–2, 165, 183, 186, 198; Obama announces intent to accept 10,000 refugees, 169; Vladimir Putin addresses UN General Assembly in New York, 185–6, 188, 192, 194–5; Russia issues *demarche* on Syria; demands clearing of airspace, 188; end of Syrian rebel training program, 163; bombing of MSF hospital in Kunduz, 180–1, 217; special operations team sent to assist Syrian rebels, 213

United States Air Force, 172, 180
United States Army War College, 19
United States Central Command, 11, 14, 16
United States Marine Corps, 18, 19, 96
United States Military Academy, West Point, 4, 12
United States Military Operations Center, 159
United States Navy, 95, 96, 172
United States Navy SEALs, 53
United States Special Forces, 41, 63, 64, 97
United States Special Operations Command, 11, 12, 53
University of Manchester, 107
urban sieges, 115, 120, 121, 125, 130, 219–27
urban warfare, 134–6, 139
urbanization, 51
useful idiots, 48, 205
Uzan, Dan, 117
Uzbekistan, 178

Valdai International Discussion Club, Sochi, 192

vehicle-borne improvised explosive devices (VBIEDs), 78
Vickers, Kevin, 114
Vieira de Mello, Sérgio, 22
Vienna, Austria, 160
vigilantism, 128

al-Wahdi, Osama al-Absi, 76
Wahhabi Islam, 60
Waleed, Iraq, 91, 92, 94, 109
Wall Street Journal, 143
War of Movement, 85, 102
War on Islam, 10
War on Terror, ix, 3, 4, 8, 26, 39, 48, 54, 112, 118, 124, 196, 197, 205, 219, 227
warlords, 175, 231
warrior mentality, 206
Warsaw Pact, 210
Washington D.C., United States, 20, 42, 118, 157
Washington Post, 72
water supplies, 20, 30, 92, 94, 134, 136, 148–9, 153
water-cannons, 169
waterfall slide, 41
weapons of mass destruction (WMD), 10, 79
Weidley, Tom, 142
welfare, 168
West Point, New York, 3–4, 12, 87
Westgate Mall shooting (2013), 120, 121, 123
White House, Washington DC, 12, 41, 79, 95, 157, 161
Wikileaks, xiii
wilayat, 3, 112, 125, 127–32, 181–3, 209, 212, 217, 220

Wilkie, Andrew, 10
Wilson, Thomas Ray, 17
Wolfowitz, Paul, 11
women's organizations, 59
Woolcock, Michael, 210
World Trade Center, New York, 3, 4, 8, 10, 26, 61, 101, 113, 117–18
World War II (1939–45), 14, 16, 17, 25, 48, 106, 144, 188, 198, 210

Yazidi people, 96–7, 98
Yekîneyên Parastina Gel (YPG), 147, 157
Yemen, 2, 8, 9, 12, 26, 49, 55, 56, 60, 61, 64, 68, 116, 118, 122, 127, 128, 129, 162, 197, 198, 203, 211, 212
Yom Kippur War (1973), 59
YouTube, 33, 55, 122, 129
Yugoslavia, 102

Zabiullah Mujahid, 178
al-Zamili, Hakim, 30
Zarif, Javad, 161, 186
al-Zarqawi, Abu Musab, 21–2, 25, 28, 29, 31–5, 40, 73, 77, 103, 116, 134–5, 158, 224
al-Zawahiri, Ayman, 8, 17, 22, 33–5, 57–8, 59, 60–2, 65, 77, 95, 159
al-Zawi, Hamid Khalil, 73
Zehaf-Bibeau, Michael, 113–14, 117, 121, 123
Zeidan, Ali, 64
Zero Day exploits, 119
Zero Option, 172, 200